The Challenge
of
Social Equality

The Challenge of Social Equality

Essays on Social Policy,
Social Development
and Political Practice

David G. Gil

SCHENKMAN PUBLISHING COMPANY
Cambridge, Mass.
02138

Library of Congress Cataloging in Publication Data

Gil, David G.
    The challenge of social equality

    Includes bibliographical references and index.
    1. Social problems. 2. Social policy. I. Title.
HN16.G5   309   76-54925
ISBN 0-87073-603-5

Copyright© 1976
Schenkman Publishing Company, Inc.
3 Mt. Auburn Place
Cambridge, Massachusetts 02138

Printed in the United States of America

To men and women of reason,
near and far in time and place,
whose thoughts and acts
have challenged my search.

To people everywhere,
who search and struggle for communities
where all are equal and free
and human potential can flourish.

D.G.G.

September 8, 1976

CONTENTS

PART III INQUIRY INTO POLITICAL PRACTICE

Introduction

The essays in this volume grew out of earlier studies reported in my books *Violence Against Children* and *Unravelling Social Policy*. Written between 1971 and 1975, most of these essays appeared separately in social science and political practice journals. In writing them I attempted to clarify several interrelated themes, and the entire set conveys the arguments and conclusions more clearly than each essay separately. The whole, in this instance, seems, indeed, greater than the sum of its parts.

The following themes were explored in the essays:
- the nature, dynamics, and evolution of social policies, social orders, policy-relevant value-dimensions, and social development; and, related to this, dilemmas of social change and time;
- the systemic roots and dynamics of specific social problems, and, related to this, contradictions and dilemmas of social control versus human welfare, amelioration versus primary prevention, and reform versus revolution;
- political practice aimed at overcoming current trends that threaten human survival, by transforming existing welf-centered, inegalitarian, problem-ridden social orders and

nation-states all over the globe into pacific, free, self-directing, humanistic communities which cooperate with one another on egalitarian terms on local, regional, and worldwide levels.

To reduce overlapping of the themes and repetition of ideas, several essays were shortened from their originally published version. However, to insure internal coherence of each essay, complete elimination of overlapping and repetition did not seem indicated. For me, in writing them, the essays were stepping stones in a search for human survival and for social orders in which the free and full development and the actualization of everyone's inherent potential should be possible—social orders in which every human being will be acknowledged as a self-directing subject of equal worth, rights, and responsibilities, rather than treated as an object or a means to someone else's ends.

This search has gradually led me to conclude that the institutions and dynamics of such social orders, and the individual and collective consciousness of their members, would have to be shaped by values of equality, liberty, cooperation, and collectivity-orientation which are diametrically opposed to the values shaping the institutions, dynamics, and consciousness of the existing social order in the United States and many other contemporary societies. Furthermore, I became convinced that transforming our prevailing social order into one conducive to survival and self-actualization for all humans everywhere is predicated upon a revolutionary process and upon political practice shaped consistently by reason and by the very same values which are to shape the new order. For that new order is unlikely to emerge from cataclysmic, violent events aimed at shifting power from currently dominant elites to new elites. Rather, its evolution seems to require the conscious use of the following, mutually reinforcing strategies:

a. challenging, piercing, and transcending the now dominant consciousness and social construction of reality which are shaped and constantly reinforced by the institutions and dynamics of the prevailing social order, and which, in turn, legitimate and sustain that order by assuring socialization into, identification with, and loyalty to it;

b. organizing movements of individuals who succeed to transcend the system-shaped consciousness, and who are committed to a revolutionary practice of helping others to transcend that consciousness so that they too may join the struggle for human liberation;

c. translating the egalitarian, cooperative, collectivity-oriented consciousness into new existential realities among members of liberation movements by creating alternative social, economic, cultural, and political institutions and correspondingly alternative life styles within, and parallel to, existing institutions.

d. establishing networks for social, economic, cultural, and political cooperation, coordination, exchange, and support among movement groups that created for themselves such new existential realities;

e. organizing conscientious refusal and active, non-armed resistance to participating in, cooperating with, and providing resources to the dehumanizing institutions and practices of the now dominant social order; such organized refusal and non-armed resistance would spread with the growth in numbers of movement-groups whose strength would derive from their solidarity with one another, and their shared commitment to humanistic goals.

As these strategies unfold and increase in intensity, the established order and its productive, distributive, cultural and governing institutions could be gradually replaced by, and dissolved into, the newly emerging order.

*   *   *   *

I was helped in exploring the ideas articulated here by discussions with students in courses and seminars at Brandeis University, Harvard University Extension, Tufts University, and Washington University (St. Louis). They are too numerous to be listed individually, but my gratitude to them must be recorded. I also wish to thank my colleagues at the Universities, my friends in political movements, my wife Eva, and my sons Daniel and Gideon with whom I explored many of the ideas discussed here. The unusual skills and help of Ms. Marianne Muscato in preparing the manuscript are gratefully acknowledged, and thanks are due to the following journals and publishers for permission to reprint essays originally published by them: *American Journal of Orthopsychiatry*, *International Social Work*, *Journal of Marriage and the Family*, *Journal of Sociology and Social Welfare*, *New American Movement*, and Basic Books.

D.G.G.

Lexington, Mass.
May 24, 1976

CONTRIBUTIONS TO THEORY AND PHILOSOPHY OF SOCIAL DEVELOPMENT

CHAPTER ONE

Thoughts on Social Equality

This essay is a modest attempt, drawing on the wisdom of past and present social philosophers, to reduce the vagueness and misconceptions which now surround the notion of social equality in public discourse in the United States. If we wish to establish a society based on social equality we need to explicate the meaning of this over-used, yet elusive, concept, and to understand the dynamics of inequality. For as long as we lack such clarity our political practice will continue to consist merely of reactions to recurrent crises, rather than of constructive initiatives aimed at systematically furthering the cause of social equality.

Social equality is one feasible organizing principle for shaping the overall quality of life and the circumstances of living of individuals and groups in a society, as well as for structuring all human relations. The principle of social equality derives from a central value premise, according to which every individual and every social group are considered to be of equal intrinsic worth, and should, therefore, be entitled to equal civil, political, social, and economic rights, responsibilities, and treatment, as well as subject to equal constraints. Implicit in this central value premise

3

is the notion that every individual should have the right and resources to develop freely and fully, to actualize his inherent human
potential, and to lead as fulfilling a life free of domination, control,
and exploitation by others as is possible within the reality of, and
in harmony with, the natural environment. He should be subject
only to the general limitation that any individual's and group's
rights to freedom and self-actualization must never interfere with
the identical rights of all other individuals and groups.

It should be stressed that social equality as conceived here
implies genuine democracy; none are to have more power than
others concerning public affairs. It implies genuine liberty, since
none are to have more liberty than others in pursuing self-
actualization nor to be subject to more constraints than others.
And it implies genuine individuality since all are to be considered
self-directing subjects and none are to be treated as objects.
Contrary to widespread fallacious assumptions, social equality
does not negate democracy, liberty, and individuality; it rather
is a sine-qua-non for overcoming obstacles to real democracy
and for reducing constraints on everyone's liberty and individuality to an absolute minimum within a societal context. Genuine
democracy, liberty, and individuality for all are simply not
feasible without social equality; opponents of social equality
are consequently also opponents of democracy, liberty, and
individuality.

Social equality as understood here, following G. B. Shaw's[1]
and R. H. Tawney's[2] most eloquent expositions of this ancient
humanistic ideal, is predicated upon social policies and institutions involving:

- rationally planned, and appropriately balanced, collective development, use, and preservation of all natural and human-
created resources;
- equality for all individuals and groups in access to statuses and
corresponding roles, prerogatives, and responsibilities within
the totality of tasks to be performed by a society;
- equality for all in civil and political rights and in rights to
material and symbolic life-sustaining and life-enhancing goods
and services.

Social equality aims at actualization of individual differences in
innate potentialities, and therefore it is not meant to be realized by
dividing all available resources into identical parts for distribution
to every member of society. Social equality does not mean monotonous uniformity. Rather, it means equal opportunity to be

oneself, and to lead as rich, rewarding, free and meaningful an individual life as is possible within a societal context.

The value premise of social equality constitutes one basic choice among alternatives, each of which results in different principles for organizing and structuring a social order and human relations within it. A diametrically opposed value premise is obviously social inequality. According to that value premise individuals and social groups differ in intrinsic worth and, hence, are entitled to different rights and to as much of available goods and services for their own use as they can gain control over through constant competition with, and exploitation of, other individuals and groups, and of the natural environment.

Neither the value premise of social equality, nor that of social inequality, and the organizing principles and institutions derived from them, can be shown to be intrinsic to human nature. Neither can be shown to be the only possible response to the universal aspects of the human condition, as is often claimed by their respective proponents.[3] Human societies throughout history have arrived at one or the other approach, or at some combination between these two antithetical principles. It seems important to emphasize in this context that the organizing principles of social orders derive from choices and decisions evolved by members and groups of a society, and that they are not consequences of natural, supernatural, or extra-societal forces. Once basic choices have been made, however, by a society in the course of its evolution, a marked tendency emerges to legitimate, perpetuate, and defend these choices and the resulting social order with all available means of socialization and social control; these include molding of minds (education) and, ultimately, the threat or actual use of physical force against non-conforming individuals and groups. As already suggested, the particular choice a society has made also tends to be rationalized, ex post facto, as reflecting human nature or the will of the gods.

It may be noted parenthetically that interpreting value choices as reflections of human nature is, in a certain sense, not entirely invalid, since human nature is plastic and can adapt to a wide range of social structures. Human nature can thus be shown to fit, eventually, almost any value choice made by a society and the corresponding institutional patterns. Furthermore, there are also circular interaction effects among the value premises and institutions of a society and the psycho-social traits of its members. For humans tend to develop personality traits best suited to the social order in which they live. It is, however, a logical fallacy, resulting from a confusion of causes and effects, to consider human traits and behavior evolved and manifested in a given social order as the only possible pattern of human behavior.

Why given human groups arrive at specific choices of values and organizing principles, rather than at others, for structuring their social systems, is a fascinating subject which cannot be pursued in this essay. Another equally fascinating question, one that has considerable philosophical and practical consequences, is whether one specific choice of values and institutions is more conducive to human survival and fulfillment than its opposite, and, hence, is also more conducive to the realization of the true, long-range survival interests of the human species. Some tentative thoughts concerning this controversial issue, with which Ruth Benedict began to struggle in her later years,[4] will be suggested at the end of this essay. But first we must sketch certain implications for social policy and political practice, of egalitarian value premises as distinguished from the non-egalitarian value premises and organizing principles which shape the existing, capitalist social order of the United States of America.

Inequality, as we know from experience in our own society, involves two subsidiary value dimensions: competitiveness and pursuit of narrowly perceived self-interest. The value cluster of inequality, competitiveness, and narrow self-interest or rugged individualism is reflected in, and reinforced by, a set of institutionalized social arrangements, including:

- private ownership and control of land, other natural resources, means of production, and many other human created goods and services;
- the right to accumulate, to will, and to inherit private property;
- the right to use one's property in free enterprise as one sees fit, subject only to limited social constraints, for purposes of generating private profits without regard to indirect social and environmental costs;
- production and distribution of goods and services for profit, mainly in accordance with the principles and dynamics of a supposedly "free" market economy and with little or no regard for human needs;
- a system of relatively stable social stratification which functions as principal mechanism of status and role allocation;
- a system of unequal rewards and constraints corresponding to differently valued statuses and roles;

- a relatively narrow scope of universal entitlements by virture of membership in society;
- a competitive, pluralistic system of formal, representative democracy, and informal political processes, in which political power tends to be highly correlated with unequal economic power;
- overt and covert controls of media of mass communication by clusters of economic power, resulting in a selective flow of information;
- a system of unequal education geared to the perpetuation of the stratification system and to systematic indoctrination of the young into the dominant ideology of the prevailing capitalist social order.

In the course of several centuries the non-egalitarian social context sustained by the foregoing institutional arrangements has resulted in an enormous concentration of wealth, income, and political power in the hands of a small fraction of the population.[5] It is utterly naive to pretend that genuine equality of civil, political, social, and economic rights is feasibe within the context of these institutional arrangements. For the very fabric of the prevailing social order involves unsurmountable obstacles to the equal exercise of these rights by all, and resists and vitiates any efforts to promote their realization.

An egalitarian social order would be characterized by value clusters and institutional arrangements radically different and diametrically opposed to those of the extant, non-egalitarian social order. Its dominant value premises would be equality, cooperation, and collectivity-orientation or societal responsibility. Land and other natural resources, and means of production, would be owned collectively and would be used for the benefit of all in order to produce life-sustaining and life-enhancing goods and services which would be distributed as universal entitlements in accordance with egalitarian principles. Processes of production would be so organized as to maintain an appropriate, dynamic balance between use and preservation of natural resources. Private ownership would be limited to goods and services used by individuals in the course of daily living. Accumulation and intergenerational transmission of wealth would be abolished, as it would be dysfunctional and unnecessary in a social order which entitled everyone to economic security and to fulfillment of his flexibly determined needs. Stratification and social segregation by class, caste, ethnicity, etc., as we know it now, would no longer exist once the dynamics of inequality would cease to operate. Functional division of labor would continue, but circumstances of living would be independent of roles performed by individuals and groups, since goods and services would be distributed to all in accordance with need as universal entitlements. Access to different statuses and to preparatory channels would be open to all irrespective of biological and social characteristics. There would also be opportunity for occupational shifts throughout an individual's life cycle, as existing artificial barriers to entry into occupations would be eliminated. Such barriers would no longer serve the vested interests of any group. Undesirable and less desirable tasks, to the extent that they could not be eliminated through automation, would be shared and rotated equitably among members of society.

Education, like other services, would be available to all throughout the life cycle in accordance with egalitarian principles and individual need. To assure actualization of innate potential of mentally or physically handicapped, disabled, or exceptional individuals, compensatory and supplementary educational processes would be developed. In general, education and media of mass communication would be geared to maximize intellectual and emotional development and creativity.

Health and personal social services would be available on a universal basis and would be oriented preventively toward maintenance of optimum physical and mental health and social functioning. Food, housing, clothing, transportation, and other essentials, could be distributed as public utilities in kind.

An intrinsic consequence of the value premises and the organizing principles of social equality is that ultimately they must transcend artificial boundaries among separate, national societies. Another intrinsic consequence is that the use of physical force for purposes of coercion, as well as all other forms of coercion, are antithetical to the philosophical essence of these principles. Let us briefly examine these corollaries of social equality. If, as noted earlier, every individual is to be considered equal in worth, and is to be equally entitled to freely actualize his inherent human potential, and to lead as fulfilling a life as possible, then humans all over the world must be given equal rights and opportunities. This means that no nation must control a disproportionate share of the world's resources, and that a system of planned resource utilization, preservation, and distribution will have to be developed on a worldwide rather than merely on a national scale within the context of equal entitlement for all. As international conflicts and wars seem to be related to the defense of existing, or the striving for new, vast inequalities in command over the world's total wealth,[6] and to massive exploitation of some nations by others, as well as to antithetical ideological commitments with respect to egalitarian and non-egalitarian values, it would seem that equalization of access to the world's real wealth should eliminate the need for armed conflicts, and the basis for the current belief of nations that for their security they must maintain military establishments and defense industries.

The use of physical force for purposes of coercion, as well as all other forms of coercion in human interaction contradict the value of equality since the context and the dynamics of coercion always involve inequalities between agents and objects of coercion. To examine the implications of this propostion would take us beyond the scope of this essay. The idea had to be mentioned, though, since it is an essential aspect of the philosophy of social equality as interpreted here.

Elimination of military establishments and of defense industries, one likely consequence of the application of egalitarian principles to the international sphere, would open up opportunities for radical, qualitative changes in the production of goods. No longer would it be necessary for nations to invest human labor and scarce natural resources and other capital in wasteful defense production and military pursuits. Instead, newly freed human energy, natural resources and other capital could be channeled into the development and preservation of real wealth needed to sustain and enhance the quality of life all over the world.

An egalitarian social order would lead to additional qualitative changes in production and in patterns of use of human and material resources besides the elimination of soldiering and defensewares. For production could be shifted from wasteful luxury items, now conspicuously consumed by few, to essential goods required for the well-being of all. Also, such profit oriented malpractices as built-in obsolescence, wasteful model changes, meaningless marginal differences, etc., could give way to emphasis on quality, durability, and truly effective and efficient use of all resources. A worldwide, open, egalitarian and rational economic system would end, also, such irrational practices as rewarding farmers for not growing food while people starve all over the world. Nor would it be necessary to create jobs for the sake of "employment" and to maintain artificially inflated levels of economic activity and economic growth with all their harmful side effects, once economic activity is no longer viewed, irrationally, as a means to profit or an end in itself, but as a means for sustaining and enhancing life; and once equal rights for all to a decent way of life are recognized as independent of an individual's particular roles and degree of participation in economic activity. There will be plenty of real work if all humans are to be adequately provided for, and, thus, there is likely to be meaningful work for all. However, the notions of "creating jobs" and of "full employment" would not be an appropriate yardstick for social policy in an egalitarian society. If the goal of self-actualization for all could be realized without "full employment," through elimination of wasteful production, sharing by all in essential production, and proper application of technological capacity, it would be foolish and dysfunctional to create unnecessary jobs and to treat work as an end in itself rather than as a means to other ends.

Social orders based on egalitarian values and principles will come into being when people everywhere will overcome the "false consciousness" which now leads them to believe their life chances are better under existing, non-egalitarian systems. While facts and figures amply demonstrate the tragic fallacy of this widespread delusion, its very existence and perpetuation constitutes a most powerful obstacle to radical social change. The central task to be undertaken, therefore, by movements intent upon promoting social equality seems to be political education; this must be aimed at unmasking the illusions which now blind people everywhere to the reality of existing social orders and to the potentialities of alternative, egalitarian systems. In this context, it should be realized that non-egalitarian, competitive social orders have disastrous consequences not only for deprived and exploited population segments, but also for privileged and middle class segments. Drug addiction and alcoholism, mental illness and crime, and such phenomena as the competitive "rat race," alienation, discontent at work, urban decay, environmental pollution and destruction, transportation crises, and endless involvement in foreign wars, demonstrate clearly the all-pervasive scope of the crisis which affects under the prevailing socioeconomic and political system all segments of our society.

A movement committed to promoting social equality by nonviolent means will have to derive its political practice from, and in accordance with, its egalitarian, humanistic philosophy. Such a movement cannot adopt the existing, manipulative and competitive model of political action which is derived from, and fits the non-egalitarian, pluralistic market philosophy, where every interest group struggles merely to maximize its own unequal shares and no group struggles for social equality for all. The political practice suggested here involves implementation of egalitarian ways of life wherever possible in the present reality, and dissemination of factual information concerning linkages between non-egalitarian values and policies, and existing disastrous social circumstances. An underlying assumption of this strategy is that the minds of enough people must and can be reached by political education aimed at *all* groups of society; they must be reached by not attacking any group of people, but by attacking value premises and organizing principles which have demonstrably destructive consequences for all, poor people, rich people, and those in between. The objective of such political practice and education is to induce value changes which are expected to result from changes in consciousness and in perceptions of self-interest. Interpretation would, therefore, have to stress and elaborate the multiple, social, psychological, and economic costs resulting from the existing, inegalitarian social order for all members of society; it would have to stress also the real advantages in terms of self-actualization which are expected to accrue to all groups and individuals from the establishment of an egalitarian social order. Changes in perceptions of self-interest and in values on the part of growing segments of the population should facilitate the gradual spreading of radical changes in social, economic, and political institutions. Such a revolution would be a process, rather than an event.[7]

This brings us back to the issue raised above when presenting the alternative value premises underlying different social systems. Can it be shown that one set of values leads to a social order which is more conducive to human survival and self-actualization for all, and which, therefore, is better suited to the true interests of the human species? From all we know from history about the performance of social systems organized on the principle of social inequality, competition, and selfishness, the record is a most dismal one when measured by the criterion of self-actualization for all. At this time many competent scientists even tell us that we may soon approach a point at which survival of the human race would no longer be assured.[8] Genuine egalitarian systems have of course never been dominant on a worldwide scale. Whatever we know about their performance from anthropologists and historians is too fragmentary to allow a definite judgment. We are thus left on the one hand with voluminous empirical evidence concerning the complete failure of non-egalitarian social systems, and on the other hand with insufficient empirical evidence concerning the potential of truly egalitarian, humanistic social systems. Logical analysis seems to suggest, however, that a worldwide order based on reason, social equality and cooperation offers a high probability for human survival and self-actualization. Is it not time, then, to give social equality a chance? If we do, we have nothing to lose but the certainty of approaching disaster.

CHAPTER TWO

Theoretical Perspectives on the Analysis and Development of Social Policies*

INTRODUCTION

The development of social policies, in American and in many other societies usually proceeds in fragmented fashion in relation to different substantive issues. I think here of issues such as economic security, housing, education, physical and mental health, social deviance, child and family welfare, aging, inter-group relations, etc. The fragmentary nature of processes of social policy formulation reflects their political nature and their roots in conflicts of real or perceived interests among diverse social groups. Were existing processes of policy development to result in social orders in which all members of a society could lead meaningful and satisfying lives, there would be little reason to explore alternative approaches. Since, however, conditions of life of large segments of most societies continue to be un-satisfactory in many respects and in varying degrees, it is im-perative to search for more constructive and effective approaches

*Presented at the Twenty First Annual Meeting of the Society for the Study of Social Problems, Denver Colorado, August, 1971. Published in International Social Work, Vol. XV, No. 3, 1972, and in *Journal of Sociology and Social Welfare*, Vol. 1, No. 1, Fall 1973; reprinted with permission.

to the analysis and development of social policies; it is important to explore potential contributions of social theory to the design of such alternative approaches. The present paper is one contribution to this search.

Analysis and development of social policies seem to be hindered at present not only by their political context, but also by inadequate comprehension of the generic function and dynamics of social policies, and of the principal variables through which these policies operate. There is, in fact, no agreement among policy analysts concerning the very meaning of the concept "social policies." To overcome these theoretical difficulties, this paper suggests a universally valid conceptual model of social policies. Such a universally valid model would enhance understanding of the general functions and dynamics of all social policies, facilitate analysis of specific social policies and their consequences, and aid in the development of alternative policies.

Implied in the general model presented below is the assumption that all those policies known as "social" are concerned with an identical underlying domain of societal existence, and are operating through the same basic processes; this is true despite the considerable variation in the substantive content, objectives, and scope of specific social policies. It follows that they are not independent, but interact with each other. All extant social policies of a given society are thus to be viewed as constituting a comprehensive system, which influences the common domain through its aggregate effects. Every specific social policy influences a certain segment of the general domain and thus contributes to the aggregate effect. It should be noted, however, that while all social policies are thus viewed as components of one system with reference to their underlying common domain, they are not necessarily assumed to be consistent with each other. Rather, considerable inconsistency tends to prevail among these policies because of their origin in conflicts of interests among a society's sub-segments.

THE COMMON DOMAIN OF SOCIAL POLICIES

Comparative, cross-cultural studies of "social policies," in American society and others throughout the world, and throughout the history of mankind, suggest that, despite variety in substance and scope, all such policies are indeed concerned with an underlying common domain. Whether in a concrete and specific sense these policies deal with any of such matters as the following—economic assistance to the poor; levying of taxes; protection of children, the aging, or the handicapped; training of manpower and regulation of working conditions; provision of housing, health care, and education; prevention and control of crime, and rehabilitation of offenders; protection of consumers; regulation of industry, commerce, and agriculture; preservation of natural resources, etc.,—in an abstract and general sense they are all dealing with one or more of the following interrelated elements of societal existence:

    a. the overall quality of life in a society;

    b. the circumstances of living of individuals and groups; and

    c. the nature of intra-societal human relations among individuals, groups, and society as a whole.

These elements constitute, therefore, the general sphere of concern, the common domain, or, in systems terms, the "output" of a society's system of social policies. They are consequently the core-elements of the proposed, universally valid conceptual model of all social policies. There is ample evidence that every human society designs policies to shape or "regulate" this general domain. Indeed, no human society could survive for long if it left the regulation of this domain to the forces of nature and of chance events, and did not attempt to influence it consistently through human-designed measures.

It should be noted also that economic factors are intrinsic aspects of the common domain of social policies as defined here, since they are important determinants of the overall quality of life in a society, the circumstances of living of its members, and their relations to each other and to society as a whole. Economic policies are included among "social policies" as they are important means for attaining ends in the social policy domain. By including economic issues within the domain of social policies, the widespread conceptual confusion resulting from the arbitrary division between economic and social policies can be avoided.

THE KEY PROCESSES OF SOCIAL POLICIES

Having identified the common domain of all social policies, the general processes by which social policies influence this domain must now be explained. These processes constitute the dynamic components of the conceptual model, for through them and their derivatives societies manage to shape the overall quality of life, the circumstances of living, and the nature of human relations. It seems that in spite of apparently unlimited diversity of the substantive provisions of social policies of different societies, at different times, they can all be reduced to one or more of the following interrelated universal processes:

1. Development of material or symbolic life-sustaining and life-enhancing resources;
2. Division of labor, or allocation of individuals and groups to specific "statuses" within the total array of societal tasks and functions, involving corresponding roles, and prerogatives intrinsic to these roles;
3. Distribution to individuals and groups of specific rights to material and symbolic life-sustaining and life-enhancing resources, goods and services through general or specific entitlements, "status"-specific rewards, and general or specific constraints.

The universality of these key processes derives from their origin in certain intrinsic characteristics of the human condition, namely, man's bio-psychological drive to survive, the necessity to organize human labor in order to obtain scarce life-sustaining resources from the natural environment, and the need to devise some system and principles for distributing these life-sustaining resources throughout a society. It is obvious that the overall quality of life of a society depends largely on its interaction with its natural setting and on the quality and quantity of resources, goods and services it generates through investing human labor into its environment. Clearly, also, the circumstances of living of individuals and groups, and their relations with each other and with society as a whole, depend largely on their specific positions or "statuses" within the total array of societal tasks and functions, and on their specific share of, or rights to, concrete and symbolic resources within the totality of those available for distribution by each society. Processes of resource development, status allocation, and rights distribution, and the interactions between these processes are consequently the underlying key variables of all social policies, and thus constitute the dynamic elements of the proposed conceptual model. The possibilities of variation in the way these processes operate and interact in different societies at different times are numerous, and so are the variations of specific social policies and of entire systems of such policies. Any specific social policy reflects one unique position on one or more of these key variables, and one unique configuration of interaction between them. Changes of policies and of systems of policies depend, therefore, on changes on one or more of these underlying key variables and in the relations between them. Desired modification in human relations, in the quality of life, and in the circumstances of living can therefore be achieved by means of appropriate modifications of one or more of these key variables of social policies. This proposition implies the frequently disregarded corollary, that significant changes in human relations and in the quality and the circumstances of life will occur only when a society is willing to introduce significant modifications in the scope and quality of the resources it develops, and in the criteria by which it allocates statuses, and distributes rights to its members. Social policies which involve little or no modification of these key variables and their interactions can therefore not be expected to result in significant changes of a given status quo with respect to the quality and the circumstances of life and the human relations in a society. Antipoverty policies during the sixties in American society are telling illustrations of this obvious fact. These policies introduced merely minor changes in resource development and in the distribution of rights and the allocation of statuses to deprived segments of the population, and thus failed to produce the promised changes in the quality and circumstances of life and in human relations. They turned out to be merely new variations on an old theme.

It should also be noted that "social problems" perceived by various groups in a society concerning the quality and the circumstances of life, or intra-societal human relations, must be understood as intended or unintended consequences of the existing configuration of social policies. Such policies are therefore viewed not only as potential solutions to specified social problems, but all past and extant social policies of a society are considered to be causally related to the various social problems perceived by its members at any point in time. This conceptualization of the relationship between social policies and social problems does not negate the significance of specific policies as potential solutions to perceived problems. Rather, it provides an expanded theoretical basis for the proposition that valid solutions of social problems require appropriate modifications of the key processes of social policies. Such modifications are viewed as potentially powerful instruments of planned, comprehensive and systematic social change, rather than merely as reactive measures designed to ameliorate specified undesirable phenomena in an ad hoc, fragmented fashion.

Limitations of space prevent further discussion and illustration of the theoretical and practical aspects of the key elements of the conceptual model of social policies and of their interactions. However, some observations seem essential concerning the linkage between status allocation and rights distribution. Many human societies, including American society, distribute many rights as rewards for status incumbency. This linkage between the distribution of rights and the allocation of statuses tends to result in considerable inequality of rights among incumbents of different statuses. It is important to note in this context that while differences in status are clearly an essential aspect of task organization in a society, once division of labor has been adopted in the course of societal evolution, inequality of rights is logically not an essential consequence of such differences in status. Many societies, including several "socialist" ones, have, however, adopted inequality of rights as if it were an essential corollary of the division of labor, and have institutionalized inequality of rewards for different statuses. From a theoretical perspective it is, of course, entirely feasible to distribute rights equally among all members of a society by means of universal entitlements, irrespective of status. Such a principle of rights distribution would be reflected in independence of rights and statuses. Any intermediate level of linkage between rights distribution and status allocation is theoretically feasible, and can be designed in practice.

The linkage of rights distribution to status allocation is usually rationalized and justified with reference to incentives and human motivation. It is claimed axiomatically that in order to recruit personnel for the diversity of statuses in a society, prospective incumbents must be attracted through incentives built into the reward system. While this may be a fairly accurate description of current human behavior, it does not explain the sources and dynamics underlying this response pattern, nor does it answer the important question whether this response pattern is biologically determined and thus the only behavioral possiblity.

Biological, psychological, and sociological research indicates that human motivation is a function of biologically given factors and socially learned tendencies. The relative importance of these two sets of factors is not known, but there seems to be little question that learned tendencies are a powerful force in human behavior. It therefore seems that existing patterns of motivation and incentive response reflect existing patterns of socialization, and that variations in these socialization patterns could produce over time different motivational attitudes and response patterns. This suggests that the patterns of human motivation used to justify the structured inequalities in the distribution of rights in most existing societies are not fixed by nature, but are open to modification by means of variations in the process of socialization. The view that man responds primarily to the profit motive is not necessarily a correct indication of mankind's social and cultural potential.

THE FORCE FIELD AFFECTING AND CONSTRAINING THE EVOLUTION OF SOCIAL POLICIES

The processes of resource development, status allocation, and rights distribution are themselves subject to the influences of certain natural and societal forces. The various forces are identified in Chart 1.

CHART 1. NATURAL AND SOCIETAL FORCES LIMITING, INFLUENCING, AND INTERACTING WITH THE KEY PROCESSES AND GENERAL DOMAIN OF SOCIAL POLICIES.

Limiting Conditions	Intra- and Inter-Societal Force Field	Constraining Variables	Social Policies	
			Key Processes	Common Domain
Physical and biological properties of a society's natural setting	Intra-societal interest group conflicts			
	Society's stage of development in cultural, economic, and technological spheres	Beliefs	Resource development	Overall quality of life
Biological and basic psychological properties of man		Values	Status allocation	Circumstances of living of individuals
	Size and institutional differentiation and complexity of society	Ideologies	Rights distribution	and groups
		Customs		Intra-societal human relations
	Personal, cultural, economic and political interaction with extrasocietal forces	Traditions		

Note: The forces represented in this chart do not exert their influence merely in a linear progression from left to right, but interact with each other in multiple and circular ways.

The physical and biological characteristics of a society's natural environment are limiting conditions with respect to the development and distribution of life-sustaining resources. Man's own biological and psychological properties affect his capacities and his motivation, his interaction with other men, and the organization of his work, and hence indirectly the key processes of resource development and rights distribution.

Societal forces affecting the evolution of social policies are traceable to man's collective response to the universal characteristics of the human condition as sketched above. Over time these responses resulted in the following significant social developments: the evolution of division of labor and of systems of social stratification based on this; the evolution of the principle of unequal rewards linked to different statuses and roles; the emerging interest of individuals and groups in perpetuating advantages accruing to them as a result of the patterned inequalities in the allocation of statuses and the distribution of rights; and the evolution of the principles of storing and accumulating surplus rewards, and transmitting them to one's offspring.

The emergence and interplay of these principles and tendencies, and the reactions to them of competing interest groups within societies seem to constitute major dynamics of the evolutionary, and at times revolutionary development of human societies and their social policies. Social policies may thus be viewed as dynamic expressions of the evolving structures and conflicts of societies; they are derived from them and in turn support the structures and spur the conflicts. Once initiated, the processes of societal evolution, and the parallel processes of social policy evolution, continue as a result of ceaseless conflicts of interest among individuals and social groups who control different levels of resources, and who differ consequently in rights and power. The processes of social policy evolution are also affected by, and in turn affect, a society's stage of development in the cultural, economic, and technological spheres; its size and its level of institutional differentiation and complexity; its interaction with extra-societal forces; and its values, beliefs, customs, and traditions.

VALUES AND SOCIAL POLICIES

The dominant beliefs and values of a society and the customs and traditions derived from them exert a significant influence on all decisions concerning the three key processes of social policies.

Consequently, any specific configuration of these processes and the resulting systems of social policies tend to reflect the dominant value positions of a society concerning such policy relevant dimensions as individualism—collectivism, competition—collaboration, inequality—equality, etc. A society's dominant beliefs and values appear thus to constitute crucial constraining variables which limit the malleability of its processes of resource development, status allocation and rights distribution, and of the social policies derived from these processes. Thus a society which stresses individualism, pursuit of self-interest, and com-petitiveness, and which has come to consider inequality of circumstances of living and of rights as a natural order of human existence, will tend to preserve structured inequalities through its processes of status allocation and rights distribution, while one which stresses collective values and cooperation and which is truly committed to the early American notion that "all men are created equal," will tend to develop a system of social policies which assure to all its members equal access to all statuses, and equal rights to material and symbolic life-sustaining and life-enhancing resources, goods and services.

While dwelling briefly on the central importance of beliefs and values for social policy analysis and development, it should be noted that public discussion of such policies in the United States tends to neglect this crucial variable. Instead, major, and often exclusive, emphasis tends to be placed on technical matters and on means, while the goals and values aimed at are pushed to the background. Technical matters are indeed important, and al-ternative means need to be evaluated in terms of effectiveness and efficiency. However, unless goals and values are clear, and are constantly kept in mind as main criteria for policy evaluation and development, the examination of means and of technologies is merely an exercise in futility.

While beliefs, values, customs, and traditions are not fixed forever in any human society, changing them is usually not a simple matter. The dominant beliefs and values of societies tend to be shaped and guarded by cultural and political elites re-cruited mainly from among their more powerful and privileged strata. Not unexpectedly, these beliefs and values seem therefore to reflect and support the interests of these more powerful and privileged social groups. It should be noted, however, that some members of cultural and political elites are recruited from less privileged strata and may represent their interests. Also, not all those members who originated in more privileged social groups are necessarily committed forever to the self-perceived, narrowly conceptualized, short-range interests of their groups of origin. Cultural elites can and often will develop comprehensive, broadly-based, long-range conceptions of societal interests. There is consequently always a potential for change in the dominant beliefs and values of societies, and in social policies, whose malleability seems limited by them. In any case, it needs to be emphasized in this context that significant changes are not likely to occur in a society's system of social policies without thorough changes in its dominant beliefs and values.

ANALYSIS AND DEVELOPMENT OF SOCIAL POLICIES[1]

Social policy analysis is a systematic, scientific process, whose purpose is to obtain valid and reliable information concerning specified societal issues, and the chain of consequences of specific policies designed to deal with them. Social policy development utilizes policy analysis in order to design alternative policies to achieve identical objectives more effectively or efficiently, or to achieve different objectives derived from different value premises. Policy evolution takes place in a political context, which needs to be considered as a significant variable in policy analysis and development, but political processes should not be confused with these. Effectiveness of social and political action can, however, be enhanced through insights derived from the conceptual model in the analysis of social policies.

Valid and reliable analysis of social policies requires considerable resources, including analysts competent in the several social and behavioral sciences and knowledgeable about the substantive issues dealt with by specific policies. Access to a variety of data concerning a population is also essential. In many instances though it may be sufficient to carry out abbreviated analyses. However, whether a comprehensive or an abbreviated analysis is conducted, all relevant analytic foci derived from the conceptual model and the forcefield surrounding policy evolution should be considered.

Before specific social policies can be analyzed or developed, or their adequacy evaluated, the relevant issues need to be clarified. Issues should be defined whenever possible with reference to the common domain of all social policies rather than in terms of specific policies and their provisions.

Policy analysis itself is to be carried out on three levels: first on that of substantive policy context, next on the social structural level, and finally on the societal forcefield level.

The first level of analysis involves specification of overt and covert policy objectives with reference to the issues dealt with, of policy relevant value premises underlying these objectives, and of theories underlying the strategy and the substantive provisions of a policy. This level also involves description of target segments of the population in qualitative and quantitative terms, and exploration of short- and long-range intended and unintended effects on target and non-target segments of the population. Finally, this level examines the extent to which policy objectives are being realized, and the overall costs and benefits of policy implementation.

The second level of analysis is derived from the conceptual model of social policies and is designed to discern implications of a policy for the structure of a society and for its entire system of social policies. It therefore aims to identify changes due to the policy in a society's development of resources, in the criteria it uses for status allocation and rights distribution, in the overall quality of life, in the circumstances of living of individuals and groups, and in the quality of human relations among its members.

The third level of analysis explores interaction effects between specific policies and the forces surrounding their development and implementation.[2] This is of special relevance for predicting the fate of given policies within a given societal context. It also reviews the history of a policy and the political forces in a society which promote or resist it.

Utilizing the conceptual model of social policies in the development of alternative policies involves determination of the nature and scope of changes which must be made in the key policy variables of resource development, status allocation, and rights distribution in order to attain selected policy objectives. These changes are then transformed into substantive program elements and are incorporated into newly generated policies. It should be emphasized again that specified policy objectives depend for their realization on specific configurations of the manner of operation of the key variables and that unless these configurations are attained by means of appropriate modifications of such variables the objectives can simply not be realized.

This abstract statement can be illustrated by a concrete example, namely, the repeated failures of policies which attempt to eliminate poverty in the United States without significantly modifying the configurations of key variables, of which poverty is an inescapable consequence. Poverty is viewed in this context as an income and wealth distribution which limits certain segments of the population to levels of command over resources, goods and services below a level defined as "sufficient" by society. In the United States this level of sufficiency is measured by the Bureau of Labor Statistics through its "Standard of Living" series. On this standard the level of annual income necessary to maintain a "low" standard of living for a family of four in the spring of 1970 was close to $7000. Obviously, poverty, as defined here, can be eliminated only by social policies which result in redistribution of purchasing power or of access to services and provisions so that all families would reach at least the level of the BLS low standard of living. Policies which do not aim to achieve this scope of redistribution of income- and wealth-related rights will do many things but will keep poverty and its destructive side effects intact.

Policy development also involves comparision and evaluation of alternative policies generated in relation to given issues. Different policies should be examined in terms of value premises, intended effects, the extent to which objectives are attained, implications for social structure and for the entire system of social policy, unintended effects, and overall costs and benefits. On the basis of these comparisons and evaluations preferred policies can be selected in terms of specified criteria which will obviously depend on one's value premises and political objectives.

IMPLICATIONS FOR SOCIAL AND POLITICAL ACTION

Let us consider the implications for social and political action of the theoretical position presented here. Social policies of a society are the product of continuous interaction among a complex set of forces, no one of which can be identified as the primary causal set. Social and political action aimed at changing the "social policy output" of a society can therefore be directed justifiably at any one of the contributing forces. Different intervention theories and the philosophical premises of different change-oriented individuals and groups will therefore lead to different intervention strategies.

One appropriate focus for intervention in terms of a non-violent change strategy, based on man's capacity for reasoned judgment of verifiable facts, is the system of beliefs and values of a society. It has been suggested earlier that such values exert a constraining influence on the malleability of its social policy system. Therefore, if policy changes are sought beyond the range set by existing value premises, these premises need to undergo change so as to widen the scope of policy options.

Changing a society's dominant value premises is, of course, a complicated undertaking, at best, since these values pervade all aspects of its culture, its institutional structure and its system of socialization. Social and behavioral sciences offer only uncertain guiding principles for value change. However, self-interest, as perceived by the majority of a population, probably provides energy for maintaining, as well as for modifying, a society's system of values. Changes in dominant values may therefore follow changes in the perceptions of self-interest of large segments of a society. Accordingly, a crucial issue to be raised and examined by groups interested in radical change of the American social policy system by way of thorough modifications of its dominant value premises, is whether the existing premises are conducive to the realization of the self-interest of the American people. Major policy relevant values in this context are the commitment to rugged individualism, competitiveness, and inequality of rights and opportunities. Characteristic features of the policy system reflecting these value commitments are attitudes and practices of exploitation towards the natural environment and towards human beings, inequalities in circumstances of living of members and groups of society, and a high incidence of alienation in human experience and relations. The question then is whether these values and these policies serve the true interests of Americans. These values and policies obviously fail to serve the interests of deprived segments of the population. Their very state of deprivation and exploitation provides sufficient evidence, their own perceptions notwithstanding. The question is consequently reduced to a consideration of the self-interest of privileged segments of the population.

Before considering, however, the extent of realization of self-interest among the privileged it may help to get some sense of the scope of deprivation in America's affluent society. If one uses the BLS low standard of living as a rough index of deprivation, one finds that approximately one-third of the American population is deprived in a material sense, for their purchasing power is below the BLS low standard of living. Furthermore, over half of the population live on incomes below the BLS "intermediate" standard, which in 1970 was $10,664. No doubt then, the real self-interests of the majority of the population, the deprived and near-deprived segments, would benefit from policy changes aimed at eliminating their deprived circumstances by truly equalizing rights and opportunities for all.

Turning to the roughly 40% of the population who constitute the non-deprived and privileged segments one realizes that material affluence in itself does not assure a satisfactory quality of life and realization of self-interest. The American middle and upper classes seem to be in a stage of social and cultural crisis. This statement could be supported with ample evidence, but space and time being limited it should suffice to mention the serious drug problems and the alienation and revolt of middle and upper class youth. These are, no doubt, symptoms of a generation in crisis. The conclusion suggested is that America's privileged classes fail under current conditions to realize their true self-interest just as the deprived classes fail to realize theirs. The existing system of social policies and its underlying value premises seem to have destructive consequences for all segments of society. Accordingly, major changes in values and in the social policies derived from them would seem to be in the true interest of the whole society. The commitment to rugged individualism, competitiveness and inequality seems detrimental to the well-being of all, the deprived and the privileged, and those in between.

This brief analysis suggests that groups interested in non-violent, yet radical, change of values and policies should engage in active political interpretation and education intended to clarify the real, underlying human interests of the vast majority, and perhaps the entire population. Such political education would have to be factual and honest, rather than manipulative, in the sense of building coalitions and gaining political support on false premises by means of inadequate information and limited comprehension of reality, and on an emotional, non-rational basis.

This leads to the tentative conclusion that workers in human service fields may choose to redefine their intervention role as political education, irrespective of the settings in which they function. This conclusion seems unavoidable as one realizes that social problems are the products of extant social policies which must be changed radically if the problems are to be erradicated, that changing these policies requires changing society's value premises, and that such change depends in turn on revisions in the perceptions of the majority of the population with respect to their true self-interest. Redefining the role of human services personnel as agents of political education raises the possibility of conflict between them and their employing organizations, all of which are linked to the existing social system, its policies and its value premises. The solution to this dilemma derives from the concept of individual responsibility for ethical action. Those who wish to assume the function of political education must become focal points of an emerging counter culture within the organizations for which they work.[3]

APPENDIX: FRAMEWORK FOR SOCIAL POLICY ANALYSIS AND SYNTHESIS

Section A: The Issues Dealt with by the Policy

1. Nature, scope and distribution of the issues
2. Causal theory(ies) or hypothesis(es) concerning the dynamics of the issues

Section B: Objectives, Value Premises, Theoretical Positions, Target Segments and Substantive Effects of the Policy

1. Policy objectives
2. Value premises and ideological orientations underlying the policy objectives
3. Theory or hypothesis underlying the strategy and the substantive provisions of the policy
4. Target segment(s) of society—those at whom the policy is aimed:
   a. Ecological, demographic, biological, psychological, social, economic, political, and cultural characteristics
   b. Numerical size of relevant sub-groups and of entire target segment(s) projected over time
5. Short- and long-range effects of the policy on target and non-target segment(s) of the society in ecological, demographic, biological, psychological, social, economic, political, and cultural spheres:
   a. Intended effects and extent of attainment of policy objectives
   b. Unintended effects
   c. Overall costs and benefits

Section C: Implications of the Policy for the Key Processes and the Common Domain of Social Policies

1. Changes in the development of life-sustaining and life-enhancing material and symbolic resources, goods and services:
   a. qualitative changes
   b. quantitative changes
   c. changes in priorities
2. Changes in the allocation of individuals and groups, to specific statuses within the total array of societal tasks and functions:
   a. Development of new statuses, roles, and prerogatives
   b. Strengthening and protection of existing statuses, roles, and prerogatives
   c. Elimination of existing statuses, roles, and prerogatives
   d. Changes in the criteria and procedures for selection and assignment of individuals and groups to statuses
3. Changes in the distribution of rights to individuals and groups:
   a. Changes in the quality and quantity of general and specific entitlements, status-specific rewards, and general and specific constraints
   b. Changes in the proportion of rights distributed as general or specific entitlements and as status-specific rewards respectively, or in the extent to which the distribution of rights is linked to the allocation of statuses
   c. Changes in the proportion of rights distributed directly, in kind, in the form of public provisions and services, and rights distributed indirectly, as right equivalents, purchasing power or money
   d. Changes in the specifications of a minimum level of rights for all members and groups of society (e.g., "official poverty line," or "fixed percentage of per capita income"), and in the extent to which the distribution of rights assures coverage of such a minimum level
   e. Changes in the relative distribution of rights throughout society, or in the degree of inequality of rights among individuals and groups
4. Consequences of changes in resource development, status allocation, and rights distribution for:
   a. the overall quality of life in society, and

    b. the circumstances of living of individuals and groups, as noted in measurements and perceptions of ecological, demographic, biological, psychological, social, economic, political, and cultural dimensions or spheres

    c. the nature of intra-societal human relations among individuals, groups, and society as a whole

Section D: Interaction Effects Between the Policy and Forces Surrounding its Development and Implementation

1. History of the policy's development and implementation, including legislative, administrative, and judicial aspects

2. Political forces in society promoting or resisting the policy prior to and following its enactment—their type, size, organizational structure, resources, overall strength, extent of interest, value premises, and ideological orientations

3. Physical and biological properties of society's natural setting, and biological and psychological properties of its members

4. Relevant other social policies

5. Relevant foreign policies and extra-societal forces

6. Society's stage of development in cultural, economic, and technological spheres

7. Society's size and institutional differentiation or complexity

8. Society's beliefs, values, ideologies, customs, and traditions

9. Conclusions and predictions

Section E: Development of Alternative Social Policies; Comparison and Evaluation

1. Specification of alternative social policies:
    a. aimed at the same policy objectives, but involving alternative policy measures
    b. aimed at different policy objectives concerning the same policy issues

2. Comparison and evaluation:
Each alternative social policy should be analyzed in accordance with this framework, and compared throughout this analysis with the original policy and other alternative policies

CHAPTER THREE

Social Policies and Social Development*

We must now explore the relationship of social policies and of policy-relevant societal values to social development. The thesis of this essay is that the scope, direction, and quality of the social development process are largely shaped by the social policies and the dominant value positions of societies.

Social scientists and others using the concepts *social policies and social development* attach different meanings to them. We begin, therefore, with an explication of my conceptions of these terms and of the societal processes to which they refer. I will first specify the value position from which my conceptions derive.

This value position I summarize as follows: All humans, everywhere, despite their manifold differences and their uniqueness as individuals, should be considered of equal intrinsic worth. Hence they should be deemed entitled to equal social, economic, civil, and political rights, liberties, and obligations. Societal institutions on local and trans-local levels, should assure and facilitate the

*Reprinted with permission from *The Journal of Sociology and Social Welfare*, Vol. 3, No. 3, January 1976.

exercise of these equal rights, and the free, autonomous, and authentic development of all humans. All humans should be considered "subjects," none should be treated as "objects" or "means." Hence no human should dominate, control, and exploit other humans.

Socially structured equality should not be interpreted, simplistically, as arithemtic equality or uniformity. Rather, it is to be understood as a guiding principle to be implemented creatively through flexible institutions, designed to assure to all humans throughout the life-cycle satisfaction of their unique needs, and actualization of their unique individuality, subject to constraints implicit in population size, aggregate wealth, and level of overall development.

SOCIAL POLICIES[1]

Social policies may be thought of as clusters of rules or as institutionalized guiding principles maintaining a social order. These rules and principles evolved throughout the history of human groups. They reflect choices and decisions made by successive generations striving to satisfy basic biological and emerging social and psychological needs as they pursued survival in the context of relative scarcities. Social policies reflect stages in human evolution beyond total dependence on instinctual dynamics and randomness in human behavior and relations. They represent significant steps beyond the trial-and-error stage of the struggle for survival. Social policies are products of the human capacity to reflect on experience and reality and on the existential imperatives encountered by all human groups, to devise systematic answers to these imperatives, and to pass these answers on from generation to generation. Eventually, social policies evolved into patterns or blueprints for societal existence, organization, and continuity.

With time, social policies, like other products of the human mind which are transmitted among generations and experienced in the course of socialization as social reality, tended to take on a life and dynamics of their own, and to exist independently of the humans whose choices created them. Consequently, social policies confront subsequent generations as powerful forces that shape life and reality and that act as constraining influences on the development of new approaches to the solution of existential problems. Their sources are no longer remembered, and the more independence they acquire with time, the more resistant to change they are likely to become. Frequently, they are not even identified as social policies but are referred to as "customs" and "traditions." Quite often, also, they are viewed as "laws of nature," as eternal and inevitable and not subject to critique and change by a present generation.

Yet humans in any generation ought to realize that behind any particular set of social policies are human choices at certain stages of history, choices which produced one possible model for organizing human existence and survival based on insights and knowledge available at the time. The choices made, and the patterns resulting from them may not have been the best possible answers even at the time they were made, nor are they necessarily the best pattern for subsequent generations including the present one. Hence, optimally, each generation should claim its right and responsibility to reexamine transmitted social policies in the light of present circumstances and knowledge, and in relation to currently held values which may differ from the value premises underlying past choices.

As for substance, social policies always represent solutions to the following fundamental, existential problems which any human group must resolve in some way:

1. What resources to select for development from the natural environment in order to assure survival and to enhance the quality of life?

2. How to organize the production of goods and services needed for survival and the enhancement of the quality of life; or, more specifically, how to design and maintain a division of labor, including preparation of individuals for, and their allocation to, specific sets of work tasks so as to assure a smooth performance of all the work necessary for generating the goods and services deemed needed by society?

3. How to divide or distribute among members of society the aggregate product of their aggregate labor, the goods and services generated for survival and for the enhancement of the quality of life; and, related to the distribution of concrete goods and services, how to distribute among members of society honor and prestige, civil liberties, and political rights?

As a society develops and, over time, institutionalizes specific solutions to these fundamental, existential issues, it determines, indirectly, the circumstances of living of every individual member, and of every group. For the circumstances of living of individuals and groups are largely a function of the activities they engage in, or the work roles they perform, the concrete goods and services they receive, and the honor, prestige, civil liberties and political rights they may claim. Furthermore, in shaping the circumstances of living of individuals and groups, social policies also determine the nature and quality of human relations in a society, since reciprocal relations among individuals and groups tend to be a function of their respective roles and rights. Finally, the overall quality of life, or the existential milieu prevailing in a society, is also shaped by its social policies since that quality may be understood as the aggregate of individual circumstances of living, the resulting quality of human relations, and the quality of the environment which, in turn, results from the interactions of humans with their natural habitat.

Summarizing then, social policies are conceived of here as rules or guiding principles for maintaining a social order. They reflect choices and decisions evolved over time concerning the selection and development of life-sustaining and enhancing resources from the environment; the division of labor or allocation of work statuses and roles in a society's aggregate system of work and production; and the distribution of goods and services, honor and prestige, civil liberties and political rights. Together, through their interactions, these developmental, allocative, and distributive decisions and processes shape the circumstances of living of individuals and groups, the quality of human relations, and the overall quality of life or the existential milieu of a society.

VALUES

A second concept which requires explication here is that of values. Theodorson's *Modern Dictionary of Sociology* defines a value as

An abstract, generalized principle of behavior to which the members of a group feel a strong, emotionally toned positive commitment and which provides a standard for judging specific acts and goals . . .

. . . they are often regarded as absolute, although the formation and apprehension of values evolve in the normal process of social interaction . . .[2]

Values may also be thought of as early layers of social policies. Their origin, evolution, and dynamics are nearly identical to those of all social policies. They differ, however, from other social policies in the level of generality and abstraction, and in the extent to which their origin in human choice is no longer realized. The sources of values are frequently projected onto non-human, supernatural powers.

Analysis of the substantive content of many values suggests that they derive from basic choices compatible with the perceived interests of entire societies, and/or the perceived interests of groups who gained influence, power, dominance, and control over the rest of society. Eventually, values evolve into powerful factors legitimating established interests and maintaining the status-quo of social orders which is shaped by these interests. Values are usually guarded and disseminated by priestly and other elites involved in processes of socialization and social control. Over time clusters of related and mutually reinforcing values became integrated into internally coherent ideological systems, which constitute constraints on, and often insurmountable barriers to, the malleability of social policies and social orders. Social policies will generally conform to prevailing ideologies and to particular constructions of social reality implicit in such ideologies, and, in turn, will reinforce the ideologies as decisive forces in society.

In studying social policies and their relationship to social development one need not concern oneself with every possible value, but only with value dimensions which are likely to affect developmental, allocative, and distributive decisions, decisions which have been identified in the preceding discussion as the key-processes of social policies. Values influencing these key-processes may be appropriately referred to as social-policy-relevant value dimensions.

The most significant value dimension from a social policy perspective is that of equality-inequality. In developing resources, a society may assign equal or unequal importance to the needs of all its members and segments. It may design a system of division of labor, and may allocate work roles within that system on the basis of equal or unequal access and assignment. And finally, it may distribute goods and services, honor and prestige, and civil liberties and political rights on equal terms as universal entitlements to all, or, on unequal terms, as differential rewards for different role and status clusters, access to which is restricted differentially.

Whether or not a society will employ equalitarian criteria in its developmental, allocative, and distributional decisions will depend on its concept of humans: Does it consider all individuals to be intrinsically of equal worth in spite of their uniqueness, and hence entitled to the same social, economic, civil, and political rights; or do individuals in the society consider themselves, and those close to themselves, of greater worth than anyone else, and hence entitled to more desirable or privileged circumstances. The former egalitarian philosophy would be reflected in institutional arrangements involving cooperative actions in pursuit of common existential interests. All individuals would be considered and treated as equally entitled subjects who could not be exploited and dominated by other individuals or groups, and whose rights to develop their individuality freely and fully would be assured and respected, subject to the same rights of all others. The latter, non-egalitarian philosophy, on the other hand, is reflected in institutional structures which encourage competitive behavior in pursuit of narrowly perceived, egotistical interests. All individuals and groups strive to get ahead of others, consider themselves entitled to privileged conditions and positions, and view and treat others as potential means to be used, exploited, and dominated in pursuit of egotistical goals.

It should be noted here that the value dimension equality-inequality is not a continuous one, for while there are degrees of inequality which may be increased or decreased, there are no degrees of equality. A distribution or allocation is either equal or unequal, and humans may be deemed equal or unequal in intrinsic worth. Therefore, the notion of "more equality" which is used frequently in political discourse by reform-minded persons is intrinsically self-contradictory. Inequality, on the other hand, is a continuous dimension and it is, therefore, appropriate to speak of increases or decreases in inequality. This distinction is important in order to avoid confusion in political thought and action, and in order not to interpret the advocacy of "more equality" as commitment to equality. More equality merely means a different level of inequality: it is thus a veiled commitment to the perpetuation of the guiding principles of inequality and privilege.

Two additional value dimensions need to be considered here because of their relevance to developmental, allocative, and distributional processes:

Cooperation—competition; and

Collectivity-orientation—self-orientation.

These two dimensions are related to, and interact with each other. They are also related to, and interact with the value dimension, equality-inequality. However, the relations among these three dimensions are not fixed. They vary in different societies and at different times in the same society.

The dimensions cooperation—competition and collectivity-orientation—self-orientation are continuous variables, which means that societies may be located at extreme or intermediate positions with reference to these dimensions. The dominant value orientations of specific societies usually involve unique combinations of cooperation and competition, and of collectivity-orientation and self-orientation in the context of equality or different levels of inequality. Different societies may thus be visualized as located at different positions in a three-dimensional value space.

Collectivity-orientation, it should be noted, is not a negation of individuality and self-actualization. It is however, a negation of "rugged individualism," which is a value orientation that disregards the rights of others to self-actualization. Collectivity-orientation may, in fact, be a necessary, though not sufficient, condition for the full and free development of everyone's individuality.[3]

SOCIAL DEVELOPMENT

Based on the conceptions of social policies and of social-policy-relevant value dimensions presented here, social development may be thought of as a specific configuration of social policies, chosen consciously by a population in accordance with egalitarian, cooperative, and collectivity-oriented value premises, aimed at enhancing systematically:

- the overall quality of life or the existential milieu of the entire society;
- the circumstances of living of all individual members and segments of the society; and
- the quality of all human relations.

Understood in this way, social development involves philosophical, biological, ecological, psychological, social, economic, and political dimensions. In contradistinction to conventional, yet by now outdated, notions of economic growth and development, the central criterion for evaluating social development is evenly shared, balanced progress of the entire population of a region, or of the globe, towards enhanced collective, segmental, and individual wellbeing. Genuine social development seems, therefore, predicated upon the conscious acceptance, and systematic implementation, of a configuration of developmental, allocative, and distributive social policies, the interaction and combined effects of which would be conducive to the comprehensive objectives specified here.

SOCIAL POLICIES FOR SOCIAL DEVELOPMENT

First among social policy clusters essential for social development is the identification, selection, and development of an appropriate range and mix of resources, sufficient in quantity and suitable in quality, to satisfy the basic biological and the social and psychological needs of the entire population. Policies for resource selection and development should preclude greedy, exploitative relations to the habitat of a population, as well as all forms of waste and destruction of real wealth which consists of land, water, wildlife, vegetation, natural raw materials, humans and human products. Such policies would involve effective measures for conservation and recycling of the natural resource basis of life while deriving sustenance from that base. Related to these policies would also be measures aimed at achieving and maintaining a dynamic balance of natural resources, the prevailing scientific and technological capacity to produce life-sustaining and enhancing goods from these resources, and the size of the population.

Next, social development is predicated upon policies conducive to effective and efficient organization of productive processes for the transformation of natural resources by means of human creativity and labor into the goods and services required to sustain and enhance the life of the population. Policies organizing the productive processes include also policies dealing with the education and preparation of society's "human capital," the release and development of the available creative physical and intellectual potential of people of all ages. Policies in this domain must also deal with the conservation, maintenance, and renewal of means of production, and with the allocation and investment of human resources and capital to the various branches of production. There is also need for policies concerning the size and location of productive units, the scope of production in various branches and units, the manner in which production and production units are controlled, and production decisions are made by those working in the units and by various local, regional, and transregional groups and institutions. Finally policies are needed to facilitate cooperation, coordination, integration, exchange, and joint planning among the separate production units, branches of production, the aggregate productive enterprise in a region, and units, branches, and aggregate economies in other regions all over the globe.

Since, by definition, social development is concerned with enhancing qualitative aspects of human existence, as much as it is concerned with quantitative aspects of production, it is predicated also on policies resulting in a division of labor that is cooperative rather than competitive, psychologically enriching rather than alienating, non-exploitative, flexible, and fair. Such a division of labor would also involve equal recognition and equal rewards for every type of work, and whenever feasible, rotation of workers among roles which differ in intrinsic rewards. Finally, such a division of labor would involve equal rights for all to participate in the productive enterprise of society, and hence would eliminate the absurdity, so prevalent in competitive, profit-motivated societies, of unemployment of workers, land, and plants while human needs remain unmet, and production is out of step with these needs.

Needless to say, social development, as conceived here, is also predicated upon flexible, egalitarian distribution to all members and segments of society of the concrete wealth produced by their labor, upon equal access to the human services a society administers, upon equal civil liberties and political rights, and upon equal recognition, honor, and prestige. It follows that implicit in genuine social development are patterns of role allocation and rights distribution which conform to the notion "to each according to need, from each according to capacity."

Finally, social development is predicated upon avoidance of exploitation and domination of humans and natural resources in other parts of the globe. All forms of exploitation and domination beyond a given society's boundaries inevitably negate and destroy internal processes of social development since foreign exploitation and domination always involve exploitative and domineering human relations within a society by powerful, ruling elites toward large segments of their own people. Internal and external exploitation and oppression complement and reinforce each other. They are manifestations of the same underlying principles and dynamics, to wit: a commitment to inequality, and hence, a readiness to use other humans as means or objects in the greedy pursuit of hegemony, privilege, and profit for oneself, one's tribe, or one's nation. Genuine social development can never result from such attitudes and actions, only imbalanced pseudo-development—illusions or caricatures of true social development. The alienating and oppressive internal milieu of societies which were, or are, practicing colonial or neo-colonial exploitation and oppression, reflects these contradictions. It demonstrates the incompatibility between social development, understood as equalitarian enhancement of the quality of life for all, and the practice of exploitation at home and abroad in pursuit of mal-distributed, imbalanced economic growth.

It should be noted here, that while foreign exploitation and domination in any form are imcompatible with genuine social development, foreign trade among societies living in different parts of the globe is not, as long as such trade involves voluntary exchanges of different types of resources on the basis of equality among trading partners. Such exchanges as well as all forms of mutual aid among neighboring and distant peoples are apt to promote the social development of all participants.

There are, of course, conceptions of social development which differ fundamentally in underlying assumptions and values from a humanistic, egalitarian, and democratic conception. Adherents of such alternative conceptions will often acknowledge humanistic, egalitarian, and democratic values as ultimate goals, but will not use these values as guiding principles and evaluative criteria when formulating policies in the present. This avoidance tends to be rationalized as being "realistic and practical," while insisting on social justice here and now is being labeled as "utopian, naive, and impractical." Such realistic and practical approaches to social development mean that, while humans would be treated as equals some time in the future, socially structured and defined inequalities are to be accepted as a given aspect of present reality. They must not be questioned or challenged on a fundamental level, but must be reckoned with, adjusted to, and incorporated into policy formulation for social development. The result of such pragmatic development policies is, at best, an illusion of social development, pursued for the benefit of relatively small, yet economically and politically powerful elite groups, through exploitation and domination of economically and politically powerless majorities of the population.

History all over the world suggests that such "pragmatic" compromise approaches to social development which acquiesce in established inequalities and injustices, do not work, however well-intentioned their advocates may be. They do not work for exploited majorities whose basic needs remain unsatisfied and who continue to be oppressed and alienated. Nor do these approaches work in terms of the real, long-range, human interest of the power-and wealth-controlling minorities. The reason for the failure of these development policies is the intensification of intra-societal conflict which usually accompanies their implementation, and which may be inevitable in view of the economic, social, and psychological dynamics generated in an inegalitarian, competitive context, and its scarcity, zero-sum mentality. The human and economic costs of maintaining an established, in-egalitarian social order tend to increase exponentially in spite of sporadic patchwork efforts to save that order from collapsing. Sooner or later this process tends to reach levels of massive breakdown. To refer to this self-defeating process as social development is, of course, absurd.

The conclusion of these considerations seems inescapable. Social development, like human freedom and dignity, is indivisible. It simply cannot be secured for segments of a population at the price of exploiting and oppressing other segments. It can be achieved only for all together, or for none at all. Either all are free and equal, brothers and sisters in a universal process towards social development, or none will gain freedom and fulfillment.

APPENDIX

The purpose of this Appendix is to present a framework which should be helpful when analyzing actual and newly proposed social policies in terms of their appropriateness for social development as conceived in this essay. The framework should be equally useful in efforts to generate appropriate alternative social policies.

The framework consists of a set of descriptive, analytic, evaluative, and synthetic items, the purpose of which is to discern the consequences of given policies and policy clusters, to examine the extent of correspondence between these consequences and the requirements of social development as articulated in this essay, and when indicated, to generate alternative policies which fit these requirements.

Since social policies differ in scope and focus, not all items of the framework will be relevant in the analysis of every policy. However, while certain items are not applicable to certain policies and would be omitted in an analysis, all social policies and policy clusters can be analyzed in terms of their suitability for social development by following the items of the framework.

FRAMEWORK FOR ANALYSIS AND SYNTHESIS OF SOCIAL POLICIES FOR SOCIAL DEVELOPMENT

A. Descriptive Section:

(1) issues dealt with by the policy; (2) policy objectives; (3) policy-relevant value positions; (4) theoretical premises; (5) population segments at whom the policy is aimed primarily; (6) short and long range, intended and unintended consequences of the policy; (7) investment costs in terms of human and other resources.

B. Analytic Section: Implications of the Policy for Developmental, Allocative, and Distributional Processes

(1) effects on the selection and development of life-sustaining and enhancing resources; (2) effects on the organization of production and the division of labour; (3) effects on the distribution of rights concerning goods and services; recognition, honour, and prestige; civil liberties and political rights; (4) consequences for: the circumstances of living of individuals and groups; the quality of human relations; the aggregate quality of life or existential milieu.

C. Evaluative Section: Correspondence Between Consequences of the Policy and the General Requirements of Social Development

(1) relevance and priority of the issues addressed by the policy, in terms of the criterion of evenly-shared, balanced progress of an entire population toward enhanced individual, segmental, and collective well-being;

(2) correspondence between policy objectives and the general objectives of social development;

(3) correspondence between value positions underlying the policy objectives and the egalitarian, cooperative, and collectivity-oriented value positions upon which genuine social development is predicated;

(4) correspondence between effects of the policy on the selection, development, utilization, and investment of resources and the requirements of social development for balanced, non-wasteful resource development, utilization, and conservation, geared to biological, social and psychological needs of people, and the size of the population;

(5) correspondence between effects of the policy on the organization of production and the quantitative, qualitative, and organizational aspects of production upon which social development is predicated;

(6) correspondence between effects of the policy on the distribution of social, economic, civil, and political rights and the requirement for flexible, egalitarian distribution of these rights;

(7) correspondence between consequences of the policy for the circumstances of living, the quality of human relations, and the aggregate quality of life and the requirement for evenly-shared and balanced progress of the entire population with respect to these dimensions;

(8) correspondence between consequences of the policy for transnational economic and political relations and the requirements of social development for avoidance of exploitation and domination of humans and natural resources in foreign lands and for equalitarian terms of foreign trade.

D. Synthetic Section: Generation of Alternative Social Policies in Conformity with the General Requirements of Social Development

CHAPTER FOUR

Resolving Issues of Social Provision*

The notion "social provision" does not have a commonly accepted meaning. The *International Encyclopedia of the Social Sciences* and other important reference works do not mention the term. A discussion of issues related to social provision must, therefore, begin with an attempt to clarify the concept.

THE SOCIETAL NATURE OF PROVISIONS

The dictionary's derivations of the meanings of "provide" and "provision" make it clear that these terms refer to fundamental aspects of the life process, and more specifically of human life, i.e. conscious life in a societal context. "Provide" and "provision" denote, according to Webster, anticipating and satisfying existential needs through foresight and forethought.

These meanings suggest certain biosocial observations. Life from the simple level of a single cell to the complex level of human societies always requires interaction and exchange between living

*Presented at the 1976 Annual Program Meeting of the Council on Social Work Education, Philadelphia, Pa., March 3, 1976.

organisms and their environment to obtain provisions for satisfying survival and other needs. Needs, experienced in the context of relative scarcities, and the pursuit of provisions to satisfy these needs, are, consequently, a major source of the evolution of human social orders. Indeed, any human social order, anytime and anywhere, be it simple or complex, can be understood as one particular response to the universal, existential imperative to provide life-sustaining and life-enhancing resources to members of the group.

The generation and distribution of provisions among humans living in groups always involve socially structured and sanctioned processes. All provisions are therefore intrinsically social, whatever their kind and manner of procurement, and whether they are used by individuals or collectively. Hence, qualifying the noun "provision" with the adjective "social," as is often done in professional and political discourse, reflects and perpetuates conceptual confusion; it implies that only certain provisions are social, while others are not. Limiting the designation "social" to selected types of provisions, e.g. provisions allocated to meet the needs of deprived segments of society, denies, by implication, that all provisions are socially sanctioned. It also denies that deprivation results from "legitimate" patterns of distribution of provisions, just as the reverse of deprivation, namely privilege, results from socially sanctioned patterns.

The current use of the notion "social provision" reflects a "blaming the victim" mentality,[1] for it implies that society needs to provide only for those who can not provide for themselves because of alleged inadequacies, imprudence, laziness, etc. Strong, industrious, thrifty, and wise individuals, on the other hand, are presumed to provide for themselves and not to require social provisions. Those who are perceived, falsely, as providing for themselves are also erroneously pictured as transferring social provisions to those identified as unable to provide for themselves, as an act of generosity, out of their "legitimate" property. In reality, however, their property is acquired, as is all property, in accordance with socially sanctioned patterns of distribution of provisions, patterns which are often grossly uneven and which thus cause the complementary conditions of deprivation and privilege.

The first issue to be settled, then, seems to be the semantic confusion implicit in the illusion-maintaining current use of the phrase "social provision." Language should convey unequivocally that all provisions of life-sustaining and life-enhancing resources in human societies are produced and distributed in accordance with socially established and sanctioned policies and processes, whether or not people are conscious of this fact, whether or not provisions are labeled "social," and whether they benefit all members of a society or merely selected individuals and groups.

UNIVERSAL ASPECTS OF SOCIAL ORDERS AND KEY ISSUES OF PROVISION

Several key issues are implicit in the societal nature of provision. These are the issues which every human group must resolve, and which therefore require appropriate solutions in our society. These issues have always been central foci of social, economic, and political development, as well as of philosophical endeavors.

As already indicated social orders of human groups are institutionalized responses to existential imperatives intrinsic to the human condition. They are products of human capacities, environmental characteristics, perceptions of the environment and of human interests, values derived from these perceptions, and human choices and decisions. Significant aspects of the human condition, of human capacities, and of the natural environment which underlie the evolution of social orders include:

—a biological drive to survive and its psychological equivalent in human consciousness;
—biological, psychological, and social needs implicit in the drive for survival;
—striving for security through a steady flow of life-sustaining, needs-satisfying provisions;
—relative scarcity of life-sustaining elements in natural environments;
—a requirement for systematic activity to secure needs-satisfying provisions;
—human capacity to perceive phenomena, "store" perceptions in the mind, reflect and reason about them, engage in abstract thought, communicate with others about perceptions, reflections, and abstract thoughts;
—human capacity to adapt to wide ranges of environmental circumstances.

Given these universal aspects of the human condition, what fundamental processes need to be dealt with by any social order to assure provisions for its members?

Choice of Kinds of Provision. Humans living in groups experience a wide range of biological and socially shaped needs. These include food, shelter, clothing; health, education, recreation; self-expression, creativity, recognition, communication, human relations; etc. These needs vary in urgency with reference to survival and other existential criteria, and they depend for satisfaction on different kinds of provisions. Human societies will, therefore, always confront fundamental choices and questions of priorities as a result of differences in type and urgency of needs, and corresponding differences in the kinds of provisions which satisfy acknowledged needs.

Stewardship of Resources and Modes of Production. The second set of issues concerns management of resources and modes of production which human societies evolve to secure provisions to match acknowledged needs. These processes affect circumstances of living, human relations, the overall quality of the existential milieu, and the flow and stock of natural resources and human products.

All production of provisions involves natural resources and human contributions. The former include solar energy, land, water, air, minerals, vegetation, wildlife, etc. The latter include the intellectual, emotional, and physical potential of past and present humans, their creativity, their accumulated stock of knowledge, and their labor. A mediating component of most productive processes is tools, which themselves are human-created products, involving natural resources, discoveries, inventions, and work.

Major choices which human societies face concerning modes of production include: ownership and control of natural resources and tools; development, transmission, ownership, and control of production technology and underlying basic science; division of labor and organization, management, and quality of work processes; quality of human relations in the workplace; location and size of production facilities; appropriate mix of human and other resources; scope of production and conservation of resources; etc.

Modes of Distribution of Provisions and Other Rights. A third set of issues concerns the patterns evolved and legitimated by human societies for the distribution of life-sustaining and enhancing material and symbolic provisions and civil, social, economic, and political rights to their members as *rewards* for undertaking specific tasks in production processes, or as *entitlements* by virtue of belonging to society or to subgroups within it. Patterns of distribution of provisions and rights also affect circumstances of living, human relations, and the quality of life.

Patterns of distribution may vary widely among societies. Provisions and other rights may be distributed equally or unequally; they may be designated for use by individuals, groups or society as a whole; accumulation of "surplus" provisions beyond levels required for needs-satisfaction may, or may not, be sanctioned; control of certain types of provisions may, or may not, be granted to selected individuals or groups; transfer of provisions through gifts, inheritance, or trade with or without profit may or may not be sanctioned; market or other mechanisms may be utilized to administer the distribution of provisions; provisions may be distributed and transferred in kind or by means of symbolic equivalents, such as money.

Modes of Decision-Making. A final set of key issues concerns procedures societies devise for making the choices and decisions implicit in the selection, production, and distribution of provisions. Issues related to decision-making transcend, of course, the domain of provision and integrate it into the overall governance of a society and the conduct of its common affairs. The manner in which decisions are made on provisions and other public matters is obviously of central importance for circumstances of living, human relations, the quality of life, and the range of freedom in a society.

Major issues to be settled in this context include criteria for participation in various types of decision; degree of openness versus secrecy of decision-making processes; manner of accountability of decision-makers to the rest of society, etc.

The key issues concerning provisions noted here have been handled in a variety of ways by different human societies. By altering approaches to these issues, consciously or unintentionally, societies have attained significant modifications in existential circumstances and human relations. These issues continue to be the crux of policy development and of political action concerned with fundamental societal choices. Issues requiring resolution in any society should, therefore, be understood and defined in terms of types of needs and kinds of provisions corresponding to these needs, modes of production and distribution of provisions, modes of decision-making, interactions among these, and desired consequences for human existence and relations.

FORCES SHAPING AND MAINTAINING SYSTEMS OF PROVISION

Many factors have affected the manner in which human societies have resolved issues of provision in the course of evolution. Fear of death, the drive for survival and security in the context of scarcity and ignorance, trial and error, discoveries and inventions, basic characteristics of humans and the environment, conscious choices of policies as well as drifting along established paths—all these and many more have played a part in this process. Solutions at any point in time reflect a society's entire material and intellectual history up to that time, or rather the history of interactions among material realities, and perceptions, ideas, and actions concerning these realities. Furthermore, these solutions reflect the history of mutual aid and cooperation among humans who developed shared perceptions and definitions, and also the history of competition and conflict among individuals and groups who differed significantly in perceptions and definitions of interest.

Finally, solutions to the key issues of provision are always influenced and constrained by dominant conceptions concerning the worth, rights, and responsibilites of humans, and dominant positions on the following value-dimensions relevant to social policy:

equality	— inequality
liberty	— domination
cooperation	— competition
collectivity-orientation	— self-orientation

In turn, solutions developed by a society for the key issues of provision will tend to reinforce dominant philosophical concepts and dominant positions on policy-relevant value-dimensions.

Humans in any society tend to take for granted the principal features of established systems of provision. They usually view these features as "constants" beyond their influence and control. The reason for the ubiquitous tendency to accept, uncritically, the principal features of prevailing systems of provision is that these features, and the ideologies justifying and sustaining them, are internalized from the earliest stages of individual consciousness through processes of socialization and social control. People, therefore, tend to be unaware of the origin of these systems in past human choices and actions. They also tend to be unaware of their own ever-present potential to transcend and transform these systems, in spite of their apparent permanence, by means of new collective choices and actions.[2]

EVALUATING THE PERFORMANCE OF SOCIAL ORDERS

Differences in the institutional arrangements of human societies result in differences of performance which can be compared and evaluated in terms of explicitly stated criteria. While the selection of criteria for the evaluation of performance is, obviously, a subjective step, it is nevertheless appropriate from a scholarly perspective, provided the criteria and the rationale for their selection are made explicit.

The criterion I tend to employ in the comparative study and evaluation of past, present, and potential future social orders is the extent to which the biological, psychological, and social needs of all members of a society are being satisfied. This criterion is derived from the proposition that social orders evolve as responses to the human drive for survival and for security of need-satisfaction in the context of relative environmental scarcities. Implicit in this performance criterion is a value premise according to which all humans belonging to a given social order should be considered of equal worth inspite of their uniqueness, and should therefore be equally entitled to satisfaction of their individual needs. By equal entitlements to needs satisfaction I do not mean monotonous sameness or uniformity since humans are unique rather than identical beings, and their individual needs will therefore vary.

The performance criterion of needs-satisfaction necessitates an elaboration of the concept of human needs. Three kinds of interacting needs seem widely prevalent among human societies. First, there are universal, biological needs and a drive for a sense of security to have these needs met. Next there are needs for reciprocal, caring social relations: not to be isolated but to belong, as a whole being, to community; to be known to, and to know others; to be acknowledged for what one is and to so acknowledge others. Finally, there are needs to discover, express, and actualize oneself through meaningful, creative and productive activity. These, in general terms, seem to be the kinds of needs which humans experience. They vary in intensity and urgency; some are more pressing than others. Also changes over time in the total existential context tend to result in changes in the experience and consciousness of human needs. Yet inspite of changes in specifics, the three general types of needs seem to endure, and their use as performance criteria for comparing and evaluating different societies seems, therefore, valid.[3]

PATTERNS OF SYSTEMS OF PROVISION

Anthropological and historical studies reveal among human societies two principal tendencies in patterning systems of provision: the egalitarian, cooperative, collectivity-oriented and the inegalitarian, competitive, self-oriented.

The Egalitarian, Cooperative, Collectivity-Oriented Pattern. In societies organized according to this tendency, life-sustaining resources such as land, water, air, vegetation, wildlife, and minerals are considered to belong to God. ["The land is mine, says the Lord".] Humans are viewed as an integral part of nature. Nature's life-sustaining resources are for everyone's use, to sustain and enhance everyone's existence. While various resources may be used by humans, individually or in groups, appropriation of natural resources is not sanctioned.

Further, work tools are available to all, and knowledge of production technology circulates freely for everyone's use. Everyone participates in accordance with individual capacity in work aimed at procuring provisions for the satisfaction of acknowledged needs. Work tends to be carried out cooperatively, in a spirit of mutual aid, and all members of society are considered equally entitled to have their legitimate needs met. Natural resources are used thoughtfully, and conservation of the ecological base of life is an ever-present concern. Exploitation, destruction, and waste of natural resources are held to an irreducible minimum. A sense of harmony, belonging, and security tends to be promoted through institutionalized mutual responsibility of all for all, through collective management of production surplus and through widespread participation in open decision-making processes.

Societies whose systems of provision reflect, more or less, this tendency include many African, Asian, and American peoples prior to European conquests of their lands, as well as many ancient European peoples prior to the expansion of Greek and Roman civilizations; many medieval European villages; various religious and secular communal settlements in Europe, Asia, and America, past and present; contemporary communes in Israel and China; etc.[4]

Philosophical concepts sustaining this pattern are that humans are intrinsically equal in worth and ought to share equally in rights and responsibilities. Postions on policy-relevant value-dimensions reflected by this pattern are close to equality, liberty, cooperation, and collectivity-orientation.

The Inegalitarian, Competitive, Self-Oriented Pattern. In societies organized according to this second tendency, appropriation by individuals and groups of life-sustaining and life-enhancing material resources is the fundamental principle around which the system of provision and the entire social order are constructed.[5] Humans are viewed as masters over nature; they may use and exploit nature for their own benefit. Humans, therefore, do not view themselves, nor do they act, as an integral, harmonious component of nature's closed system, but as a unique species destined (by God) to rule this system.

The acquisitive, accumulative principle reflects the notion that all men are responsible to provide for themselves and their kin out of resources over which they manages to establish control. This notion usually gives rise to the desire to increase one's share of the aggregate available resources, as any increase in property is perceived as an increase in existential security. Collective responsibility for procurement of provisions to satisfy the needs of all members of society is usually not acknowledged under this pattern, as everyone is expected, and presumed to be able, to provide for one's own needs. As long as population size does not exceed the resource base and everyone controls sufficient resources to support himself by working with these resources, these expectations and presumptions correspond to reality.

However, an acquisitive mentality tends to result, over time, in increasing concentration of control over real wealth among decreasing numbers of owners and in an increase in the number of individuals whose share in the wealth of society decreases. This is the inevitable outcome of competitive dynamics in the context of limited resources: there are winners and losers. Eventually, large segments of the population end up without property, and thus without resources to provide for themselves. When this stage is reached they may either emmigrate in search of new, uncontrolled territories and resources, choose to die for want of needed provisions, or work on property controlled by others on disadvantageous terms set by the owners. They become tenants, serfs, slaves, or wage-laborers and are forced to live on minimal provisions, as major portions of the products they create by their labor are appropriated by the owners, on whose property they work. The wealth of the latter continues to grow through constant appropriation of surplus produced by the former.

In a later stage of this pattern, tools and factories and even knowledge of production technology and skills are gradually appropriated and controlled by owners of wealth and their agents. By then the majority of the population owns little more than labor-power, often untrained and unskilled, which it is forced to supply to the owners in return for limited provisions. There usually are more property-less seekers of employment in the labor market than vacant work places. The share of the product allocated to workers can therefore be kept at a relatively low level.

During early stages of this process, society as a whole does not interfere to counteract evolving imbalances in control over life-sustaining resources, nor to assure provisions for the losers in the acquisitive race. On the contrary, the usual inclination is to blame the losers and to admire and reward the winners, especially since the latter tend to attain control over political institutions along with their growing control over society's basic wealth. Later on, various schemes are devised, e.g. charity and welfare, to allocate limited shares of essential provisions to disowned population segments, and to assure their survival and labor power, while checking rebellious tendencies and reinforcing the legitimacy of property rights and privileges.[6]

The mentality and dynamics of acquisitiveness tend to be reflected not only in exploitative attitudes towards other humans, who are perceived and treated as means towards further accumulation of wealth through profit, but also in equally exploitative attitudes towards the natural environment. As a result, irreplaceable resources are destroyed without concern for long-range consequences for future provisions and for human survival.

As a result of this pattern, human relations become increasingly competitive and antagonistic. Alienation, isolation, and various forms of deviance spread. The incidence of destructive and violent acts against property and people increases, and real security and personal fulfillment become unattainable. Eventually, increasing amounts of accumulated resources are channeled into futile efforts to defend the established order against internal and external challengers of privilege in order to regain an illusion of security.

Societies whose systems of provision reflect, approximately, the inegalitarian, competitive, self-centered, acquisitive, and exploitative pattern are ancient, medieval, and modern empires and would-be empires; slave-owning, feudal, and capitalist economic-political systems; and modern, industrial, urbanized, centralistic "welfare-states" of the pseudo-democratic, oligopoly-capitalist version, and the pseudo-socialist, state-monopoly-capitalist version.

Philosophical concepts which evolve along with this pattern and sustain it are that humans are intrinsically unequal in worth and hence entitled to unequal shares of rights and responsibilities. Essentially, they are entitled to what they manage to grab. Positions on policy-relevant value-dimensions reflected by this pattern are close to inequality, domination, competition, and self-orientation.

The two tendencies of provision systems sketched here have rarely, if ever, existed in a pure form. Different human societies reflect varying combinations of these tendencies and can be imagined as located on a continuum. Comparative studies of actual societies suggest the hypothesis that in a society approximating the egalitarian, cooperative, collectivity-oriented pattern of provisions, it is more likely that biological, social, and psychological needs of its members will be satisfied through sharing in the production and distribution of adequate provisions, and through participation in decisions affecting them. In such societies, it is also less likely that humans and natural resources will be exploited, wasted, and destroyed, and that people will feel insecure and alienated.[7]

Societies organized in accordance with inegalitarian, competitive, self-oriented, acquisitive, and exploitative tendencies have made important scientific and technological contributions and have achieved a large productive potential. But a study of societies approximating the egalitarian-cooperative pattern in the past, and also in the present, e.g. collective settlements in Israel and in contemporary Chinese society, reveals significant scientific and technological achievements as well as impressive levels of agricultural and industrial productivity. These have been attained at a lesser cost in human and natural resources, and at a higher level of evenly distributed human fulfillment, than in societies reflecting opposing tendencies in their structures and dominant values.

PROVISION IN MODERN, HIERARCHICAL, CENTRALIZED, INDUSTRIAL STATES

Before turning to issues of provision in our own society, some observations are indicated on certain attributes of provision systems in modern, hierarchical, centralized, industrial states, be they of the "democratic," oligopolist-capitalist or the "socialist," state-monopoly-capitalist version. In such states, most people are not self-directing, individually or collectively, in their lives and work, but are subject to controls of large, impersonal organizations with respect to many domains of existence, including production, consumption, health, education, leisure, etc. They work, usually for wages, in hierarchically managed enterprises. They have no meaningful share in the ownership and control of natural resources and production settings, nor do they play significant roles in determining the nature and quality of products and production processes, or of their share of the fruits of labor. Irrespective of legal definitions concerning ownership and control of resources and means of production, and irrespective of dominant political ideologies, the actual experience of people is not that of masters over their own lives and over production and consumption. What people do while creating provisions, and the scope of provisions to which they are eventually entitled, is determined largely by distant decision-makers, somewhere up the ladder of organizational command. As producers of provisions, workers usually lack a sense of mastery, creativity, pride, accomplishment, and fulfillment; they are not as fully human as they can become, being alienated in the deepest sense of this term. As consumers of services such as health, education, communications media, and recreation, and of mass-produced, standardized goods, people's relation to provisions is even less under their control, as it tends to be shaped by impersonal, political, and economic forces.

What is true for workers as producers and consumers is even truer for individuals and groups who, because of age, health, education, occupational, and personal qualifications, do not participate in the "work force," some of whom are at times considered and treated as surplus populations. Their relations to provisions are determined entirely through processes beyond their influence, and often beyond their grasp.

PROVISION SYSTEMS AND IDEOLOGIES IN CAPITALIST WELFARE STATES

Systems of provision in welfare states of the oligopoly-capitalist version involve varying combinations of elements of the principal tendencies sketched above, contradictions due to the pull of these tendencies, and conflicts which cannot be resolved unless the contradictions are overcome at their philosophical and institutional roots.

There are historical, philosophical, material, and institutional differences among democratic, capitalist welfare states in Western Europe, America, and other parts of the world, which are reflected in important differences in their respective systems of provision. However, in spite of these differences, all these societies sanction appropriation and control of important shares of natural resources, productive facilities, and human-created wealth by individuals, families, business enterprises, and other private formations. Humans are perceived as masters over nature, and an acquisitive, exploitative, competitive, selfish, and inegalitarian philosophy and mentality shape all social institutions and relations of humans to one another and to the environment. Wealth and political power tend to be correlated and concentrated. The majority of the population are practically propertyless; they possess few skills and limited knowledge. Their principal route to secure a meager share of provisions is through wage labor.

These societies expect all persons to provide for personal and family needs out of resources they own and work they do on these resources, or out of employment for wages on someone else's resources. However these societies also acknowledge with varying degrees of conviction that every human is entitled to a minimum of provisions to assure survival, and that such minimum provisions should be derived from taxes on wealth, income, production, trade, consumption, etc. This notion of societal responsibility for the survival and even well-being of all citizens has emerged gradually from many contradictory roots and has led to many controversies throughout the history of Europe and societies shaped by European civilization.

The roots of the welfare state notion include residues of communal tendencies toward mutual aid and collective responsibility; the Judeo-Christian beliefs in the sacredness of life, the brotherhood of all humans and their equality before God, and neighborly love as the ideal model for all human relations; monarchic and feudal, paternalistic traditions concerning responsibility for the life of one's subjects; the common-sense notion that basic human needs of a population ought to be satisfied, so that a stable and reliable work force and dependable military forces should be available on a regular basis; the realization that privilege tends to arouse challenge from deprived groups, and that rebellious tendencies might be pacified by assuring tolerable standards of existence to these groups; the relatively recent notion that a satisfied and well-trained population may, in fact, be an asset in the acquisitive drive of propertied groups, rather than an obstacle, and that, therefore, eliminating poverty in its worst forms may actually serve the interests of wealth; a vague sense of guilt for success in the competitive struggle of all against all; etc.

Controversies have centered on such issues as the following—what level of provision constituted an appropriate minimum that would assure survival but would not become a disincentive to unattractive, low-wage work? Should everyone in need be entitled to have his needs met by society or only the "deserving poor," to wit, individuals belonging to specified categories, e.g., children, aged, blind, handicapped, and sick persons, who lacked provisions through no fault of their own? Should strangers in need be assisted or only local residents? Should aid be provided by religious and other voluntary agencies or by government? From what sources should provisions for aiding poor people be derived, and who should shoulder that burden? Should provisions be made available in kind or in the form of purchasing power (i.e., money)? How thoroughly should applicants for aid be investigated before aid is granted; how much control should be exercised over the lives of those who receive aid; how should they be treated, and what should be expected of them? What kind of administrative and technical mechanisms would be most effective and efficient to achieve the ends of public welfare and what, actually were these ends?

Gradually these roots and controversies and the opposing tendencies crystallized into two philosophical-ideological positions concerning provisions for deprived groups in the population. These positions are labeled "liberal" and "conservative," respectively. These philosophies and ideologies continue to shape the politics, social policies, and programs of democratic, capitalist welfare states.

The "liberal" position. Present-day liberalism in the United States has little in common with 18th century liberal or "laissez-faire" philosophy which stressed individual freedom and free-enterprise in a truly competitive market, with minimal government intervention into the affairs of freely contracting parties. Liberal-ism now suggests an open, progressive mind-set on public issues, a fair, sympathetic, and humanistic attitude towards deprived population groups, and support for comprehensive government action to alleviate suffering and deprivation and to strengthen and stabilize economic activity. The modern liberal position in the United States seems, in many respects, akin to that of European social-democratic labor parties, who are committed to massive government intervention into capitalist economies to assure a wide range of health, education, and welfare services as well as transfers of purchasing power to population segments that fail to secure these services and a minimal income through conventional market mechanisms.

Liberals, during this century, have gradually come to ac-knowledge the roots of poverty and other social and economic problems in the unequal distribution of wealth and income. How-ever, in spite of such understanding, liberals usually do not suggest strategies to overcome the social-structural roots of these prob-lems. They tend to promote instead reforms aimed at ameliorating the symptoms through government-administered social services and financial assistance to those directly affected, and through "stimulating the economy"—a euphemism for channeling re-sources to owners of wealth whose investments are expected to cause benefits to "trickle down" to unemployed and poor persons.

Examples of liberal policies are the "New Deal" and "Great Society" programs, including Social Security, unemployment compensation, public housing, public assistance, Medicare and Medicaid, the War on Poverty, Headstart, Model Cities, etc. Clearly, these policies created mechanisms for the transfer of provisions to needy and deprived individuals and groups, to ameliorate their circumstances, but not to eliminate the structural inequalities which gave rise to, and continue to perpetuate, these circumstances. Besides, these programs generated huge, impersonal bureaucracies which became ever-present factors in the lives of people whose access to provisions they control.

Examples of another major type of liberal policies are fiscal and monetary interventions into the economy by government in accordance with theories developed in the twenties and thirties by the British economist John Maynard Keynes. These reforms, too, are essentially symptom-focused and ameliorative. They are meant to compensate for instabilities intrinsic to the existing economic order such as business cycles, unemployment, inflation, recessions, and depressions, but not to overcome the systemic roots of these instabilities and their unsettling consequences for the flow of provisions to the population.

The "conservative" position. This stance, in spite of its label, is actually closer than modern liberalism to eighteenth century liberalism. What conservatives seem eager to conserve are the sanctity and freedoms of property rights, and privileges resulting from the prevailing distribution of control over natural resources and productive facilities. Hence they tend to oppose, on principle, government intervention into the economy and into the no longer free play of market forces, especially when this intervention involves taxation for purposes of providing health and welfare services and purchasing power to deprived groups.

Conservatives believe, in spite of contrary evidence, that under the prevailing capitalist order everyone could provide for his own needs through work, savings, investments, and acquisition of property. They consider people who fail to do so unfit, lazy, and inferior, and hence deserving of blame rather than entitled to help from government and honest, hard-working taxpayers. In the view of conservatives, helping those who fail merely encourages others to avoid efforts to support themselves, and to depend instead on provisions from the government.

The conservative position usually disregards and denies structural sources of social and economic problems and interprets such problems as due primarily to individual shortcomings and faults. Policies derived from this position involve either "benign neglect" or measures to promote adjustment of individuals to prevailing realities, rather than adjustment of the social and economic order to the needs of people. Conservative policies will often also reflect authoritarian and punitive tendencies, and elements of crisis response, rather than prevention. Finally, conservatives prefer voluntary, charitable aid to government programs.

While conservatives tend to oppose government programs on behalf of deprived groups, they are no longer opposed to massive government intervention into the economy when such intervention is designed to improve the "business climate," to provide subsidies to industry and tax cuts for business investments, or otherwise to benefit the interests of owners of wealth.

The ideological positions sketched here which dominate political discourse on welfare state policies and provisions clearly do not confront the roots of social and economic problems in the prevailing inegalitarian distribution of ownership and control over natural resources, productive facilities, and human products, and of rights derived from such ownership and control. They also fail to deal with questions of human liberation, genuine human relations, and self-actualization.

The conservative position denies the existence of systemic roots. It perceives correctly, though for wrong reasons, the futility of symptom-oriented interventions, and objects to the creation of programs and bureaucracies, which are doomed to fail because of inadequate causal and intervention theories. However, though usually correct in their criticism of liberal welfare state policies and programs, conservatives do not offer a valid alternative.

A consistent, conservative position would have to acknowledge, as Karl Hess has done in a recent book,[8] that the prevailing system of provision excludes the majority of the population from sharing in natural resources and productive facilities, prevents them from providing for their own needs through self-directed work, and forces them, consequently, to depend for necessary provisions on government-controlled welfare state mechanisms until such time that natural resources and productive facilities will be freely available for everyone's use.

Liberals, too, do not challenge the all-prevasive inequalities which underlie our persistent social and economic problems, and tend to disregard the needs of people for self-actualization through meaningful work and genuine self-direction of their lives. Welfare state programs, however generous, remain subject to bureaucratic controls. Thus, while liberal reforms can and do reduce deprivation significantly, they can not bring about conditions essential to a free, fulfilling, and creative existence, for they avoid solving the key issues of control over life-sustaining and life-enhancing resources, self-direction at work, and participation by all in decisions affecting their lives.

It follows that in spite of important differences, the liberal and conservative positions serve a common function, to wit, to preserve the capitalist state, and the inequalities, privileges, and deprivations intrinsic to its social, economic, and political dynamics and system of provision. Whether, following the conservative position, dysfunctional aspects of capitalism are denied and attributed to the victims, or whether, in accordance with the liberal position, massive governmental programs for ameliorative intervention are devised, conservatives and liberals alike are committed to maintain the status quo, and their ideologies are conducive to the defense, legitimation, and perpetuation of capitalism.

SOCIAL SERVICES IN CAPITALIST WELFARE STATES

Social services and education for social service practice have evolved over recent centuries into widely accepted institutions in capitalist welfare states. Liberals and conservatives may favor different models of social services; yet every important group within the political spectrum of capitalism will approve some form of social services to distribute limited shares of provisions when market mechanisms fail to do so. This general acceptance of social services makes good sense within the internal logic of capitalist societies in view of the concrete benefits they now provide for many groups throughout society, and in view of the socialization, social control, and stabilization functions they perform on behalf of the prevailing social order by reinforcing the institutions, ideologies, and the entire symbolic universe.

Implicit in the social services in capitalist welfare states, and in the education for social service practice, is a tacit affirmation and legitimation of prevailing patterns of control over resources—i.e. over property rights, status allocation, and rights distribution—and of the consequences of these institutions for human relations and the existential milieu, for privilege and deprivation, and for individual, social, and economic problems rooted in privilege and deprivation. Paradoxically, then, implicit in the social services is the affirmation of oppression and exploitation of humans by humans, and the negation of equality of rights, responsibilities, and dignity and of genuine liberty and self-actualization for all. The social services are thus revealed not as part of the solution of issues of provision in our society, but as a factor in the maintenance of the human problems they pretend to treat and prevent.

Intervention theories implicit in our social services frequently derive from the erroneous notion that social problems are functions of shortcomings of the very individuals and groups who suffer from these problems, rather than functions of prevailing social policies. In accordance with these faulty theories, services aim to change people rather than social institutions. The latter are taken for granted; they are considered "constants" to which people are being helped to adapt or conform. Furthermore, along with other professions and academic disciplines, the social services are organized as if social problems such as unemployment, poverty, crime, addiction, mental illness, etc., were discrete phenomena, each with a specific "professional" solution based in theory and involving skills which "experts" transmit through sophisticated educational processes. Obviously, such a fragmentary conception of social problems and corresponding practice disregard the common roots of those problems in prevailing social values, structures, and dynamics.

Professionals in the social services in modern, industrial capitalist welfare states tend to identify with the earlier sketched "liberal" ideology which, while never challenging the capitalist order, favors large-scale government programs to compensate for chronic and acute ills of that order, so as to ameliorate resulting suffering. In identifying with the ideologies and political efforts of liberals, social service professionals and their educators also accept, uncritically, the notion that more and larger social service programs within the capitalist system can overcome its multiple social problems. Having adopted this fallacious notion, social service professionals usually act in accordance with it, manifesting in doing so a high degree of faith and genuine commitment. They become planners, researchers, adminstrators, consultants, and staff and line workers of constantly growing service bureaucracies. Once involved in the agencies and programs, professionals are subject to the usual illusions and the social and psychological dynamics of large organizations. They come to believe in the validity of what they are doing in order to maintain their own sanity, and they develop blinders against the abundant evidence of constant failure. They will explain failures as due to inadequate budgets and staff shortages, and they will overlook the fact that the reported incidence of social problems tends to rise along with the growth of social service agencies, and that no social service agency has ever eliminated a social problem. The best one can reasonably expect of such agencies on the basis of past performance is some measure of amelioration.

The foregoing observations are by no means new to social service professionals who have experienced a sense of failure and futility for a long time. Furthermore, they are usually not unaware of being used to socialize and to control deprived human beings, and to administer often inhumane and oppressive services in the interest, not of their "clients," but of population groups whose privileged circumstances are the real source of the clients' deprivation and problems. And yet, social service professionals and educators continue the futile task of administering and reorganizing their services, designing forever new variations on the old theme of injustice, although, by and large, they are caring and thoughtful human beings. The reason for this contradiction is that social service professionals, like nearly all humans, are trapped in the institutional realities, the economic necessities, and the false consciousness of our society. They need their jobs to survive. Hence they develop illusions about, and vested interests in, the organizations which employ them; they are afraid to confront these organizations head on, and instead end up as apologists for them.

RESOLVING ISSUES OF PROVISION: A PHILOSOPHICAL AND POLITICAL TASK

Analysis in this essay, so far, leads to one unambiguous conclusion. Resolving issues of provision in a fundamental sense is not, as is often assumed, a professional task involving technical innovations and adjustments within existing societal systems. Rather, it is a philosophical and political task, requiring strategies aimed at radical transformations of values, consciousness, and social institutions. The history of recent centuries all over the globe has demonstrated that there are no solutions to issues of provision in a manner that would satisfy the biological, psychological, and social needs of all humans within the framework of capitalist welfare states, since the values, structures, and dynamics of such states negate equality of rights and responsibility, genuine liberty, and self-actualization for all. Capitalism and other inegalitarian and oppressive systems, whatever their official designations may be, will have to be overcome and transformed thoroughly by philosophical and political means in order to assure the emergence of new value systems, consciousness, social structures, and dynamics conducive to an egalitarian, free, and non-exploitative existence for all. Fundamental solutions to issues of provision need therefore be discovered and realized through philosophy, political theory, and practice.

CURRENT TRENDS OF PROVISION SYSTEMS AND HUMAN PROSPECTS

The objectives of systems of provision in the future are the same as they were in the past: survival, enhancement of the quality of life, and self-actualization for humans everywhere. Yet present provision systems all over the world are shaped largely by zero-sum dynamics, by competitive, self-centered mentality, and by conflict models. These, plus the inegalitarian and selfish values from which they derive, and which they, in turn, reinforce, have brought humankind face to face with the possibility of extinction, at a time when scientific and technological development make a previously unattained quality of human life possible on a world-wide scale. Selfish, ethnocentric, narrow, and short-range perspectives and policies of major societies have caused, and continue to accelerate, critical conditions. Among these are those concerning population trends, production and distribution of food and other life-sustaining goods and services, waste and destruction of non-renewable, essential natural resources, chemical, thermal, and radioactive pollution of the biosphere, and the spread of thermonuclear and conventional armaments. Scholars with impeccable credentials have documented these interrelated, critical conditions, their sources and dynamics, and their likely consequences in countless reports.[9] They have also suggested courses which could lead humankind away from disaster toward survival and fulfillment for all. Yet prevailing political consciousness, dominant social values, short-sighted perceptions of interest, universal mistrust and fear, and existing institutional structures and dynamics constitute massive obstacles to bringing about fundamental transformations in attitudes and actions. Without these, humankind cannot overcome the multiple crises threatening its survival.

THE NEED FOR A NEW RENAISSANCE

When our planet was sparsely populated and societies existed in relative isolation from one another, solving issues of provision in accordance with selfish and ethnocentric principles may not have been just and satisfying to all, but it did not constitute a threat to survival. However, a densely populated planet in which human societies are in close contact with one another and in which levels of interdependence and of material and cultural exchanges are high can no longer solve these issues in this way. Satisfying one's needs and the needs of those close to one while remaining indifferent to the needs of others, or worse still, satisfying one's needs by exploiting and depriving others, accelerates the momentum of reciprocal processes which cause a constant decrease of need satisfaction for all societies and individuals. This is true whatever the level of development of these societies and however privileged they may be. To overcome this ultimately suicidal trend, sophisticated and comprehensive perceptions and definitions of self-interest are called for in the modern, crowded world.

In order to solve issues of provision effectively and satisfyingly, locally and globally, we need today a worldwide New Renaissance of egalitarian, libertarian, cooperative, and collective values and institutions shaped by these values. These are the conclusions reached in recent decades by progressive thinkers such as Martin Buber, Paulo Freire, Erich Fromm, Martin Luther King, Herbert Marcuse, Julius K. Nyerere, George Wald, and also by consistent, libertarian-conservative thinkers such as Karl Hess and George Cabot-Lodge.

To discover the essential elements of such a New Renaissance, we need to think through how issues of provision will have to be resolved locally and globally to assure not only survival, but also evenly shared enhancement of the quality of life, and free and full development and self-actualization for humans everywhere. Solutions to issues of provision today need to transcend prevailing political boundaries among communities, nation-states, and power blocks, since solutions which satisfy the needs of some parts of human-kind by exploiting and depriving others are merely pseudo-solutions; they constitute part of the very problems and obstacles which must be overcome.

Yet, while the global scope of issues of provision must serve as the frame of reference, solutions must be developed on different geographic and political levels, always with proper regard for issues of provision on more inclusive levels, so that local solutions should not constitute obstacles to trans-local and world-wide solutions. The search for solutions must be oriented, simultaneously, to one's own needs, the needs of one's group, and the needs of all groups, everywhere. Satisfying the needs of everyone, everywhere—the needs of the "generalized other"—thus becomes the criterion, and the condition, for satisfying the needs of the self and of the immediate group to which the self belongs. Self-interest, to fit the realities of the twentieth century and centuries to come, will have to be redefined to include the existential interests of all humans, everywhere, living now and in the future.

Solutions to issues of provision require a coherent set of interacting values and principles so as not to contradict the objectives of survival, evenly shared life enhancement, and self-actualization for humans everywhere. Such a set is suggested below:

—All humans and groups of humans ought to be considered intrinsically equal in worth in spite of differences among them.

—All resources, i.e. natural resources, human potential, and human material and non-material products, ought to be used, judiciously, to satisfy everyone's acknowledged needs, holding waste and destruction of resources to an irreducible minimum.

—All humans ought to be equally entitled to have their biological, social, and psychological needs acknowledged and satisfied, allowing, however, for differences in priorities related to types and urgency of needs, and for limitations in the aggregate of available need-satisfying resources.

—All humans ought to be equally entitled to participate in, and be responsible for, processes of production and decision-making; these processes ought to be cooperative, collectivity-oriented, open, and non-secretive, and ought to preclude exploitation, domination, and control of humans by other humans.

Some comments seem indicated here to avoid misunderstandings concerning the value cluster of equality, cooperation, and collectivity orientation. Equality does not mean monotonous sameness or uniformity, but involves flexible consideration of individual uniqueness and individual needs. Furthermore, socially structured equality is not a contradiction to freedom but an essential condition for the maximization of human freedom in societies. Absolute individual freedom is not possible in a social context, for life in society involves always, certain limitations on freedom. A central problem of social philosophy has therefore, always been to identify social designs which minimize interference with individual freedom. Since socially sanctioned inequalities tend to reduce the range of freedom not only of deprived segments of a society but also, indirectly, of privileged segments, it appears that social orders based on principles of equality would reduce limitations on individual freedom to a minimum level for all members and segments of a society.

Just as equality appears to be a necessary, though not sufficient, condition for maximizing, rather than obstructing, liberty in societies, so do cooperation and collectivity-orientation appear to be necessary, though not sufficient, conditions for maximizing, rather than obstructing, individuality, creativity and genuine self-interest. When societies are shaped by dynamics of selfishness and competition, material and non-material needs of humans are likely to be frustrated and self-actualization would be blocked. On the other hand, when dynamics of cooperation and collectivity-orientation shape societies, biological, psychological, and social needs tend to be satisfied, which means that, full and free development of everyone's individuality and creativity become possible, and the genuine self-interest of humans and their self-actualization are no longer blocked.

FROM VALUES AND PRINCIPLES TO SOCIAL POLICIES AND INSTITUTIONS

The discussion of trends which threaten human survival, of the need for a New Renaissance to overcome that threat, and of the values and principles upon which such a renaissance is predicated, suggests that solutions to issues of provision are unattainable through merely marginal adjustments of the existing systems. What is needed, therefore, is a radical transformation of these systems. Centralized, nationalistic, militaristic states, which rule hundreds of millions of alienated and competitive individuals at home, and which strive to maintain privileges abroad through pragmatic, unprincipled power politics, must be transformed into decentralized, humanistic, pacific commonwealths, federations of truly democratic, self-governing, self-reliant, egalitarian communities in which all humans can attain autonomy and authenticity through cooperation and mutuality. How would such commonwealths resolve issues of provision, and what would be their institutional structure?

Natural and Human-Created Wealth as Public Trust. The primary institution of a commonwealth of democratic, self-governing, self-reliant, egalitarian communities is a permanent Public Trust of all natural resources, productive facilities, scientific knowledge, and technological skill. These material, intellectual, natural, and human-created resources and products, the wealth or capital of all the people, would no longer be owned, controlled, transferred, exchanged, saved, invested, wasted, and destroyed by a small segment of the population to secure privileged circumstances of living for owners, their managers and professional aides—the propertied, bureaucratic, and intellectual elites. Nor could these currently powerful elites continue to exclude the remainder of the population from access to and use and enjoyment of natural and human-created wealth, and to exploit their productive potential by continuous appropriation of newly produced wealth. Instead, suitable shares of natural resources and productive facilities would be made available for use, not ownership, by all people, individually or in groups, to work with and to derive their livelihood from them. Scientific knowledge and technological skills would be freely available for use, enjoyment, and further development.

The Public Trust would have to be administered judiciously, in a manner assuring everyone's participation throughout life as equally acknowledged and entitled decision-maker, producer, and consumer. Everyone's potential and talents would be used fully, satisfying common and unique needs, subject to overall limitations on available resources and to the equal right of all others to satisfy their common and unique needs. There would be prevention, so far as possible, of the waste and destruction of resources. Private ownership would be limited solely to items destined for personal use, such as clothing, homes, household equipment, etc.

The concept of the Public Trust, according to which everyone is equally entitled to use natural and human-created wealth, to derive livelihood from this use, and thus be truly free, is radically different from the welfare state concept. According to the welfare state concept, the sanctity of private ownership and control of capital—the permanent, dynamic source of inequalities and deprivation—is preserved essentially unchanged, while parts of income from capital and labor are allocated for transfers and government-administered human services to various groups in the population. Obviously, under this concept wealth-holding segments of the population continue their privileged circumstances, and the remainder of the people are not liberated from their dependence on government and on the elites that monopolize the control over all natural and manufactured wealth.

Production of Provisions to Be Geared to Need, Not Profit. Allocation of productive resources out of the Public Trust will have to be guided by flexible priority rules to assure that goods and services corresponding to the essential needs of the entire population are produced in appropriate quantities and quality before less essential items are produced. Furthermore, policies are required to balance population size and needs against ecological considerations and the reality of ultimate limits of natural resources by adjusting birth rates and by avoiding waste and destruction of human potential and other natural wealth. Such waste and destruction may be intrinsic to production processes shaped by the drive for profit and the accumulation of privately controlled wealth. When production is geared systematically to match population needs with high-quality, long-lasting goods and services, producers will not need to engage in irrational economic practices which are now induced by the competitive scramble for market shares and profits. Among these irrational economic practices are artificially inflated and manipulated patterns of consumption, model changes involving marginal variations rather than real improvements, built-in obsolescence, deceptive advertising, etc.

An effective system of provision also requires balanced integration of agricultural and industrial production and of rural and urban settlements. Reliable supply of high-quality food is obviously a *sine-qua-non*. Accordingly, policies ought to be avoided which impede food production and debase the quality of rural life by shifting human and material resources toward urban industrial centers primarily for the benefit of wealth-holding and other powerful groups. Such policies tend to result in mass migration from potentially healthy rural communities into urban slums, traditional breeding grounds for human misery, exploitation, and manifold individual and social pathology.

Industry must not be an end in itself, nor a means for the creation of privately controlled wealth. It must be a powerful instrument to promote the well-being of the entire population. Policies should therefore facilitate dispersion of industry to where people and natural resources are, and should steer industrial capacity toward high priority needs of the population and away from wasteful production of non-essentials.

Restructuring Processes of Production, Distribution, and Consumption. Once natural and human-created wealth are liberated for the use of all people, the modes of production, distribution, and consumption can be radically transformed. Everyone, regardless of sex, age, and other personal characteristics, will be entitled, as well as expected, to participate in the aggregate labor needed by communities to assure survival of the community and to enhance the quality of life for all. The manner of participation in work will be related to capacities, talents, and interests. Whether the amount of labor deemed needed by a community is large or small, it will be shared evenly by all. Human unemployment, including forced retirement, the exclusion of youth, and other forms of discriminatory exclusion from work, would thus be abolished. So also would be the waste, the deprivation, and the alienation which now result from such exclusion and unemployment.

All work deemed needed within a rationally designed system of provision should entitle workers to equal social recognition or prestige and to roughly equal claims against a community's aggregate product, adjusted flexibly to differences in individual needs. This policy reflects the fact that in a rational system of provision, "work" means activities required by communities for collective and individual well-being of all members. All such activities should be considered of equal worth and should, therefore, entitle workers to equal circumstances of living.

The experience of individuals engaging in different occupations would, nevertheless, vary widely in quality. Moreover, different individuals will also develop preferences for different types of work. Hence, different work roles will result in different levels of intrinsic satisfaction. Yet people should be entitled not only to equal social recognition for their work and to satisfaction of their material needs, but also to equal opportunities for subjective satisfaction, self-expression, and self-actualization in the process of production. Appropriate social policies are therefore required to compensate for differences inherent in occupations and in people, and also to overcome other potentially conflicting objectives intrinsic to processes of production, distribution, and consumption. A set of such policies is suggested below.

Firstly, all work should be directed by the workers engaged in it, whether it is carried out collectively or by an individual working alone. Next, production processes should not be split into minute, meaningless tasks; thus there would not be destruction of opportunities for expressing individual craftsmanship and creativity, and for deriving a sense of pride and accomplishment while producing goods and services of high quality and aesthetic value. Thirdly, unhealthy, dangerous, heavy, unpleasant, and routine work should be performed by machines before other, more desirable work is mechanized and automated. Work considered less desirable, or undesirable, that cannot be mechanized for various reasons but is nevertheless essential to a community's well-being ought to be shared evenly by all. This could be accomplished by assigning everyone during specified stages of the life cycle to the performance of such less desirable tasks, or by taking turns in undertaking these tasks throughout life. Fourthly, opportunities ought to be provided for all to change occupations at various stages of life, to engage in different occupations at the same time, or to rotate among different roles over time. Special efforts are imperative to overcome the prevailing, nearly absolute separation between physical and mental work, and the differential social valuation of these work domains. Fifthly, access to all occupations, and to preparatory channels for all occupations, ought to be completely open to all, and vestiges of role allocation by way of sex, age, caste, or class must be eliminated. Finally, societal structures which now bring forth competitive attitudes and practices at work must be transformed into structures conducive to cooperative attitudes and mutual aid in the course of production.

The distribution of provisions, or of shares of the aggregate product of the community, ought to be administered independently of the division of labor, once all work is considered of equal worth and hence the basis for equal entitlements. Provisions ought to be made available as needed and as universal entitlements, rather than through task-specific, differential wages and nonmaterial rewards. Everyone will thus be entitled to an appropriate share of the aggregate product to satisfy all socially acknowledged needs throughout life by virtue of being a contributing member of a community, irrespective of the type and amount of one's work. Entitlement to provisions in accordance with individual needs is different from the welfare state concept, according to which welfare provisions represent transfers from privileged to deprived groups. Entitlements under the provision system discussed here are not one-way transfers but reciprocal exchanges over the life-cycle on the basis of equality and mutuality. For, with everyone entitled to use communal capital out of the Public Trust, and to derive a livelihood from such use, the goods and services created by self-directing, cooperating producers will be the peoples' to consume and exchange by right. Individuals will create only a limited range of products, but exchanges among producers whose labor is considered equal in worth will assure that everyone's needs are met. Everyone will be an equally entitled consumer.

Decision-Making, Coordination, Governance, Leadership. How would decisions be made, how would local, trans-local, and global needs be coordinated, and what governance structures are suited for humanistic, egalitarian, self-directing, and self-reliant communities? Choices and decisions affecting relations and circumstances of living ought to be arrived at in a thoroughly democratic fashion. Everyone who may be affected by a decision should be informed fully about all relevant aspects, and have an "equal voice," that is, equal rights, opportunities, and power in determining the outcome. Representative democracy, when practiced in an essentially inegalitarian context of interest group competition, inevitably falls short of these criteria. Hence it will have to be transcended, and replaced by political institutions conducive to genuine, participatory democracy.

The basic units of participatory democracy would not be isolated individuals, but self-governing communities. They would be small enough to permit personal relations, yet large enough to assure economic viability and social continuity. The communities would share social, economic, cultural, child-rearing, educational, and recreational functions and concerns. They would vary in size and in patterns and life-styles. They would be linked in local and trans-local networks or federations, which in turn would form more encompassing, democratic commonwealths. Coordination and integration would be achieved through local, regional, trans-regional, and global representative assemblies designed in a manner that would assure full and informed participation of all units and levels in decisions shaping their existence. Administrative units would be selected by and accountable to these assemblies. Issues for deliberation and decision could originate at any level, but would always have to be examined on all levels so that local and trans-local perspectives would be taken into consideration and reconciled before decisions are reached.

Such a multi-level, political-administrative system of decentralized, yet federated, coordinated, and integrated, self-governing communities could not function effectively unless every unit is guided by, and committed to egalitarian and collectivity-oriented value premises. These premises would have to be primary decision criteria for internal and external issues, and there would have to be avoidance of competitive interactions derived from a scarcity mentality and a "zero-sum" model. Egalitarian values, non-competitive attitudes, and cooperative practices in sharing and allocating productive resources and in producing and distributing goods and services will set in motion and sustain a process of "plus-sum" dynamics.

Egalitarian-democratic institutions require widespread political awareness and conscientious involvement in public affairs; these would be facilitated by an unobstructed flow of relevant information. Hence, such political institutions must not sanction secrecy and confidential, privileged communications concerning public issues. If people are to be their own masters, and if they are to share equally responsibilities and entitlements, then individuals undertaking representative and administrative public service roles must under no circumstances be permitted to withhold information from the sovereign people. Behind all claims for secrecy and privileged communications lurks an evil purpose involving either the defense of existing unfair and unjust conditions, or the intent to create, and benefit from, such conditions. Just and fair objectives and purposes, on the other hand, can always be discussed and confronted openly among equals.

Leadership in an egalitarian-democratic commonwealth means service to people, not control and rule over people. It involves performance of certain tasks deemed necessary to maintain and enhance life. The social value of these tasks is equal to that of all other tasks deemed necessary by communities. Hence individuals assigned for a time to the performance of leadership functions should not be entitled to privileged circumstances of living, but should share the same life style and the same rights to goods and services as other members of their community. Once leadership roles are defined as service functions that do not entitle individuals performing them to special rewards in the form of additional goods, services, and prestige, people will be less eager to assume these roles and to hold on to them. It may even become difficult to recruit volunteers for leadership roles, as their performance would require commitment of extra time and effort. Hence, these roles may eventually have to be filled by assigning everyone to take a turn.

Qualifications for leadership roles are not as extraordinary and as rare as people in inegalitarian, competitive societies assume and as leaders and their promoters pretend. In such societies, leaders invariably come from or are selected by, and represent the perceived interests of, wealthy and powerful population segments. Furthermore, leadership roles in such societies entitle those who perform them to considerable privileges. They are a source of patronage and corruption. Once secrecy and confidential, privileged communications are abolished, and with them the monopoly on information about public affairs, individuals who keep informed on public affairs and who will participate in the study and disposition of public issues will soon develop the skills necessary for dealing with such issues, for representing their communities, and for assuming leadership positions. As with many other tasks that are monopolized in the prevailing social order by various powerful groups, the real issue concerning leadership roles seems to be access and opportunity rather than unique qualifications and abilities. It should also be emphasized that in an egalitarian-democratic and pacific commonwealth the nature of leadership roles will be less complex than in a centralized, nationalistic and militaristic world power. The political institutions of egalitarian, participatory democracy will be designed in a manner which will preserve the right and responsibility of the people to make all decisions on policy in their communities and in their representative assemblies on local and trans-local levels. Accordingly, the responsibility of leaders will be the faithful execution of the people's decisions. They will be administrators, not rulers.

Global Relations. A commonwealth of federated, egalitarian-humanistic, and pacific communities is predicated upon avoidance of exploitation and domination of humans and natural resources in other parts of the globe. All forms of exploitation and domination abroad inevitably negate and destroy a just system of provision and of human relations at home; foreign exploitation and domination involve always exploitative and domineering human relations between powerful ruling elites and large segments of people. Internal and external exploitation and oppression complement and reinforce each other. They are manifestations of the same underlying principles and dynamics, to wit, commitment to inequality and hence readiness to use other humans as means or objects in the greedy pursuit of hegemony, privilege, and profit for oneself, one's family, one's tribe, or one's nation and state.

While foreign exploitation and domination in any form are incompatible with an egalitarian system of provision and of human relations, trade among communities living in different parts of the globe is not, as long as such trade involves coordinated, voluntary exchanges of different types of resources on the basis of equality among trading partners. Such exchanges as well as all forms of mutual aid among neighboring and distant peoples are apt to enhance the quality of life for all participants.

It is however not enough to avoid exploitation and domination of humans and natural resources beyond one's own community. This is an essential first step, but human survival on a global scale requires that the concept of Public Trust be applied to the entire human species and to the whole planet earth. Every human being should be equally entitled to make use of, and to derive a livelihood from, the total natural and human-created capital of the planet, to participate in processes of production, distribution, and consumption of provisions, and to participate in decision-making and governance. There are many technical problems of coordination and exchange to be worked out in transforming greedy and competitive nation-states into a world-wide, egalitarian, humanistic, democratic commonwealth. Reason suggests, though, that this is the logical course of sophisticated self-interest if there is to be a future for the human species. The right of every human being to a meaningful existence should no longer be left to chance and to determination by circumstances of birth. Human cooperation, and solutions to issues of provision derived from the principles and values sketched above, would enable us to overcome chance and parochialism by making full use of available natural and human-created resources, scientific knowledge and technology, and the power of reason and reflection. Narrow selfishness, tribalism, and ethnocentricity have run their disastrous course and have brought humankind to the brink of self-destruction. Sophisticated, humanistic self-interest can now guide us away from the abyss toward life and a meaningful existence for all.

A Unifying Philosophy. The suggestions presented here for solving the key issues of provisions in our society are not isolated fragments. In fact, they complement one another. Their combined impact should bring about the fundamental transformations of social values, structures, and dynamics implicit in the notion of a New Renaissance for survival of humankind and an enhanced quality of life for all. What unifies these policies is the underlying humanistic, egalitarian, democratic philosophy. According to this, all humans are intrinsically of equal worth, are entitled to equal rights in every sphere of life, and may not be exploited or dominated by other humans. The policies were developed by consistently applying these values and principles to the major domains of human existence and social organization, namely, the stewardship and allocation of all natural and human-created wealth, the design of productive processes and criteria for production priorities, the division of labor and the organization and valuation of work, the distribution of rights and claims to shares of the aggregate social product, and finally, the design of local and global political institutions.

REFORM AND RADICAL TRANSFORMATION: SHORT-RANGE AND LONG-RANGE TIME PERSPECTIVES

Solving issues of provision in a manner assuring the survival and the free and full development of humans everywhere has been shown to be predicated upon a New Renaissance involving a radical transformation of currently dominant selfish, competitive, oppressive, and inegalitarian values and institutions into community-oriented, cooperative, libertarian, and egalitarian ones. In the modern, crowded, and interdependent world, freedom, security, and self-actualization are simply not attainable for any individual or group unless they become available for all individuals and groups. Sophisticated self-interest must therefore pursue conditions conducive to survival, freedom, and fulfillment for all humans.

Such comprehensive transformations are obviously not realizable in one magic master stroke. A worldwide cultural revolution, without which the necessary institutional transformations can not become reality, requires consistent efforts by a liberation movement over an extended period of time. The movement must achieve massive reorientations of currently dominant ideas, perceptions of reality, and consciousness and corresponding fundamental redefinitions of self-interest among steadily growing segments of the population in our own and many other societies.

The time dimension implicit in this transformation process poses the difficult question of what to do in the meantime about acute human needs, suffering, and oppression, and more specifically, how to respond to now feasible reform measures. A valid solution to this dilemma seems to be not to reject the use of symptom-oriented, ameliorative reforms when they provide relief to suffering and oppression, but to expose openly and honestly their inadequacies and faulty assumptions, and their futility in terms of overcoming systemic causes of suffering and oppression. To reject reductions in suffering and oppression which can be obtained now through welfare state reforms would be cruel, inhuman, and unethical. Human suffering should never be used manipulatively in a humanistic strategy toward radical transformations.

Yet, misrepresenting reform measures which conform to the logic and institutions of capitalism as real solutions to the basic and complex existential needs of people, as promoters of reforms often do in political discourse, and refraining from exposing clearly their inadequacies in terms of the requirements of fundamental transformations, seems definitely counterproductive. Such mis-representations and lack of openness and clarity will invariably strengthen the illusions and false consciousness which are essential to the perpetuation of the existing destructive societal order. On the other hand, unravelling the real nature and dynamics of now feasible reform measures, and openly criticizing their systems-maintenance function while using them to their limits, can even be turned into stepping stones in the struggle for fundamental transformations. Such activities can fit into a strategy of spreading consciousness of the dynamics of oppression and deprivation and of alternative value premises and institutions. Such a consciousness would be conducive to real liberation and to the prevention of further suffering and oppression. In this manner, reform measures designed and initiated for the defense of the status-quo can be turned into tools for its subversion, while being used at the same time for reducing the scope of deprivation inherent in that status quo.[10]

To move toward radical transformations by enhancing consciousness around the use of ameliorative reforms may not be entirely satisfactory, especially with regard to the time dimension. This is only one element of a comprehensive strategy, although it is an important one for many severely deprived and oppressed human beings. Impatience with the alienating, oppressive status quo is understandable, and so is the yearning for an immediate fundamental solution, if need be, by way of armed struggles. Yet studies of world history, of human psychology, and of societal institutions and dynamics have a sobering effect. Such studies reveal that quick social revolutions are unlikely to be thorough enough in terms of real changes in values and institutions. Human institutions and consciousness have evolved to their current stage over very long periods of time, and fundamental changes, while they can certainly be accelerated through systematic and consistent, politically conscious efforts and practice, inevitably require much time. All we can do is to carry on the movement and the struggle and give it the intellectual and material resources at our disposal. To become involved in that movement and struggle through our studies, teaching, practice, and life-style, and to help others understand the context of this movement and struggle and the personal choices which they must face in connection with their own involvement in the movement for human liberation—these actions constitute, in my view, important contributions toward the solution of issues of provision in our society.

PART

II

EXPLORING ROOTS
OF SOCIAL PROBLEMS

CHAPTER FIVE

Institutions for Children *

We propose to examine here institutional care for dependent and neglected children in the United States and social policies[1] implicit in this care. Social policies are not always fully comprehended even by the people involved in implementing them. Therefore, we will be exploring possibly unexpected questions such as the social issues dealt with by the institutional type of child care, its social functions, purposes, and value premises, and its multi-faceted consequences.

THE SCOPE OF INSTITUTIONAL CARE FOR CHILDREN

According to the 1970 White House Conference on Children,[2] about 74,000 children were living in child welfare institutions for neglected, dependent, and emotionally disturbed children in 1969.

*Reprinted with permission from Alvin L. Schorr, Editor, *Children And Decent People*. New York, N.Y.: Basic Books, Inc. 1974. Tables are not revised here mainly because comparable updated information is not available.

This consitutes a rate of 1 per thousand children under age 18. One generation earlier, in 1933, 144,000 children, or 3.4 per thousand children, lived in such institutions. Although institutional care for children has clearly decreased, the rate of decline appears to have slowed in recent years.

The change appears to be primarily the result of a shift in child welfare philosophy toward foster family care rather than of a decrease in the number of children cared for away from their own homes and families. The number of these children in placement increased between 1933 and 1969 from 249,000 to 323,000 children. As the number of children in the population increased, the rate per thousand of children in placement decreased only moderately during this period—from 5.9 to 4.5. In 1933, children's institutions accounted for 58 percent of children in child welfare placements; in 1969 institutional care accounted for 23 percent of such placements. Comparative figures are provided in Table 1.

TABLE 1

CHILDREN UNDER AGE 18 IN FOSTER FAMILY CARE AND IN CHILD WEL-
FARE INSTITUTIONS FOR NEGLECTED, DEPENDENT, AND EMOTIONALLY
DISTURBED CHILDREN (NUMBERS AND RATES PER 1,000 CHILDREN)

Year	TOTAL		FOSTER FAMILY CARE		INSTITUTIONAL CARE	
	Number	Rate	Number	Rate	Number	Rate
1933	249,000	5.9	105,000	2.5	144,000	3.4
1969	323,000	4.5	249,000	3.4	74,000	1.0

Source: *Profiles of Children*, 1970 White House Conference on Children (Washington, D.C.: Government Printing Office, 1970), p. 147, Table 107.

It needs to be noted, however, that neglected, dependent, and emotionally disturbed children now constitute less than 25 percent of all children in institutional care. In 1960, nearly 62,000 children lived in various types of "correctional institutions" (training schools, jails, diagnostic and reception centers, and so on); over 78,000 lived in institutions for mentally handicapped, in mental hospitals, and in residential treatment centers; and nearly 25,000 lived in institutions for physically disabled children.[3] While the number of neglected, dependent, and emotionally disturbed children in institutions has been declining steadily, the number in correctional institutions and in institutions for mentally disabled children has been increasing significantly.[4]

We have not, as yet, revealed the entire scope of institutional care for children in the United States. Children residing in private boarding schools ought to be included in the total number of children in institutional care. It seems significant in this context that the Census Bureau does not count private boarding schools as institutions. This point will be commented on below. Systematic data are not available on the numbers and characteristics of children in private boarding schools. Incomplete statistics of the U.S. Office of Education suggest, however, that about 150,000 children resided in private elementary and secondary boarding schools in 1961.[5]

The scope of institutional care for children in the United States can now be summarized. On any day in 1960 about 400,000 children under age 18 resided in some type of institutional setting. About 20 percent were in institutions for neglected, dependent, and disturbed children, about 15 percent in correctional institutions, about 20 percent in institutions for the mentally disabled, about 6 percent in institutions for the physically disabled, and about 38 percent in private boarding schools.

The 1970 census of the institutional population is not available, as this is written. Assuming that the population of child care institutions has increased at about the same rate as the total population of children,[6] it may be estimated that on any day in 1970 about 432,000 children were in institutional care. That is, there were 70,000 children in correctional institutions, 100,000 children in institutions for the mentally disabled, 27,000 in institutions for physically disabled children, 162,000 in private boarding schools, and 73,000 in institutions for neglected, dependent and disturbed children. An overall rate of institutional care, including child welfare, correctional, and private institutions, works out to about 6.2 per thousand children. Chances are, the 1970 census will show that correctional institutions and institutions for mentally disabled took slightly larger proportions of children, institutions for the physically disabled and private boarding schools took about the same proportion, and institutions for neglected, dependent, and disturbed children took a somewhat smaller proportion of institutionalized children.

Several questions are suggested by the foregoing review of trends in institutional care for children. What is the meaning of, or how "real" is, the decline in the number of neglected, dependent, and disturbed children in child welfare institutions while their numbers increase in other types of institutions? Are children labeled "neglected and dependent" and children in correctional institutions different? Is institutional care bad for the first, but good for the second? How do children in private boarding schools differ from those in institutions for neglected and dependent children? Why is private institutional care still considered suitable when child welfare institutions are increasingly viewed as inappropriate? Why are private boarding schools never mentioned in the professional literature of child welfare?

Some quantitative information about children's institutions themselves seems now in order. The best existing source is a census of children's residential institutions conducted in 1966.[7] Tables 2, 3, and 4 summarize some findings of this census.[8] In short, there were 3,763 residential institutions for children in the United States, about half under charitable auspices, a third public, and the remainder operated for private profit. Institutions for dependent and neglected children were largely under voluntary, nonprofit auspices. Public institutions accounted for the largest number of facilities for delinquent children, as might be expected. Proprietary institutions were largely devoted to mentally retarded children. The federal government has little role in children's institutions of any sort; states and counties support most of them. The large majority of voluntary, nonprofit institutions are under religious auspices.

The authors of this census surveyed over 2,300 of these institutions. Although they secured an extensive range of information, no data were secured on the ethnic or socioeconomic background of the children, the goals or finances of the institutions, or the outcome of placement. Such information is essential; its omission seems significant.

SELECTION OF CHILDREN BY INCOME AND SOCIAL STATUS

The scarcity of systematic social information concerning the children in residential care seems strange in a society as data-hungry as ours. We know that boarding schools of the U. S. Bureau of Indian Affairs held about 5,000 children in 1960 and that private boarding schools cater, by and large, to families who can pay substantial amounts. Beyond that we have no aggregate data on the total population of these boarding schools.

TABLE—2

TYPES AND AUSPICES OF CHILDREN'S RESIDENTIAL INSTITUTIONS IN THE UNITED STATES—SEPTEMBER 1965

| | AUSPICES AND NUMBER OF INSTITUTIONS ° | | | |
Type of Institution	Public	Volun-tary	Propri-etary	Total †
Maternity homes for unmarried girls				
Separate facilities	2	170	1	174
Facilities joint with infant or child care ‡	—	38	—	38
Institutions for dependent and neglected children				
Nurseries joint with maternity homes ‡	—	36	—	36
Temporary shelters	45	37	—	82
Institutions for dependent and neglected	244	1,090	63	1,397
Institutions for delinquent and predelinquent children				
Detention facilities	242	5	—	247
Institutions for delinquents and predelinquents	276	103	21	400
Institutions for emotionally disturbed children				
Residential treatment centers	5	141	18	166
Psychiatric inpatient facilities	119	17	12	149
Institutions for handicapped children				
Facilities for mentally retarded	152	128	416	701
Facilities for physically handicapped	136	202	31	373
Total institutions	1,221	1,967	562	3,763

Source: Shirley A. Star and Alma M. Kuby, *Number and Kinds of Children's Residential Institutions in the United States*. U.S. Department of Health, Education, and Welfare, Children's Bureau (Washington, D.C.: Government Printing Office, 1967), Table 2.
° Includes Puerto Rico and the Virgin Islands.
† Includes 13 institutions of private, but otherwise unknown, auspices not shown in preceding detail columns.
‡ Figures for these two categories would be identical except for the fact that two of the maternity homes are joint with facilities for mentally retarded children.

As for institutions serving dependent, neglected, and delinquent children, we can only infer that the families of children in these institutions are poor or in marginal economic circumstances. This may be deduced from a 1966 study of the financing of public services prepared for the Joint Economic Committee of Congress. Contributions of families to the cost of care in such institutions ranged from less than 4 percent in institutions serving delinquents to about 6.5 percent in institutions for dependent children.[9] These so-called "user charges" may be taken as a rough

TABLE—3

TYPES AND AUSPICES OF PUBLIC CHILDREN'S RESIDENTIAL INSTI-
TUTIONS IN THE UNITED STATES—SEPTEMBER 1965

Type of Institution	AUSPICES AND NUMBER OF PUBLIC INSTITUTIONS °				
	Federal	State	County	Muni-cipal	Total Public †
Maternity homes for unmarried girls					
Separate facilities	—	2	—	—	2
Facilities joint with infant or child care	—	—	—	—	—
Institutions for dependent and neglected children					
Nurseries joint with maternity homes	—	—	—	—	—
Temporary shelters	2	4	34	5	45
Institutions for dependent and neglected	98	28	108	10	244
Institutions for delinquent and predelinquent children					
Detention facilities	—	8	226	8	242
Institutions for delinquents and predelinquents	2	211	56	7	276
Institutions for emotionally disturbed children					
Residential treatment centers	—	3	2	—	5
Psychiatric inpatient facilities	1	114	1	3	119
Institutions for handicapped children					
Facilities for mentally retarded	—	149	1	2	152
Facilities for physically handicapped	4	122	3	6	136
Total public institutions	107	641	431	41	1,221

Source: Shirley A. Star and Alma M. Kuby, *Number and Kinds of Children's Residential Institutions in the United States*. U.S. Department of Health, Education, and Welfare, Children's Bureau (Washington, D.C.: Government Printing Office, 1967), Table 3.
° Includes Puerto Rico and the Virgin Islands
† Includes one institution of public, but otherwise unknown, auspices not shown in preceding detail columns.

measure of the economic capacity of the families of these children.

In view of the marginal family income of children in child welfare institutions, it is not surprising that nonwhites are over-represented. According to a 1960 study:

. . . the rate of institutionalization of nonwhite children in these types of institutions was 6.3 per 1,000, which was 58 percent above the rate of 4.0 white children per 1,000. Although nonwhite children

TABLE—4

TYPES AND AUSPICES OF VOLUNTARY CHILDREN'S RESIDENTIAL
INSTITUTIONS IN THE UNITED STATES—SEPTEMBER 1965

Type of Institution	AUSPICES AND NUMBER OF VOLUNTARY INSTITUTIONS°					
	Protes-tant	Cath-olic	Jewish	Secular	Unspec-ified	Total Voluntary
Maternity homes for unmarried girls						
Separate facilities	56	43	2	64	5	170
Facilities joint with infant or child care †	4	20	—	12	2	38
Institutions for dependent and neglected children						
Nurseries joint with mater-nity homes †	4	18	—	12	2	36
Temporary shelters	10	6	2	15	4	37
Institutions for dependent and neglected	397	273	24	337	59	1,090
Institutions for delinquent and predelinquent children						
Detention facilities	—	—	—	5	—	5
Institutions for delinquents and predelinquents	15	61	1	22	4	103
Institutions for emotionally disturbed children						
Residential treatment centers	34	24	11	62	10	141
Psychiatric inpatient facilities	—	3	3	11	—	17
Institutions for handicapped children						
Facilities for mentally retarded	16	36	2	68	6	128
Facilities for physically handicapped	9	19	3	162	9	202
Total Institutions	545	503	48	770	101	1,967

Source: Shirley A. Star and Alma M. Kuby, *Number and Kinds of Children's Residential Institutions in the United States*, U.S. Department of Health, Education, and Welfare, Children's Bureau (Washington, D.C.: Government Printing Office, 1967), Table 4.
° Includes Puerto Rico and the Virgin Islands.
† Figures for these two categories would be identical except for the fact that two of the maternity homes are joint with facilities for mentally retarded children.

then comprised 13 percent of the nation's children they comprised 20 percent of children residing in child welfare institutions. The great majority of the nonwhite children in institutions were Negro (89 percent), but 8 percent were American Indian and 3 percent were of other races.[10]

Tables 5 and 6 show the racial distribution for different types of institutions, the rate of institutionalization by age, and a comparison of these data for 1950 and 1960. It is noteworthy that, in Low's words, "the largest proportion of nonwhite children is found in the class of correctional institutions (33 percent)."[11] "More than half of all nonwhite children in institutions reside in correctional institutions (as compared with about one-fourth of the white)."[12]

The overrepresentation of nonwhites in child welfare institutions increased considerably between 1950 and 1960. Whereas the rate per thousand for white children decreased during the 1950s from 4.8 to 4.0, the rate for nonwhite children increased from 5.3 to 6.3. "In correctional institutions the number of nonwhite children rose 92 percent during the decade, more than double the increase in white children."[13] As for institutions for dependent and neglected children, the number of nonwhite children in these institutions increased during the 1950s by 48 percent, while the number of white children declined during this same period by 30.6 percent.[14]

Scanty as the foregoing aggregate information is, it seems clear enough: public and charitable institutions serve poor and minority children, whereas private boarding schools serve the affluent. We will discuss the meaning of those findings shortly. Many studies of local institutions, of the characteristics of children cared for in these institutions, and of placement practices, lend support to the foregoing conclusions. The following quote from Kadushin's comprehensive book[15] on child welfare services is illustrative:

> . . . the Howard University School of Social Work conducted a study of the reasons for placement of a sample of 376 children at Junior Village, an institution for dependent and neglected children in Washington, D.C. As the report indicates: "Over half of the children were admitted because of the destitution of the person caring for them; 20 percent, because of the inadequacies of this person, usually a parent; about 15 percent, because of parental illness; and less than 4 percent, because of the child's behavior."
>
> The general hypothesis of the study that placement of the children was the result of the "destitution of the parent rather than the result of unsatisfactory parental functioning"—was sustained. Nine of ten children in the sample were Negroes, and more than half were under six years of age when placed in the institution. A disconcerting tendency was that children placed in the institution because of family poverty were likely to remain there even longer than those placed

TABLE—5

RATE OF INSTITUTIONALIZATION OF CHILDREN, BY RACE AND BY AGE, 1960 and 1950 (RATES PER 1,000 CHILDREN)

Age	1960		1950	
	White	Nonwhite	White	Nonwhite
Under 5	0.7	0.9	1.1	0.8
5-9	2.4	2.0	3.8	1.8
10-14	5.1	7.4	7.3	5.5
15-19	8.9	19.0	8.6	14.1
20	8.6	21.7	7.8	17.6
Total	4.0	6.3	4.8	5.3

Source: Seth Low, *America's Children and Youth Institutions, 1950—1960—1964*, U.S. Department of Health, Education, and Welfare, Children's Bureau (Washington, D.C.: Government Printing Office, 1965), Table 2.

because of parental inadequacy. Family poverty was defined "not as the simple absence of money, but a poverty compounded of poor education, poor health, poor housing, . . . unemployment and low wages."[16]

SOCIAL ISSUES DEALT WITH BY RESIDENTIAL CHILDREN'S INSTITUTIONS

In every human society situations may occur when some children cannot, or should not, live with their parents. Residential children's institutions are one of several possible responses to such eventualities. Other responses are adoption, foster family care, indenture, slavery, abandonment, infanticide, and so on. These various responses may overlap. For instance, foster family care may include elements of indenture, and institutional care may include elements of abandonment or of slow infanticide.

The circumstances under which children will be separated from their parents may vary. Definitions of these circumstances will at times be quite precise, for example, "orphanhood," and at other times quite vague, for example, "emotional disturbance," "delinquency." Such factors as age, sex, social caste and class, economic circumstances, and minority status may affect the definitions. In present-day American society, for instance, a child of black working-class parents will more likely be separated from his parents for truancy than will a child of white, professional parents.

TABLE—6

NUMBER OF CHILDREN UNDER 20 YEARS OF AGE IN INSTITUTIONS, BY RACE AND BY TYPE OF INSTITUTION, 1960 AND 1950ᵃ

Type of Institution	1960					1950				
	NUMBER OF CHILDREN			PERCENT DISTRIBUTION		NUMBER OF CHILDREN			PERCENT DISTRIBUTION	
	Total	White	Nonwhite	White	Nonwhite	Total	White	Nonwhite	White	Nonwhite
All institutions	282,571	229,289	53,282	81.1	18.9	240,782	210,464	30,318	87.4	12.6
Welfare	75,060	66,538	8,522	88.6	11.4	101,239	95,491	5,748	94.3	5.7
Homes for dependent and neglected children	70,164	62,307	7,857	88.8	11.2	95,073	89,771	5,302	94.4	5.6
Homes for unwed mothers	2,631	2,227	404	84.6	15.4	2,291	2,101	190	91.7	8.3
Homes for the aged and dependent	2,265	2,004	261	88.5	11.5	3,875	3,619	256	93.4	6.6
Correctional	87,323	58,593	28,730	67.1	32.9	56,664	41,691	14,973	73.6	26.4
Training schools for juvenile delinquents	43,793	29,940	13,853	68.4	31.6	34,742	26,884	7,858	77.4	22.6
Prisons and reformatories	19,421	12,828	6,593	66.1	33.9	12,531	8,368	4,163	66.8	33.2
Local jails and workhouses	13,091	8,321	4,770	63.6	36.4	6,944	4,550	2,394	65.5	34.4
Detention homes	9,790	6,648	3,142	67.9	32.1	2,447	1,889	558	77.2	22.8
Diagnostic and reception centers	1,228	856	372	69.7	30.3	—†	—†	—†	—†	—†

Mental disabilities	92,821	81,542	11,279	87.8	12.2	57,228	51,945	5,343	90.7	9.3
Homes and schools for the mentally handicapped	73,664	65,768	7,896	89.3	10.7	46,265	43,230	3,035	93.4	6.6
Mental hospitals and residential treatment centers	19,157	15,774	3,383	82.3	17.7	11,023	8,715	2,308	79.1	20.9
Physical disabilities	27,367	22,616	4,751	82.6	17.4	25,591	21,337	4,254	83.4	16.6
Homes and schools for the physically handicapped	21,588	18,974	2,614	87.9	12.1	17,973	15,935	2,038	88.7	11.3
Tuberculosis hospitals	4,287	2,579	1,708	60.2	39.8	6,753	4,652	2,101	68.9	31.1
Chronic disease hospitals	1,492	1,063	429	71.2	28.8	865	750	115	86.7	13.3

Source: Seth Low, *America's Children and Youth Institutions, 1950—1960—1964*, U.S. Department of Health, Education, and Welfare, Children's Bureau (Washington, D.C.: Government Printing Office, 1965).
° This table relates to children under 20 years of age (rather than under 21) in order to make possble a comparison of 1960 and 1950 data. Alaska and Hawaii are excluded.
† Not available.

Circumstances for separating children from parents are not always defined in terms of social, biological, or psychological deviance. Placement in residential institutions may be a normal procedure under specified circumstances in certain social groups. Thus, British and American aristocratic and upperclass families tend to transfer child-rearing responsibilities for their adolescent children to elite boarding schools, and many collective settlements in Israel tend to rear even their infants in residential children's institutions. Consequently, many successful members of the ruling elites in Great Britain, the United States, and Israel have spent part or all of their childhood in child care institutions.

Since the beginning of colonization of the New World in the sixteenth century, residential care of children has been used for a variety of normal as well as deviant circumstances. Perhaps the first use of this method of socialization was boarding schools for American Indian children operated by Christian missionaries. In 1512 King Ferdinand of Spain promulgated a law according to which "all the sons of the caciques [Indian nobles appointed by the Spanish government] who are under 13 years of age are to be handed over to the friars of the Order of St. Francis so that the said friars teach them how to read and write and all things pertaining to Our Holy Catholic Faith; [the friars] are to keep these children for four years and then shall return them to their ecomenderos [Spanish colonists] so that they will teach other Indians."[17] About a century later, in 1609, Virginia Company officials authorized the "kidnapping" of Indian children in order to bring them up as Christians.[18] King Ferdinand's law and the Virginia Council's instructions to its resident governor reflect the arrogant, self-righteous, and cruel attitudes that underlie the practice, now in its fifth century, of placing American Indian children and youth in residential institutions, often against the wishes of their families and tribes, in order to acculturate them to the values of the foreign conquerors of their lands.

After the war of independence of the United States and a long series of nearly genocidal wars of the young republic against Indian tribes, child care institutions or boarding schools were used with increasing frequency as important tools of an oppressive colonial-type policy, referred to euphemistically as "civilization of Indians."[19] These residential schools were operated by private organizations, mainly missionary societies, with subsidies from the federal government. Gradually the government took over

direct operation of these facilities. The twentieth-century variation
on this sad and destructive theme is the boarding schools of the
U.S. Bureau of Indian Affairs, nearly 100 of which were still in
operation in 1965. Bremner, after reviewing the government's
efforts concerning the education of Indian children, concludes
that "the broad impact of institutions under government contol
or influence on children of minority groups was to enforce an
alien way of life and a degrading conception of themselves, incompatible with growth and fulfillment."[20]

Efforts to conquer the minds of Indian youth were not always overtly oppressive. A more subtle and humane attempt to
"civilize the infidel savages" is reflected in the establishment
during the seventeenth century of preparatory boarding schools
for Indians at Harvard College in Massachusetts[21] and at the
College of William and Mary in Virginia.[22] Dartmouth College
was established in 1754 as an "Indian Charity School" by the
Reverend Eleazar Wheelock. It was transferred in 1769 from
Lebanon, Connecticut, to its present campus in New Hampshire.
When it failed to attract Indian youngsters,[23] it was gradually
transformed into a college for European settlers. Harvard and the
College of William and Mary were also unsuccessful in attracting
Indian youth and eventually relinquished these missionary efforts.

Another important type of residential institution for children
and youth originated in colonial times to serve educational and
socialization needs of top and upper-middle social strata. A study
of private schools of colonial Boston mentions several tutors who
established boarding schools in their homes for sons and daughters
of wealthy families and instructed them in classical and modern
languages, mathematics, sciences, and religious teachings.[24] Residential grammar and preparatory schools were established also in
conjunction with the early institutions of higher learning, including
Harvard College, soon after 1636,[25] and the College of William
and Mary, early in the eighteenth century.[26] Several prestigious
boarding schools were established in the eighteenth and nineteenth
centuries: Governor Dumner Academy, 1763; Phillips Academy,
1778; Phillips Exeter Academy, 1781; Lawrence Academy, 1793;
Mercensburg Academy, 1836; Groton School, 1884; The Ursuline
Academy for Girls, 1727; the Moravian Seminary for Girls, 1742;
and Abbot Academy for Girls, 1829.[27] At present the number of
private boarding schools on the elementary and secondary level
throughout the United States exceeds several hundred. Comprehensive guides are published annually to help wealthy families in

selecting boarding schools suited to the needs of their children.[28] Private boarding schools pride themselves on their graduates' high rate of college admission, especially to the private high-prestige universities. With racial and social class integration in public schools, increased enrollment in private boarding schools may be expected as a way of protecting the exclusive and segregated socialization process of upper-middle-class youngsters.

A third type of institutional care, the evolution of which is traceable to prerevolutionary days, is residential settings dealing with a variety of circumstances regarded as being outside the range of normalcy. These include orphanhood, abandonment, illegitimacy; serious physical and mental disabilities; behavioral patterns defined as undesirable, such as laziness, vagrancy, and truancy; and various parental incapacities. Such circumstances were more likely to result in placement when associated with destitution.[29] Such institutions came into widespread use only in the nineteenth century. In earlier days such children shared institutional facilities with adults. These facilities, known as almshouses, or workhouses, provided shelter for the entire range of "surplus" populations, irrespective of sex, age, and type or cause of dependency.

The care of dependent children in almshouses was considered progressive and humane during the latter half of the eighteenth century. Prior to that time, dependent children were often auctioned off to the highest bidder ready to pay for the right to keep and exploit them, or they were "indentured" or "bound out" by the courts to farmers, craftsmen, or tradesmen who considered them a source of cheap labor. Even after the widespread adoption of the poorhouse system, children continued to be bound out as soon as they were old enough to work for their keep. Humane considerations no doubt played a part in arrangements for the care of dependent children. The historical record suggests, however, that efforts to economize carried a decisive weight in public choices about children who were, after all, only the offspring of "inferior segments" of the population.

During the nineteenth century, the public became concerned with the conditions of children vegetating in almshouses. Charitable and religious organizations established institutions for the care of orphans and other dependent children, as well as for the physically handicapped, the mentally retarded, and juvenile delinquents. Gradually, also, state legislatures realized the shocking conditions of children in public poorhouses and provided support to privately operated institutions. When this method of subsidy proved inadequate, states, counties, and municipalities began to erect their own child care institutions. Simultaneously, laws were enacted in state after state requiring removal of children from the poorhouses and placement in specialized children's institutions.

The nineteenth century was a century of institution building. Social reformers promoted a wide range of theories concerning the redemptive potential of highly structured institutional living.[30] However, public enthusiasm and support were eventually followed by disappointment when exaggerated claims remained unfulfilled. Furthermore, in spite of the allocation of public funds to child care facilities, they usually operated on quite limited budgets. The ideas of reform-minded designers and administrators were thus never fully implemented and tested. Consequently, by the end of the nineteenth century, child care institutions were once more viewed as failures. The stage was set for several decades of heated debate between defenders of institutional care and opponents who advocated foster family care or even care of "dependent" children in their own families.[31]

The controversy still continues and has been reflected in child welfare literature throughout the twentieth century. By now, extreme positions for and against institutional care have become more flexible. Kadushin has summarized prevailing thinking as follows:

> Child welfare workers developed a hierarchy of preferences in making decisions regarding what was most desirable for the child: the child's own home, even if inadequate in many respects, was felt to be better than the best boarding home; a boarding home, even if inadequate in many respects, was felt to be better than the best institution. More recently, however, the controversy regarding the relative merits of the boarding home and the institution has been redefined in different terms. The institution is no longer viewed in terms of a hierarchy of preferences but, rather, in terms of its appropriateness for certain groups of children who cannot be served by any other kind of facility. Institutions and boarding homes are currently seen as complementary, rather than competitive, resources. Each is necessary and appropriate for different groups of children, and each has a particular place in the total pattern of child care services.[32]

But throughout the long and often bitter controversy about different means of child care, little consideration has been given to the most crucial variables in terms of eventual outcome. These are the social function, the definition of the social context, and the developmental expectations implicit in that definition, of a child care system. Let us turn to these questions.

SOCIAL FUNCTION OF RESIDENTIAL CHILDREN'S INSTITUTIONS

All residential children's institutions may be understood as means of socialization. Their general function is to aid in the preparation of children for their eventual roles as adults. Children's institutions are thus important components of a society's stratification system. Different social strata tend to evolve different preparatory processes and experiences. It is therefore not surprising that residential children's institutions vary in relation to the statuses and roles for which they serve as preparation and that admission is not random, but is controlled by rigid criteria.

The three types of children's institutions reviewed in the preceding section—boarding schools for American Indian children, private boarding schools for children from affluent families, and institutions for dependent children—reflect different specializations within the overall socialization function. Each institutional type was developed to carry out unique societal functions, and its social context has been defined accordingly. Likewise, expectations concering the adult statuses and roles of children brought up in these institutions vary considerably.

Since early days, the objective of institutions for Indian children has been to undermine the indigenous cultures of these tribes, to destroy their own socialization processes, and to acculturate children to the alien lifestyles that surround them. Tribal cultures were defined in these schools as "primitive" and "savage," while the white man's culture was presented as intrinsically superior. Indian children were induced to believe themselves and their tribes to be inferior, uncivilized, and underdeveloped. At the same time, they were not encouraged to enter white American society as equals. They were expected, instead, to return to their tribes and become exponents of the racist ideology of their arrogant though, at times, well-intentioned oppressors.

The function of private boarding schools for children whose families belong to the social, professional, economic, and political elites of the nation is very different. Built into the fabric of these preparatory schools is the expectation that students will move on to prestigious colleges and will eventually achieve positions of leadership and power. These institutions then serve as conveyor belts, or escalators, for children who are "programmed to succeed" by criteria of the dominant culture, and to fill superior statuses. Access tends to be selective and is controlled largely by the simple mechanism of tuition fees. The more prestigious a school, the more selective and restrictive its admission policies tend to be.

The social context and function of residential institutions for dependent children is defined differently. Just as the expectation of social success has been built into the very fabric of private boarding schools, so the expectation and acceptance of failure or, at best, mediocrity has been built into institutions for dependent, neglected, and delinquent children.[33] The history of these institutions here and in Europe reveals a constant function, irrespective of changes in structure, administration, professional theories, or labels. Statements from well-intentioned child welfare administrators, professionals, community leaders, and politicians notwithstanding, this function has been to "process" lower-income and dependent children into inferior or deviant social and economic statuses and roles as adults; and to do so at least possible cost to the public treasury.[34]

We see now the significance of the failure of the census to define private residential schools as "institutions," excluding their children from the enumeration of "immates of institutions," while residents of institutions for dependent, neglected, and delinquent children are included.[35] The former group are said to be excluded because these children have a "usual residence elsewhere," but of course most dependent, neglected, and delinquent children have also a "usual residence elsewhere." To justify this inconsistency, the Census Bureau cites the "demand for statistics" on the part of health and welfare administrators and social scientists, an argument that merely seems to beg the question. It does reveal, however, that the biases of administrators and social scientists help to decide who is defined in and out of the usually stigmatizing category "inmate of institutions." In truth, statistical information on children in private boarding schools would be needed for somewhat the same purposes as information on residents in child welfare institutions. The real, yet covert, reason for treating children in private boarding schools differently in the census seems to be that the privileged and affluent are entitled to privacy, and their affairs are not to become "statistics." These children are defined as normal, even though they are in institutional care. Poorer children are not entitled to the same privacy, and their affairs are subjected to public scrutiny and scientific analysis.

A striking differentiation between the two types of institutions is absence of professional and theoretical linkages between them. These facilities are usually not inspected, licensed, and accredited by the same agencies. Their staff members rarely belong to the same professional organizations, do not attend the same conferences, are not trained in the same disciplines and schools, and do not share common educational and psychological theories. It was observed earlier that an extensive survey of child welfare institutions did not trouble to secure background data on the children or on the objectives of the institutions. If these two systems are to be kept apart, how convenient that we should not have to know *what* is being kept apart!

The differences seem very revealing. Child welfare specialists working with dependent children have for decades maintained that institutional placement of children is intrinsically harmful and should be avoided. This view, which was never shared by the private boarding schools, was based primarily on a set of vague psychological concepts, for example, "separation trauma," and "maternal deprivation." These complex phenomena were blamed for a variety of undesirable side effects and consequences of institutional placement.[36] Yet children in private schools thrived and seemed to be relatively immune to these dangers. No doubt, the radically different social context and expectations of private schools must have neutralized whatever negative forces were operating in institutional living, and the boarding schools were thus able to continue processing generation after generation of social elites. Similar evidence concerning the crucial importance of the definition of the social context for the eventual outcome of institutional placement is available from Great Britain's Public Schools and from children's houses in Israeli Kibbutzim.

The constructive experiences of many children in congregate educational settings in the United States and other countries support the hypothesis that there are no intrinsically destructive aspects in child care institutions. Such institutions are essentially neutral tools which may be used constructively or destructively, depending on the particular mix of social, economic, educational, and psychological ingredients. If their social purpose derives from egalitarian and humanistic values and, hence, is aimed at maximizing every child's inherent developmental potential, and if economic provisions and educational and psychological measures match that purpose, then children will thrive in the setting. If, on the other hand, the social purpose reflects a non-egalitarian, discriminatory, and punitive philosophy, and if economic, educational, and psychological measures match that purpose, then children are likely to be thwarted in their development. This proposition brings us to the all-important issue of the value premises underlying the programs of our various children's institutions.

VALUE PREMISES AND IDEOLOGIES

It is now possible to identify the value premises, ideologies, and theoretical postions that shape the dynamics and the professional practice in residential child care. The implicit view seems to be that children from different segments of society are of different intrinsic worth. Indian children are worth less than children of middle-class white families, and children dependent on the public for support are worth less than children from families who pay their own way.

In brief, social inequality seems to be part of the brick and mortar of our children's institutions. To put it bluntly may shock devoted child welfare practitioners and administrators and may strike them as slanderous. After all, Americans pride themselves on being an egalitarian, democratic, and child-centered society. Yet in spite of our ritualistic commitments to, and sincere yearnings for, an egalitarian social order, inequalities are thoroughly structured into the fabric of our society.[37] Our system of residential child care has never been, nor is it today, an exception. Humanistic and egalitarian values have been reflected here and there, yet their influence has never had a dominant effect.

The ideology of social inequality is reflected today in such concepts as the "indigenous culture of poverty."[38] These concepts underlie theoretical positions that shape our social services—including child welfare services and social reforms such as the war on poverty,[39] and the Model Cities Program.[40] The central theoretical theme is that poor persons are responsible for their own state.[41] Hence, it is they who need to be changed rather than the social order and its premises of inequality, competition, and rugged individualism.

The premises and theories are reflected prominently in the socialization processes of residential children's institutions. As we have seen, they are geared to maintain social stratification. Private boarding schools prepare children of elite groups for creativity and leadership and elite positions. Boarding schools for children of Indian tribes and child welfare institutions prepare their charges for "adaptation" and "adjustment" and inferior statuses.

LIFE IN RESIDENTIAL CHILDREN'S INSTITUTIONS

What is life like for children residing in various types of children's institutions? This important question cannot be answered reliably, for systematic national information about the quality of children's experience in residential institutions has never been collected.

Several reports on life in institutions have been published by professionals working in the institutions, by social scientists observing them, and also by former inmates.[42] Such studies are unusual, and institutions engaging in them may not be representative. On the other hand, muckraking reports on scandalous conditions in children's institutions which, every now and then, make headline news may also not represent general conditions. All that is attempted here is to deduce qualitative aspects from available quantitative data of one national study.

Perhaps the most significant criterion of the quality of life of institutional children is the extent to which an institution's milieu facilitates individuation rather than regimentation. Actualization of every child's developmented potential and human worth—the professed goal of child welfare services—requires that children be individualized in interaction with truly caring adults, adults who respect them, hold out standards for their development, and stimulate self-respect and aspirations in the children. And the objective of child development requires that children have the material and symbolic resources necessary for realizing these expectations. To what extent do conditions in our children's institutions permit this kind of individuation? The 1966 census of children's institutions[43] may throw light on this question.

During 1965 over half the children residing in public and charitable institutions were living in institutions caring for more than 100 children, nearly one-third in institutions with over 250 children, and over 12 percent in institutions with more than 500 children. Institutions caring for delinquent children tend to be large, whereas institutions for emotionally disturbed children tend to be smaller.[44] To the extent that bigness suggests regimentation, the majority of children must have suffered from it.

The way institutional staffs perceive their children is important, because, however valid, it is a real aspect of the children's milieu. In 1966, staffs in child welfare institutions judged that three out of four children were emotionally disturbed or exhibited disordered behavior.[45] This would require a broad scope of individual attention, not to mention treatment. Prior to admission, nearly all children received physical examinations, 70 percent had dental checkups, 56 percent were tested by psychologists, and 31 percent were evaluated by psychiatrists. But only 18 percent of children admitted to institutions for the neglected and dependent and 35 percent of children entering institutions for delinquents were evaluated psychiatrically.[46]

The primary treatment strategy for children in institutions is individual therapy or counseling by psychiatrists, psychologists, and social workers.[47] However, only 6 percent of all children received regular treatment from psychiatrists during 1965. Most of these children were in psychiatric inpatient units and institutions for emotionally disturbed children. In institutions for dependent and neglected children, less than 3 percent received psychiatric treatment, and in institutuions for delinquents such treatment was provided to less than 6 percent. Treatment by social workers—a very vague term indeed—was available in 1965 to 42 percent of all institutionalized children. In institutions for dependent and neglected children 32 percent were receiving social work treatment, while in institutions for delinquents nearly 50 percent received such treatment. Individual counseling or treatment by psychologists, chaplains, probation-parole workers, physicians, psychiatric nurses, and others was provided to 15 percent of all children in institutions.[48]

Two-thirds of school-aged children living in institutions attend schools operated by the institutions, while one-third go to regular community public schools. Attendance at public schools is especially low for children in institutions for delinquent children, about 5 percent, while 60 percent of children in institutions for the dependent and neglected go to public school.[49] Separate educational facilities may result in isolation of children and may have negative effects on their self-image. Rarely does such separate education mean better education, although at times separate, specialized education is geared to the unique needs of children in institutions.

Children in institutions are likely to require special help with their academic studies. Only 17 percent of all children in institutions receive individual tutoring. Among delinquent children the need for such help may be greatest. Only 15 percent of children in institutions for delinquents receive individual tutoring.[50] These low percentages raise serious questions concerning the "individuation" goal and suggest that children's institutions tend to have low aspirations for the academic achievement of inmates. Getting by with a C seems to be considered success. Twenty-seven percent of children in institutions participated in "remedial education." In institutions for dependent and neglected children less than 20 percent benefited from remedial education, while 35 percent received such educational aid in institutions for delinquents.[51]

The encouragement of special interests and talents of children is a meaningful indicator. Nearly half the institutions have no programs whatsoever in art, music, creative dancing, and so forth and less than 40 percent of all institutionalized children are reported to take part in such programs.[52] Programs for physical education are not available at all in 45 percent of the institutions, and 65 percent of children are said to participate. In institutions for dependent and neglected children 54 percent participate in physical education.[53]

Is low emphasis on academic studies accounted for by a strong emphasis on vocational education? Less than 31 percent of all children in institutions and less than 21 percent in institutions for dependent and neglected children participated in vocational training, while half the children in institutions for delinquents received some vocational training. Sixty-four percent of all institutions had no programs available for vocational training.[54]

In 1965, there were 161 social workers, 82 teachers, 58 psychiatrists and psychologists, 126 physicians and dentists, and 132 other professionals for every thousand children. There were 192 full-time and 68 part-time child care workers per thousand children. Institutions for dependent and neglected children had 134 full-time child care workers per thousand children; institutions for delinquents had 181.[55] Directors of nearly half of all public and charitable children's institutions had graduate degrees. The proportion of graduate degree holders was lower among directors of institutions for dependent and neglected children (39 percent) and institutions for delinquent children (42 percent). Fourteen percent of all institutions had directors without a college degree, and 10 percent had directors with only a high school education or less. In over half the institutions employing social workers, these positions were held by workers lacking a graduate degree. About one-third of all the institutions did not employ social workers.

Fifty-six percent of the institutions had no minimum educational requirements whatsoever for child care staff. This proportion was higher in institutions for neglected and dependent children (65 percent), but lower in institutions serving delinquent children (48 percent). Indeed, 17 percent of the institutions had child care staff who had never attended high school. Eleven percent of institutions for delinquent children had child care workers who had not even finished grammar school.

The poor educational level of child care staff has frequently been commented upon; yet progress seems unimpressive. In few public and charitable children's institutions in the United States are child care workers considered as professional colleagues, a status to which many of them aspire and which has been attained in some European countries. The limited education of child care workers tends to be reflected in low salaries, low social prestige, high turnover, and, worst of all, low morale. Men and women who work with children of low social status are treated as if they too were of little worth. The implicit attitudes are not conducive to enhancing the development of the children. Because child care staff serve as role models for the children, the children's aspirations are in turn depressed. Thwarted themselves, child care workers are, by and large, ill-equipped to stimulate children toward creativity and self-actualization. As a reaction, moreover, child care staff are often embroiled in severe conflicts with professional co-workers. These conflicts are known to obstruct treatment efforts of some of the most sophisticated institutions.[56]

Because of the staffing patterns sketched above, child care tends to deteriorate in many institutions into emphasis on routines, discipline and chores—a custodial milieu that lacks imagination, joy of living, and constructive stimulation. The emphasis on obedience and discipline is often reflected in punitive and manipulative approaches that involve also the use of cruel and violent measures. At the same time, a chronic problem of underfinancing leads to overcrowding and a deteriorating physical environment.[57]

We conclude with judgments obtained from the directors of the institutions themselves. In the directors' collective judgment, they cared for about 70,000 children who would have been better off elsewhere. That is, at least one in three children should not have been retained in those institutions. In the same year, ironically, the directors had to reject, for lack of space, staff, or facilities, some 55,000 children whose needs, they thought, could have been matched in their institutions.[58]

The directors' collective judgment implies an answer to the question whether existing children's institutions facilitate optimal development. The answer seems to be "no." If the directors themselves feel they are not meeting the needs of one in three children, then something in the institutional system must be terribly wrong.

The quality of life in an institution is not necessarily determined by specific details, although details are important, but rather by underlying attitudes and values. The details are merely functions or indicators of these underlying attitudes and values. From the details reviewed here, we can only assume that children in the main receive custodial care—care that does not facilitate individuation or child development.

No systematic information is available on the quality of life and education in private boarding schools. It may be suggested that attitudes and values implicit in the milieu of private boarding schools are likely to be much more conducive to individuation and self-actualization of children than in public and charitable institutions. This assumption is supported by evidence reflected in the results of the two institutional systems.

CONCLUSIONS

The social policies underlying institutional care for dependent, neglected, and delinquent children seem to be conducive to low-quality ameliorative services. The potential impact of these services on structural causes of dependency, neglect, and delinquency seems worse than naught. These programs not only fail to attack causes, but actually perpetuate them by processing children for adult positions of low social status and limited rights. In other words, public and charitable residential institutions maintain inequalities intact and fail to equip graduates to participate equally in civil, political, social, and economic rights and responsibilities.

In concluding, I should like to reemphasize that residential child care can be constructive and liberating as well as destructive and oppressive. The use to which private boarding schools are put demonstrates this. Our child welfare institutions could be transformed into channels for equality, freedom, and creativity if, and when, we redefine their social purpose in these terms. To achieve this requires a broad commitment to the intrinsic and equal worth of every child. Such a commitment would remove built-in obstacles in the operation of our child welfare institutions. We would then establish a single child care system, specialized according to children's needs rather than their social background. We could be guided in this quest by John Dewey's dictum, "What the best and wisest parent wants for his own child, that must the community want for all of its children."[59] We have the professional, scientific, technological, and economic capacity to carry out such a radical reform of our children's institutions. What has been lacking to activate this capacity is the political will. It is time we face up to this simple truth.

CHAPTER SIX

Violence Against Children*

American society has often been described as child-centered. This idealized image seems, however, contradicted by various destructive aspects of child life in the United States such as widespread poverty, hunger, malnutrition, neglect and exploitation; stultifying education and inadequate health care; and an ample measure of physical violence inflicted upon children in their homes, in schools, in child care facilities, and in various children's institutions. There can be little doubt that all these phenomena tend to block opportunities for growth and development of many millions of children, and that they prevent the realization of their innate human potentialities.

Physical violence against children has attracted considerable

*This paper is based on the author's book *Violence Against Children—Physical Child Abuse in the United States*. Cambridge, Massachusetts: Harvard University Press, 1970. (A Commonwealth Fund Book). The series of nationwide studies summarized here were conducted by the author between 1965 and 1969 with support from the Children's Bureau, U.S. Department of Health, Education, and Welfare.

interest during recent decades in this country and overseas among pediatricians, psychiatrists, social workers, lawyers, public authorities, communications media, and the general public. Yet in spite of this widespread interest and concern, which is reflected in numerous studies and demonstration projects, conferences, seminars, articles and books, the underlying dynamics of physical child abuse are still insufficiently understood, and its real incidence and prevalence rates throughout the population and among various population segments are unknown.

The somewhat sensational concern with individual cases of child abuse seems, at times, to have a quality of "scapegoating," for it enables the public to express self-righteous feelings of anger, disgust, resentment, and condemnation toward an individual abusing parent while the entire society is constantly guilty of massive acts of "societal abuse" of millions of children, about which relatively little is said, and even less has been done in recent decades.

One consequence of the extensive interest in child abuse seems to have been the now widely held assumption that its incidence was on the increase. This claim, however, can neither be substantiated nor refuted since no systematic data are available in the form of time series on incidence. One other consequence of the professional and public concern with child abuse was the swift passage throughout the United States of legislation requiring or urging physicians, hospitals and others to report child abuse incidents to appropriate local public authorities. This legislation had been initiated and promoted vigorously by the United States Children's Bureau in order to protect children who had been abused, and to prevent further abuse of these same children and of others in their families. However, since the dynamics of child abuse were not adequately understood at the time reporting legislation was enacted, no proven strategies and policies for prevention and treatment were incorporated into these laws, and their impact on incidence rates is consequently not expected to be significant.

The failure of clinical investigators and of various professional groups to unravel the complex underlying dynamics of violence against children in American society seems due mainly to a significant, built-in bias of the social and behavioral sciences, and of the general system of beliefs of our society. This bias is the deeply rooted, yet untested, assumption that behavioral manifestations which are viewed by the majority of society as "deviant" are the result of personal characteristics, failings, problems, maladjustment, or dysfunction. Whatever label is used, the source of all deviance is conceived to be in the individual or his primary group, his family, rather than in characteristics of the society. This general conception of the dynamics of deviance seems to derive from a politically "conservative" premise, according to which American social structure is basically sound except, perhaps, for a few minor, necessary adjustments. Since the design and the findings of social and behavioral research tend to depend on the questions and hypotheses investigated, and since these questions and hypotheses in turn tend to be generated within the framework of the general assumptions of a scientific discipline and its societal context, it is not surprising that most investigations of child abuse in the United States were clinically oriented, and found this phenomenon to be the result of psychological disorders of the perpetrators or, at times, of the abused children themselves, and/or certain pathological aspects of family relationships. This interpretation of the causal context of child abuse is matched logically by intervention strategies aimed mainly at changing the disorders of individuals and the pathology of families, rather than aspects of the social context in which these "disordered" individuals and "pathological" families live.

The series of nationwide studies of physical child abuse discussed here tried to avoid the limitations inherent in the foregoing assumptions concerning the "individual as source" of behavioral deviance. The causal model guiding these investigations was that behavioral phenomena perceived to be deviant tend to result from interaction effects of societal and individual forces rather than from one or the other of these sets of forces acting independently of each other. The corresponding intervention model or social policy perspective of these studies is that intervention at the societal level is likely to be more effective in terms of prevention than intervention at the individual level since intervention aimed at modifying the societal force field can be expected to have a more far-reaching impact on the causal context of deviance posited here. This intervention model does, of course, not preclude direct protection and treatment of individuals and family groups involved in incidents of child abuse or in other deviant phenomena.

STUDY DESIGN AND DEFINITION OF SUBJECT

The general causal model of deviance sketched here led to a comprehensive psycho-social-cultural conception of child abuse. To study this phenomenon from such a perspective required an epidemiologically oriented survey design involving systematic review of large numbers of child abuse incidents from all over the country rather than a clinically oriented design involving intensive analysis of small samples in specified settings and localities. Accordingly, the nationwide surveys gathered standardized information on every incident of child abuse reported through legal channels throughout the United States during 1967 and 1968, nearly 13,000 incidents. This broadly-based survey was supplemented by more comprehensive case studies of nearly 1400 incidents reported during 1967 in a representative sample of 39 cities and counties. Further data sources, especially concerning the cultural roots of child abuse, were interviews in October of 1965 with 1520 adults from across the country selected at random so as to be representative of the entire U. S. adult population, and a six months survey during 1965 of daily and periodical newspapers and magazines published throughout the United States.

Studies of child abuse were hampered in the past not only by a certain preconception of the causal context but also by the lack of an unambiguous definition of the phenomenon itself. Definitions were usually derived from observable consequences of violent acts against children rather than from the acts themselves and the underlying behavioral dynamics. However, consequences of abusive acts seem to be an inappropriate basis for developing a conceptually valid definition since such consequences are likely to be affected by chance factors as much as by the intentional behavior of perpetrators, and since their evaluation depends on subjective standards or judgments.

In an effort to minimize ambiguity in defining physical abuse of children, the following conceptual definition was developed. This definition is based only on the behavior of perpetrators, rather than on the variable consequences of such behavior.

> "Physical abuse of children is intentional, non-accidental use of physical force, or intentional, non-accidental acts of ommission, on the part of a parent or other caretaker in interaction with a child in his care, aimed at hurting, injuring, or destroying that child."

The foregoing definition seems sound conceptually, but is not completely satisfactory as an operational definition since it may not' always be possible to differentiate between intentional and accidental behavior. Also, the presence of intentional elements in the behavior of perpetrators does not imply complete absence of chance elements. An added difficulty is the fact that behavior which appears to be accidental may be determined in part by "unconsciously intentional" elements. Thus, while the boundary between "pure" accidents and physical abuse can be drawn clearly on a conceptual level, it may, at times, be difficult to differentiate between them without examination of the motivations which underlie manifest behavior in given incidents.

Apart from the difficulty of ascertaining the presence of elements of intentionality, which, by definition, constitute a *sine qua non* of child abuse, the definition reduces ambiguity by including *all* use of physical force and *all* acts of omission aimed at hurting, injuring, or destroying a child, irrespective of the degree of seriousness of the act, the omission, and/or the outcome. Thus, the relativity of personal and community standards and judgments is avoided.

SELECTED FINDINGS FROM THE NATIONWIDE SURVEYS

The Scope of Child Abuse

During 1967 child abuse registries throughout the United States received 9,563 reports. The number of reports rose to 10,931 in 1968. Screening the reports against the conceptual definition of physical child abuse resulted in the elimination of over 37 percent of the 1967 cohort and of over 39 percent of the 1968 cohort, leaving 5,993 children for 1967 and 6,617 for 1968. The post-screening nationwide reporting rate per 100,000 children under age 18 was thus 8.4 in 1967 and 9.3 in 1968.

Analysis of reporting rates state by state suggests that the increase in reporting from 1967 to 1968 reflects primarily changes in legal, administrative, and professional services patterns. The net increase of 624 reports for the country as a whole resulted from an increase of 1,157 reports in 23 states and territories and a decrease of 533 reports in 28 states and territories. No changes in reporting levels were reported from two states. The group of states which reported increases had strengthened their procedures between the two years when compared with the group of states which reported decreases.

There were significant differences in reporting rates per 100,000 children under age 18 among the states ranging from 0.0 to 24.0 in 1967, and from 0.0 to 31.2 in 1968. Reporting rates within the states appeared to be associated with legal, administrative, and professional practices. The more effective these practices were the higher tended to be the reporting rates.

It may be of interest to compare the foregoing reporting levels with a rough estimate of actual incidence of physical abuse of children resulting in some degree of injury. On the basis of a nationwide survey of public knowledge, attitudes and opinions about physical child abuse, the maximum incidence during 1965 was estimated to have been between 2.53 to 4.07 million cases. The actual figure is likely to have been somewhat lower. It should be noted that this figure includes all kinds of injuries from minimal through serious to fatal. The figure would certainly be larger if incidents of abuse which did not result in injury were added.

It is easily seen that official reporting figures bear no relation whatsoever to actual incidence. However, since severity of injury is likely to be one important decision criterion in reporting, reported incidents as a group are likely to constitute the more severe segment of a spectrum of cases ranging from no injury to fatality.

One further comment on reporting patterns concerns reports from metropolitan and non-metropolitan areas. Reporting rates in SMSAs during 1967 and 1968 were markedly higher than in areas outside SMSAs. While less than 70 percent of the U.S. population live in SMSAs, approximately 80 percent of all reports originated in communities within SMSAs. This concentration of reports in metropolitan areas supports the view that administrative and professional factors are likely to be reflected in reporting patterns.

Characteristics of Legally Reported Abused Children

Slightly more than half the children reported as abused during 1967 and 1968 were boys. Boys outnumbered girls in every age group under age 12, but were outnumbered by girls among teen-aged victims of child abuse. Shifts in the sex distribution during different ages seem to reflect culturally determined attitudes. Girls are viewed as more conforming than boys during childhood and physical force tends to be used less frequently in rearing them. However, during adolescence parental anxieties concerning dating behavior of girls lead to increasing restrictions, conflicts, and use of physical force in asserting parental control. With boys physical force tends to be used more readily prior to adolescence. However, during adolescence, as the physical strength of boys begins to match their parents' strength, the use of physical force in disciplining boys tends to diminish.

The age distribution of the reported children indicates that physical abuse is not limited to early childhood. Over 75 percent of the reported victims were over two years of age, and nearly half of them were over six years. Nearly one-fifth were teen-agers. Age distribution was similar for all ethnic groups.

Non-white children were over-represented in the study cohorts. Nationwide reporting rates per 100,000 white children were 6.7, and per 100,000 non-white children 21.0. This over-representation of non-white children seems due partly to reporting bias but mainly to the higher incidence of poverty and poverty related social and psychological deviance, and to the higher rate of fatherless homes and large families among non-white population segments, all of which were found to be strongly associated with child abuse. Finally, the possibility of real differences in child rearing practices among different ethnic groups cannot be ruled out as a contributing factor to observed differences in reporting rates. Such differences in the use of physical force in child rearing may reflect the violence inflicted upon many generations of non-white minorities in American society.

About 29 percent of the children revealed deviations in social interaction and general functioning during the year preceding the abusive incident, nearly 14 percent suffered from deviations in physical functioning during the same time span, and nearly eight percent revealed deviations in intellectual functioning. Among the school-aged children over 13 percent attended special classes for retarded children or were in grades below their age level. Nearly three percent of the school-aged children had never attended school. Nearly 10 percent of children in the sample cohort had lived with foster families sometime during their lives prior to the incident, and over three percent had lived in child care or correctional institutions. Over five percent had appeared before Juvenile Courts on other than traffic offenses. Taken together, these items suggest a level of deviance in excess of the level of deviance of any group of children selected at random from the population at large.

Over 60 percent of the children had a history of prior abuse.

It thus seems that physical abuse of children is more often than not an indication of a prevailing pattern of caretaker-child interaction in a given home rather than of an isolated incident. This impression is supported also by data on involvement in previous abuse by parents, siblings, and other perpetrators.

The Families of Abused Children

Nearly 30 percent of the abused children lived in female-headed households. The child's own father lived in the home in 46 percent of the cases, and a stepfather in nearly 20 percent. Over two percent of the children lived in foster homes, and 0.3 percent lived with adoptive parents. The child's own mother was not living in his home in over 12 percent. Ten percent of the mothers were single, nearly 20 percent were separated, divorced, deserted, or widowed, and over two-thirds were living with a spouse. The homes of non-white children were less frequently intact than those of white children. The data on family structure suggest an association between physical abuse of children and deviance from normative family structure, which seems especially strong for non-white children.

The age distribution of parents of abused children does not support observations according to which parents tend to be extremely young.

The proportion of families with four or more children was nearly twice as high among the families of the reported abused children than among all families with children under 18 in the U.S. population, and the proportion of small families was much larger in the U.S. population. The proportion of larger families among non-white families in the study was significantly higher than among white families.

Educational and occupational levels of parents were markedly lower than of the general population. Non-white parents ranked lower on these items than white ones. Nearly half the fathers of the abused children were not employed throughout the year, and about 12 percent were actually unemployed at the time of the abusive act. Unemployment rates were higher for non-white fathers. Table 1 shows the distribution of income for all sample families, for white, black and Puerto Rican families in the sample, and for all families in the United States.

Compared to all families in the United States, the income of families of abused children was very low and that of families of

TABLE I. FAMILY INCOME 1967

| Income in $ | Percent of Sample Cohort | | | | Percent of all U.S. Families* |
	All families	White	Negro	Puerto Rican	
under 3,000	22.3	17.7	24.8	34.5	12.5
3,000 to 4,999	26.1	21.9	28.6	41.9	12.8
5,000 to 6,999	16.2	18.5	14.1	9.7	16.1
7,000 to 9,999	12.7	15.9	11.7	5.4	24.3
10,000 to 14,999	2.6	3.1	1.9	1.1	22.4
15,000 and over	0.4	0.9	0.2	0.0	12.0
unknown	19.8	22.2	18.6	7.5	0.0
	N=1380	N=536	N=630	N=93	N=49,834,000

*Consumer Income, Bureau of the Census, Current Population Reports, Series P-60, No. 59, April 1969.

non-white abused children even lower. At the time of the abusive incident over 37 percent of the families were receiving public assistance. Altogether nearly 60 percent of the families had received public assistance at some time preceding the abusive incident.

Data concerning the personal history of the parents of the reported abused children suggested a level of deviance in areas of psycho-social functioning which exceeds deviance levels in the general population.

The Incidents and the Circumstances Surrounding Them

In nearly 50 percent of the incidents a mother or stepmother was the perpetrator and in about 40 percent a father. However, since about 30 percent of the homes were female-headed, the involvement rate of fathers was actually higher than that of mothers. Two-thirds of incidents in homes with fathers or stepfathers present were committed by fathers or stepfathers, while mothers or stepmothers were the perpetrators in less than half the incidents occurring in homes with mothers or stepmothers present. Over 70 percent of the children were abused by a biological parent, nearly 14 percent by a stepparent, less than one percent by an adoptive parent, two percent by a foster parent, about one percent by a sibling, four percent by other relatives, and nearly seven percent by an unrelated caretaker. Fifty-one percent of the children were abused by a female perpetrator.

TABLE 2. TYPES OF INJURIES SUSTAINED BY
CHILDREN IN REPORTED ABUSE INCIDENTS

Injury	Percent of Children
Bruises, Welts	67.1
Abrasions, Contusions, Lacerations	32.3
Wounds, Cuts, Punctures	7.9
Burns, Scalding	10.1
Bone Fractures (excluding skull)	10.4
Sprains, Dislocations	1.9
Skull Fractures	3.7
Subdural Hemorrhage or Hematoma	4.6
Brain Damage	1.5
Internal Injuries	3.3
Poisoning	0.9
Malnutrition (deliberately inflicted)	4.2
Freezing, Exposure	0.1
Other Injuries	5.4
No Apparent Injuries	3.2
Type Unknown	2.2

The percentages in this table do not add up to 100 since many
children sustained more than one injury.

Perpetrators tended to have little education and a low socio-
economic status. About 61 percent of them were members of
minority groups, 56.8 percent had shown deviations in social
and behavioral functioning during the year preceding the abuse
incident and about 12.3 percent had been physically ill during
that year. Nearly 11 percent showed deviations in intellectual
functioning, 7.1 percent had been in mental hospitals some time
prior to the incident, 8.4 percent before Juvenile Courts, and
7.9 percent in foster care. Under 14 percent had a criminal record.
About 11 percent had been victims of abuse during their childhood, and 52.5 percent had been perpetrators of abuse prior to
the current incident.

The types of injuries sustained by the children are shown in
Table 2.

The foregoing tabulation of injuries is based on medical veri-
fication in 80.2 percent of the cases and the reliability of the
diagnoses is therefore quite satisfactory. The injuries were considered to be "not serious" in 53.3 percent. They were rated
"serious, no permanent damage expected" in 36.5 percent, "serious
with permanent damage" in 4.6 percent, and fatal in 3.4 percent.
It is noteworthy that 90 percent of the reported incidents were
not expected to leave any lasting physical effects on the children,
and that over half the incidents were not considered to be serious

at all. Even if allowance is made for under-reporting, especially of fatal cases, one must question the view of many concerned professional and lay persons, according to which physical abuse of children constitutes a major cause of death and maiming of children throughout the nation.

Analysis of the relationship between severity of injury and age reveals that injuries of children under age 3 were serious or fatal in 65 percent of the cases while injuries of children over age 3 were serious in 35 percent of the cases only.

Severity of injuries was also found to be related to ethnicity. The injuries of white children were judged not serious in 61.6 percent and serious or fatal in 35.2 percent. The injuries of Negro and Puerto Rican children were judged not serious in 47.3 percent and serious in 52.0 percent.

While severity of injury was thus associated with the age and the ethnic background of the victim, it was found not to be associated with the victim's sex. Severity of injury was about equal for boys and girls.

Several less pronounced associational trends were revealed concerning the severity of injuries sustained by abused children. Severe injuries were more likely to be inflicted by parents and other perpetrators under age 25 than by older ones, by women than by men and especially by single women. Parents who had appeared before Juvenile Courts and who experienced some form of foster care were more likely than other parents to inflict serious injury. Finally, injuries were more likely to be serious or fatal in families whose annual income was under $3,500.

The extent of medical treatment is another crude indicator of the degree of severity of physical abuse sustained by children. The injuries of nearly 60 percent of the children did not seem to require hospitalization, and in nearly 25 percent no medical treatment seemed indicated at all. Of those requiring hospitalization, over 41.7 percent were discharged in less than one week. Hospitalization beyond one week was required by 21.3 percent of the children, and this group seems to represent the segment of severe injury of the child abuse spectrum.

Official Actions Following Abuse

While public and voluntary social welfare agencies were a third choice as an initial source for help following abusive incidents, they carried major responsibility in dealing with and caring for the abused children and their families later on. Social welfare agencies were involved to some extent in 86.9 percent of all cases. Courts were involved in 45.8 percent, the police in 53.1 percent, and District or County Attorneys in 19.1 percent.

Over 36 percent of the abused children were placed away from their families after the abuse incidents. In 15.4 percent of the cases, not only the victims but also siblings living in the same homes were placed away from their families. Placement away from the child's home was more likely to be used when injuries were serious and when children had been abused before. Homemaker service was made available to 2.2 percent of the families, and counseling services were made available to 71.9 percent.

The suspected perpetrators were indicted in 17.3 percent of the incidents. They were convicted in 13.1 percent and jailed in 7.2 percent. Court action was more likely to be taken when children were seriously or fatally injured.

A TYPOLOGY OF CHILD ABUSE

Based on observations throughout the study, the conclusion was reached that physical abuse of children is not a uniform phenomenon with one set of causal factors, but a multi-dimensional phenomenon. In order to explore the many possible contributing causal contexts which may precipitate incidents of physical abuse of children, lists were prepared of circumstances which may or may not have been present in any given case. The items on the checklist were not designed to be mutually exclusive. Associations between two or more types were therefore expected in many incidents. Responses concerning the circumstances of abuse of 1,380 cases of a sample cohort suggest the following observations concerning types of physical child abuse:

One major type involves incidents developing out of disciplinary action taken by caretakers who respond in uncontrolled anger to real or perceived misconduct of a child. Nearly 63 percent of the cases were checked as "immediate or delayed response to specific act of child," and nearly 73 percent were checked as "inadequately controlled anger of perpetrator."

A second important type seems to involve incidents which derive from a general attitude of resentment and rejection on the part of the perpetrator towards a child. In these cases, not a specific act but the "whole person," or a specific quality of the person such as sex, looks, capacities, circumstances of birth, etc., are the object of rejection. In these cases, too, specific acts of the child may precipitate the acting out of the underlying attitude of rejection. The item "Resentment, rejection of child . . ." was checked in 34.1 percent of the cases. This type was associated with "Repeated abuse of same child by perpetrator," and also "Battered child syndrome".[1]

A third type is defined by the item "Persistent behavioral atypicality of child, e.g., hyperactivity, high annoyance potential, etc." Cases checked positively on this item may be considered as child-initiated or child-provoked abuse. This item was checked in 24.5 percent of the cases. This type was found to be associated with "Misconduct of child."

A fourth type is physical abuse of a child developing out of a quarrel between his caretakers. The child may come to the aid of one parent, or he may just happen to be in the midst of a fight between the parents. Sometimes the child may even be the object of the fight. The item reflecting this type was checked in 11.3 percent of the cases. It was associated with "Alcoholic intoxication of perpetrator."

A fifth type is physical abuse coinciding with a perpetrator's sexual attack on a child. This item was checked in 0.6 percent of the cases. It was found to be associated with the sixth type, "Sadistic gratification of the perpetrator."

The seventh type may be referred to as sadism sublimated to the level of child rearing ideology. The item was worded on the checklist: "Self-definition of perpetrator as stern, authoritative disciplinarian." It was checked in 31.0 percent of the cases, and was associated with the first type.

Type Number 8 was called "Marked mental and/or emotional deviation of perpetrator." It was checked in 46.1 percent of the cases and was associated with "Mounting stress on perpetrator."

Type Number 9 is the simultaneous occurrence of abuse and neglect. Contrary to observations of many investigators who consider abuse and neglect as mutually exclusive phenomena, this type was checked in 33.7 percent of the cases. It was associated with type Number 2, "Resentment, rejection . . ."

"The battered child syndrome" constitutes type Number 10. This item was checked in 13.6 percent of the cases.

"Alcoholic intoxication of the perpetrator at the time of the abusive act" constitutes type Number 11. It was checked as present in 12.9 percent of the cases and was associated with "Caretaker quarrel," and Mother temporarily absent—perpetrator male."

A very important type is Number 12, "Mounting stress on perpetrator due to life circumstances." It was checked as present in 59.0 percent of the cases and was associated with "Mental, emotional deviation of perpetrator."

Type Number 13 is an important "typical constellation" which frequently tends to precipitate physical abuse of a child. The mother or substitute are temporarily absent from the home, working or shopping, or for some other reason, and the child is left in the care of a boyfriend or some other male caretaker. This type was the context for the abuse in 17.2 percent of the cases and seems to deserve special attention in preventive efforts. It was found to be associated with "Physical and sexual abuse coincide," "Sadistic gratification of perpetrator," and "Alcoholic intoxication."

The last type, Number 14, is similar to type Number 13, but quantitatively much less important as a typical context for child abuse. It is the temporary absence of the mother or substitute during which the child is cared for and abused by a female babysitter. This item was checked in 2.7 percent of the cases.

The foregoing typology is quite crude. However, it may be of interest to note that this typology seems to have successfully covered most of the circumstances of abuse observed by social workers who completed the checklists. This is reflected in the fact that a residual item—"other circumstances"—was checked only in 2.7 percent of the cases.

Data underlying the foregoing empirically derived typology were subjected to a factor analysis. The final results of this analysis, shown in Table 3, suggest that the typology can be reduced to the following underlying seven factors of legally reported physical child abuse:

1. Psychological Rejection
2. Angry and Uncontrolled Disciplinary Response
3. Male Babysitter Abuse
4. Personality Deviance and Reality Stress
5. Child Originated Abuse
6. Female Babysitter Abuse
7. Caretaker Quarrel

In a certain sense, the seven factors of the spectrum of legally reported physical abuse of children summarize the findings of the nationwide surveys by reducing them into a concentrated paradigm which reflects the underlying structure of the phenomenon. A more comprehensive conceptual summation of these

TABLE 3. FACTOR ANALYSIS OF CIRCUMSTANCES OF CHILD ABUSE
ROTATED FACTOR LOADINGS (ORTHOGONAL VARIMAX, ROTATION
BY VARIABLE)

Type of Circumstances	Factors							Commu-nality
	1	2	3	4	5	6	7	
1. Perpetrator response to child's act	-.069	.739*	-.100	-.032	.253	.013	.208	.670
2. Misconduct of child	-.266	.235	.051	-.122	.714*	-.074	.128	.676
3. Inadequately controlled anger	-.050	.805*	-.170	.115	-.009	-.119	-.129	.724
4. Resentment, rejection of child	.620*	.003	-.092	.192	-.083	-.022	-.060	.440
5. Repeated abuse of same child	.729*	.200	.084	.059	.039	-.135	.058	.605
6. Persistent behavorial atypicality	.071	.069	-.007	.053	.797*	-.048	.044	.652
7. Physical abuse and sexual attack coincide	.022	-.235	.673*	-.060	.165	.074	-.143	.565
8. Abuse resulting from caretaker quarrel	-.004	-.068	.057	-.020	-.078	-.048	-.880*	.791
9. Battered child syndrome	.675*	-.148	.051	-.110	-.029	-.015	.027	.494
10. Abuse and neglect coincide	.431+	-.328	.068	.340	.026	.050	-.001	.417
11. Mental, emotional deviation of perpetrator	.306	.019	.188	.675*	-.256	.025	-.004	.651
12. Sadistic gratification of perpetrator	.445+	.017	.546*	.135	-.110	.251	-.080	.595
13. Alcoholic intoxication of perpetrator	-.036	.039	.493*	.148	-.103	.022	-.499*	.529
14. Perpetrator stern disciplinarian	.212	.522*	.369	-.178	.167	.098	.042	.525
15. Mounting stress on perpetrator	-.031	.003	-.121	.813*	.124	-.062	-.040	.697
16. Mother absent; perpetrator male	-.274	.031	.554*	-.087	-.389	-.365	.267	.746
17. Mother absent; perpetrator female	-.143	-.052	.108	-.051	-.105	.899*	.059	.861
Sums of Squares	2.075	1.762	1.566	1.403	1.547	1.071	1.214	10.638

*high loadings
+moderately high loadings

findings, and a set of recommendations derived from them, are
presented below.

A CONCEPTUAL MODEL OF PHYSICAL CHILD ABUSE

a. Culturally Sanctioned Use of Physical Force in Child Rearing

One important conclusion of the nationwide surveys was that
physical abuse of children as defined here is not a rare and unusual

occurrence in our society, and that by itself it should therefore not be considered as sufficient evidence of "deviance" of the perpetrator, the child, or the family. Physical abuse appears to be endemic in American society since our cultural norms of child rearing do not preclude the use of a certain measure of physical force toward children by adults caring for them. Rather, such use tends to be encouraged in subtle, and at times not so subtle, ways by "professional experts" in child rearing, education, and medicine; by the press, radio and television; and by professional and popular publications. Furthermore, children are not infrequently subjected to physical abuse in the public domain in such settings as schools, child care facilities, foster homes, correctional and other children's institutions, and even in juvenile courts.

Strong support for considering child abuse as endemic in American society was provided by the public opinion survey, which revealed that nearly 60 percent of adult Americans thought that "almost anybody could at some time injure a child in his care." That survey also indicated that several millions of children may be subjected every year to a wide range of physical abuse, though only several thousands suffer serious physical injury and a few hundred die as a consequence of abusive attacks. Against the background of public sanction of the use of violence against children, and the endemic scope of the prevalence of such cases, it should surprise no one that extreme incidents will occur from time to time in the course of "normal" child rearing practices.

It should be noted that in most incidents of child abuse the caretakers involved are "normal" individuals exercising their prerogative of disciplining a child whose behavior they find in need of correction. While some of these adults may often go farther than they intended because of anger and temporary loss of self-control, and/or because of chance events, their behavior does, nevertheless, not exceed the normative range of disciplining children as defined by the existing culture. Moreover, their acts are usually not in conflict with any law since parents, as well as teachers and other child care personnel, are in many American jurisdictions permitted to use a "reasonable" amount of corporal punishment. For children are not protected by law against bodily attack in the same way as are adults and, consequently, do not enjoy "equal protection under the law" as guaranteed by the XIVth Amendment to the U.S. Constitution.

While, then culturally sanctioned and patterned use of physical force in child rearing seems to constitute the basic causal dimension of all violence against children in American society, it does not explain many specific aspects of this phenomenon, especially its differential incidence rates among different population segments. Several additional causal dimensions need therefore be considered in interpreting the complex dynamics of physical child abuse.

b. Difference in Child Rearing Patterns Among Social Strata and Ethnic Groups

Different social and economic strata of society, and different ethnic and nationality groups tend to differ for various environmental and cultural reasons in their child rearing philosophies and practices, and consequently in the extent to which they approve of corporal punishment of children. These variations in child rearing styles among social and economic strata and ethnic groups constitute a second set of causal dimensions of child abuse, and are reflected in significant variations in incidence rates among these strata and groups. Thus, for instance, incidence rates tend to be negatively correlated with education and income. Also, certain ethnic groups reveal characteristic incidence patterns. Some American Indian tribes will never use physical force in disciplining their children while the incidence rates of child abuse are relatively high among American blacks and Puerto Ricans.

Lest the higher incidence rates among black and Puerto Rican minority groups be misinterpreted, it should be remembered that as a result of centuries of discrimination, non-white ethnic minority status tends to be associated in American society with low educational achievement and low income. The incidence rates of child abuse among these minority groups are likely to reflect this fact, as much as their specific cultural patterns. Furthermore, exposure of these minority groups to various forms of external societal violence to which they could not respond in kind, is likely to have contributed over time to an increase in the level of frustration-generated violence directed against their own members. Relatively high rates of homicide among members of these minority groups seem to support this interpretation.

Higher reporting rates of physical child abuse, and especially of more serious incidents, among the poor and among non-white minority groups may reflect biased reporting procedures. It may be true that the poor and non-whites are more likely to be reported than middle class and white population groups for anything they do or fail to do. At the same time there may also be considerable under-reporting of reportable transgressions not only among middle class and white population groups but also among the poor and the non-white minorities. The net effect of reporting bias and of overall and specific under-reporting with respect to child abuse can, at this time, not be estimated.

It should not be overlooked, however, that life in poverty and in minority group ghettoes tends to generate many stressful experiences which are likely to become precipitating factors of child abuse by weakening a caretaker's psychological mechanisms of self-control and contributing, thus, to the uninhibited discharge of his aggressive and destructive impulses toward physically powerless children. The poor and members of ethnic minority groups seem to be subject to many of the conditions and forces which may lead to abusive behavior toward children in other groups of the population and, in addition to this, they seem to be subject to the special environmental stresses and strains associated with socioeconomic deprivation and discrimination. This would suggest that the significantly higher reporting rates for poor and non-white segments of the population reflect a real underlying higher incidence rate among these groups.

It should also be noted that the poor and non-whites tend to have more children per family unit and less living space. They also tend to have fewer alternatives than other population groups for avoiding or dealing with aggressive impulses toward their children. The poor tend to discharge aggressive impulses more directly as they seem less inhibited in expressing feelings through action. These tendencies are apparently learned through lower class and ghetto socialization, which tends to differ in this respect from middle class socialization and mores.

Middle class parents, apparently as a result of exposure to modern psychological theories of child rearing, tend to engage more than lower class parents in verbal interaction with their children, and to use psychological approaches in disciplining them. It may be noted, parenthetically, that verbal and psychological interaction with children may at times be as violent and abusive in its effects, or even more so, than the use of physical force in disciplining them. Life in middle class families tends to generate tensions and pressures characteristic of the dominant individualistic and competitive value orientations of American society, and these pressures may also precipitate violence against children. However, middle class families are spared the more devastating daily tensions and pressures of life in poverty. They also tend to have fewer children, more living space, and more options to relax, at times, without their children. All this would suggest a lower real incidence rate of physical child abuse among middle class families.

Deviance and Pathology in Bio-Psycho-Social Functioning of Individuals and Families

A further set of causal dimensions of violence against children involves a broad range of deviance in biological, psychological, and social functioning of caretakers, children in their care, and of entire family units. This is the causal context which had been identified and stressed by most clinical investigators of child abuse. It is important to note that this dimension of child abuse is by no means independent of the basic cultural dimension discussed above. The choice of symptoms through which intra-psychic conflicts are expressed by members of a society tends to be influenced by the culture of that society. Symptoms of personality deviance involve often exaggerated levels of culturally sanctioned trends. It would thus seem that violent acts against children would less likely be symptoms of personality disorders in a society which did not sanction the use of physical force in rearing its young.

The presence of this third dimension of child abuse was reflected in findings from our surveys, which revealed relatively high rates of deviance in bio-psycho-social circumstances and functioning of children and adults involved in many reported incidents. Often manifestations of such deviance had been observed during the year preceding an incident. Deviance in functioning of individuals was also matched by high rates of deviance in family structure reflected in a high proportion of female-headed households, and of households from which the biological fathers of the abused children were absent.

Environmental Chance Events

A final, but not insignificant causal dimension of child abuse is environmental chance events which may transform "acceptable" disciplinary measures into serious and "unacceptable" outcomes. It is thus obvious that physical abuse of children, like so many other social problems, is a multidimensional phenomenon rather than a uni-dimensional one with a single set of causal factors. This multidimensional conception of child abuse and its dynamics suggests a corresponding multidimensional approach to the prevention or reduction of the incidence rate of this destructive phenomenon.

IMPLICATIONS FOR SOCIAL POLICY

Violence against children constitutes a severe infringement of their rights as members of society. Since distribution of rights in a society is a key aspect of its social policies, modifications of these policies are necessary if the rights of children to physical safety are to be assured.[2] For social policies to be effective they must be based on a causal theory concerning the etiology of the condition which is to be corrected or prevented. Accordingly, social policies aimed at protecting the rights of children to bodily safety should be designed around the causal dimensions of child abuse presented in the conceptual model of this phenomenon.

Since cultural sanctions of the use of physical force in child rearing constitute the common core of all physical abuse of children in American society, efforts aimed at gradually changing this aspect of the prevailing child rearing philosophy, and developing clear-cut cultural prohibitions and legal sanctions against such use of physical force, are likely to produce over time the strongest possible reduction of the incidence and prevalence of physical abuse of children.

Suggesting to forego the use of physical force in rearing children does not mean that inherently non-social traits of children need not be modified in the course of socialization. It merely means that non-violent, constructive, educational measures would have to replace physical force. It needs to be recognized that giving up the use of physical force against children may not be easy for adults who were subjected to physical force and violence in their own childhood and who have integrated the existing value system of American society. Moreover, children can sometimes be very irritating and provocative in their behavior and may strain the tolerance of adults to the limit. Yet, in spite of these realities, which must be acknowledged and faced openly, society needs to work toward the gradual reduction, and eventual complete elimination, of the use of physical force against children if it intends to protect their basic right of security from physical attack.

As a first, concrete step toward developing eventually comprehensive legal sanctions against the use of physical force in rearing children, the Congress and legislatures of the states could outlaw corporal punishment in schools, juvenile courts, correctional institutions and other child care facilities. Such legislation would assure children the same constitutional protection against physical attack outside their homes as the law provides for adult members of society. Moreover, such legislation is likely to affect child rearing attitudes and practices in American homes, for it would symbolize society's growing rejection of violence against children.

To avoid misinterpretations it should be noted here that rejecting corporal punishment does not imply favoring unlimited permissiveness in rearing children. To grow up successfully, children require a sense of security which is inherent in nonarbitrary structures and limits. Understanding adults can establish such structures and limits through love, patience, firmness, consistency, and rational authority. Corporal punishment seems devoid of constructive educational value since it cannot provide that sense of security and nonarbitrary authority. Rarely, if ever, is corporal punishment administered for the benefit of an attacked child, for usually it serves the immediate needs of the attacking adult who is seeking relief from his uncontrollable anger and stress.

The multiple links between poverty and racial discrimination and physical abuse of children suggest that one essential route toward reducing the incidence and prevalence of child abuse is the elimination of poverty and of structural social inequalities. This objective could be approached through the establishment of a guaranteed decent annual income for all, at least at the level of the Bureau of Labor Statistics "low" standard of living. No doubt this is only a partial answer to the complex issue of preventing violence toward children, but perhaps a very important part of the total answer, and certainly that part without which other preventive efforts may be utterly futile. Eliminating poverty by equalizing opportunities and rights, and by opening up access for all to all levels of the social status system, also happens to be that part of the answer for which this nation possesses the necessary know-how and resources, provided we were willing to introduce changes in our priorities of resource development, and to redistribute national wealth equitably.

Deviance and pathology in biological, psychological, and social functioning of individuals and of family units were identified as a third set of forces which contribute to the incidence and prevalence of physical abuse of children. These conditions tend to be strongly associated with poverty and racial discrimination, and, therefore, eliminating poverty and discrimination are likely to reduce, though by no means to eliminate, the incidence and prevalence of these various dysfunctional phenomena. The following measures, aimed at the secondary and tertiary prevention, and amelioration of these conditions and their consequences, and at the strengthening of individual and family functioning, should be available in every community as components of a comprehensive program for reducing the incidence of physical abuse of children, and also for helping individuals and families once abuse has occurred:

a. Comprehensive family planning programs including the repeal of all legislation concerning medical abortions: The availability of family planning resources and medical abortions are likely to reduce the number of unwanted and rejected children, who are known to be frequently victims of severe physical abuse and even infanticide. It is important to recall in this context that families with many children, and female-headed households, are overrepresented among families involved in physical abuse of children.

b. Family life education and counseling programs for adolescents and adults in preparation for, and after marriage: Such programs should be developed in accordance with the assumption that there is much to learn about married life and parenthood which one does not know merely on the basis of sexual and chronological maturity.

c. A comprehensive, high quality, neighborhood based, national health service, financed through general tax revenue, and geared not only to the treatment of acute and chronic illness, but also the promotion and maintenance of maximum feasible physical and mental health for everyone.

d. A range of high quality, neighborhood based social services geared to the reduction of environmental stresses on family life and especially on mothers who carry major responsibility for the child rearing function. Any measure which would reduce these stresses would also indirectly reduce the incidence rate of child abuse. Homemaker and housekeeping services, mothers' helpers and baby-sitting services, family and group day-care facilities for pre-school and school age children are all examples of such services. It should be recognized, however, that unless a decent income is assured to all families, these social services are unlikely to achieve their objectives.

e. Every community needs also a system of social services and child care facilities geared to assisting families and children who cannot live together because of severe relationship and/or reality problems. Physically abused children belong frequently to this category.

The measures proposed herewith are aimed at different causal dimensions of violence against children. The first set would attack the culturally determined core of the phenomenon; the second set would attack and eliminate major conditions to which child abuse is linked in many ways; the third set approaches the causes of child abuse indirectly. It would be futile to argue the relative merits of these approaches as all three are important. The basic question seems to be, not which measure to select for combating child abuse, but whether American society is indeed committed to assuring equal rights to all its children, and to eradicate child abuse in any form, abuse perpetrated by individual care-takers, as well as abuse perpetrated collectively by society. Our affluent society certainly seems to possess the resources and the skills to eradicate the massive forms of abuse committed by society collectively as well as the physical violence perpetrated by individuals and societal institutions against children in their care.

CHAPTER SEVEN

Holistic Perspective on Child Abuse and its Prevention*

INTRODUCTION

In recent decades, child abuse has come to be considered a social problem of significant scope and has, therefore, attracted intense public and scholarly interest. Yet, in spite of efforts by scholars, professionals, government agencies, concerned individuals and organizations, and the media of public communications, clarity eludes us concerning the sources and dynamics, and concerning effective approaches to the primary prevention, of this destructive phenomenon. Several obstacles seem to cause these gaps in our knowledge and in our ability to design effective policies and programs for the primary prevention of child abuse.

OBSTACLES TO UNDERSTANDING AND TO POLICY AND PROGRAM DEVELOPMENT

Perhaps the most serious obstacle to understanding and to effective intervention is the prevailing conception of social problems as

*Presented at a conference at the National Institute of Child Health and Human Development, June 17, 1974. Reprinted with permission from *The Journal of Sociology and Social Welfare*, Vol. 2, No. 2, Winter 1974; and the *American Journal of Orthopsychiatry*, Vol. 45, No. 3, April 1975, which published a shortened version of this paper entitled "Unraveling Child Abuse."

isolated, fragmented phenomena, rather than as consequences of the societal context in which they evolve, and as related to, and interacting with, other social problems generated in the same societal context. This symptom, rather than source, oriented conception of social problems has caused scholars and social planners to consider child abuse as a separate and unique entity, to study it in isolation, and to design around it specialized policies, programs, and bureaucracies. We tend to deal in the same way with all social problems, such as alcoholism, drug addiction, crime, mental illness, corruption in public affairs, urban decay, poverty, etc. The frustrating results of this fragmentary approach to social problems which are deeply rooted in the total fabric of our society, are too well-known to require detailed discussion: the problems tend to persist unchanged, or even to increase in scope, while the bureaucracies which study and deal with them tend to grow with time into major, separate industries, each of which would face serious "unemployment," were its "house-problem" overcome. Thus, one cannot help wondering whether these specialized, symptom-focused agencies are, indeed, committed to the eradication of their problems, or whether, perhaps out of their symbiotic relationship with the problems and their myopic perspective on them, the agencies themselves become factors contributing to the perpetuation of the problems.

Another, equally serious, obstacle to understanding and over-coming social problems is the tendency to interpret their causation and dynamics along single dimensions such as biological, psychological, social, economic, political, etc. The explanatory dimensions frequently tend to correspond to the academic discipline or the professional field of the investigators who put forth an interpretation. Thus, one suspects that the interpretations reflect the credentials of investigators rather than the multi-dimensional nature of the phenomena. The long-standing controversy whether child abuse is caused by individual psychopathology of perpetrators or by societal forces is an illustration of the futility and absurdity of the single-dimensional approach to the causal interpretation of social problems. Such rigid, explanatory paradigms are derived from relatively closed thought structures of academic disciplines and professional groups, and reflect the "trained incapacities" and the vested research and practice interests of these disciplines and groups. They are unlikely to be correct representations of real human phenomena which are always multi-dimensional and which, therefore, do not fit neatly into the conventional division of labor among academic disciplines, university departments, and programmatic agencies.

It should be noted in this context that observations of cases which can be shown, reliably, to result from a specific factor, e.g. psychopathology, must not be interpreted as evidence against the possible operation of other causal factors, in other cases showing the same symptoms, or even as contributing factors to the observed cases. Such inferences would obviously not be logical.

One more obstacle may be understood as a special manifestation of the just discussed fallacious tendency to interpret social problems along single dimensions. In our society, this tendency seems definitely weighted in favor of individual, rather than social interpretations. William Ryan has referred to this process very aptly, "blaming the victim."[1] By positing individual factors as causal agents of such social problems as poverty, crime, corruption, addiction, and child abuse, attention is diverted away from likely sources in the social fabric. Intervention programs are consequently designed to change individuals involved in or affected by the problems, rather than possibly pathogenic aspects of the social order. By blaming individual victims, or groups of victims, for the social problems they experience, and turning them thus into scapegoats, society as a whole is easily absolved from all blame and responsibility. No doubt, this conception of the dynamics of social problems is highly functional for the protection and maintenance of the social status-quo.

The last obstacle to be noted here is the tendency to define social problems too narrowly, in descriptive rather than in analytic-dynamic terms. Such descriptive definitions are of limited utility in guiding investigations into the etiology of phenomena, and in developing measures for primary prevention, the effectiveness of which depends on a penetrating analysis of the sources and dynamics of the problems, and the identification and elimination of causal agents. It should be noted also in this context that definitions of social problems ought to incorporate explicit value premises in order to be conducive to the design of socially significant research, and to the generation of effective intervention measures.

A HOLISTIC DEFINITION OF CHILD ABUSE

In developing a holistic perspective on child abuse, freed of the

obstacles discussed in the preceding section, one must first redefine this phenomenon in a comprehensive, dynamic manner.
I have formulated such a definition for testimony I presented on
March 26, 1973, before the Sub-Committee on Children and
Youth of the U.S. Senate, at hearings on the "Child Abuse Prevention Act" (S. 1191). This definition, which is quoted here from
the record of the hearings, includes also specifications of value
premises and of the rights of children. Abuse is viewed as inflicted deficits, or gaps, between the rights and the actual circumstances of children, irrespective of the source or agents of the
deficits:

> "Every child, despite his individual differences and uniqueness is to
> be considered of equal intrinsic worth, and hence should be entitled
> to equal social, economic, civil, and political rights, so that he may
> fully realize his inherent potential and share equally in life, liberty,
> and happiness. Obviously, these value premises are rooted in the
> humanistic philosophy of our Declaration of Independence."

> "In accordance with these value premises then, any act of commission
> or omission by individuals, institutions, or society as a whole, and
> any conditions resulting from such acts or inaction, which deprive
> children of equal rights and liberties, and/or interfere with their
> optimal development, constitute, by definition, abusive or neglectful
> acts or conditions."[2]

In this definition, the dimensions of child abuse derive logically
from the stated egalitarian value premises and the related position
concerning the rights of all children to optimal development and
self-actualization. If different value premises and a correspondingly
different position on children's rights were specified in a definition,
the dimensions of child abuse would be modified accordingly,
for abuse is conceived of here as an inflicted deficit between the
specified rights of children and their actual circumstances of
living, no matter who the source or agents of the deficit may be.

ANALYTIC CONCEPTS

The holistic definition of child abuse presented above suggests
the use of two related analytic concepts for studying the nature of
child abuse and for developing effective policies and programs
for its prevention. These concepts will be referred to here as
"levels of manifestation" and "levels of causation" or "causal
dimensions." The levels of manifestation identify the agents and

the settings in which children may experience abuse, or, in terms of the holistic definition, in which the inflicted deficits between their rights to develop freely and fully and their actual circumstances become manifest. The levels of causation unravel the several causal dimensions, the interactions of which result in abusive acts and abusive conditions at the levels of manifestation. The distinction implicit in these analytic concepts, between the levels at which abuse occurs and the forces that underlie the occurances is important, for these levels and forces are not the same. They do, however, complement each other and interact with each other in multiple ways. Moreover, interaction takes place also among the levels themselves, and among the forces. Clarifying the nature of child abuse means essentially to trace these multiple interactions among the levels of manifestation and the causal dimensions.

LEVELS OF MANIFESTATION

Three levels of manifestation of child abuse may be distinguished. The most familiar one is abusive conditions, and abusive inter-action between children and caretakers in the home. Abuse in this setting consists of acts of commission or omission by in-dividuals which inhibit a child's development. The perpetrators are parents, permanent or temporary parent substitutes, or others living in a child's home regularly or temporarily. Abuse in the home may be intentional and conscious or unintentional and also unconscious. Abuse may result from supposedly constructive, disciplinary, educational attitudes and measures, or from negative and hostile feelings toward children. Abusive acts in the home may be one-time events, occasional incidents, or regular patterns. So far, this level of manifestation of child abuse has been the dominant focus of scholarly, professional, and public concern with this destructive phenomenon.

A second level at which child abuse may occur is the institutional level. This includes such settings as day care centers, schools, courts, child care agencies, welfare departments, correctional and other residential child care settings, etc. In such settings, acts and policies of commission or omission which inhibit or insufficiently promote the development of children, or which deprive children of, or fail to provide them with material, emotional, and symbolic means needed for their optimal development, constitute—in accordance with the holistic definition—abusive acts or conditions.

Such acts or policies may originate with an individual employee of an institution, such as a teacher, a child care worker, a judge, a probation officer, a social worker, or they may be implicit in the standard practices and policies of given agencies and institutions. In the same way as in the home, abusive acts and conditions in institutional settings may be intentional and conscious, or unintentional and unconscious. They may also result from supposedly constructive, or from negative and hostile attitudes toward children, and they may be one-time or occasional events or regular patterns.

Institutional child care settings such as schools are often perceived by parents as bearers of cultural norms concerning proper child rearing practices and discipline. Hence, when school and other child care settings employ practices not conducive to optimal child development, e.g. corporal punishment and other demeaning and threatening, negative disciplinary measures, they convey a subtle message to parents, namely, that such measures are appropriate, as they are sanctioned by educational authorities and "experts." Influence flows, however, also in the other direction, from the home level to the institutional level. Teachers and child care personnel will frequently adopt child rearing practices and disciplinary measures similar to those practiced in the homes of children in their care, on the assumption that this is what the children are used to, what they expect, and to what they respond. In this way, methods conducive, or not conducive, to optimal child development tend to be transmitted back and forth, and reinforced, through interaction between the home and the institutional levels.

When child abuse is viewed as inflicted deficit between a child's actual circumstances and circumstances that would assure his optimal development, it seems to be endemic in most existing institutional settings for the care and education of children, since few of these settings facilitate the actualization of the human potential of all children in their care. Further analysis of institutional child abuse reveals that this form of abuse is not distributed randomly through our population. Schools and institutions serving children of minority groups, children from deprived socio-economic backgrounds, handicapped, and socially deviant children are less likely to facilitate optimal development of the children's inherent potential than schools and institutions serving children of majority groups, "normal" children, and children from affluent families and neighborhoods. However, even settings

serving children from such privileged backgrounds rarely encourage the optimal development of all children in their care.
They, too, tend to inhibit spontaneity and creativity, and to
promote conformity rather than critical, independent thought.
Only rarely will children in these settings develop all their inherent
faculties and their unique individuality.

Worse though than the educational system with its frequently
mind-stifling practices, its widespread use of corporal punishment
and other demeaning and threatening forms of discipline, is the
legally sanctioned, massive abuse of children under the policies
and practices of the public welfare system, especially the "Aid to
Families with Dependent Children" (AFDC) program. This
system of grossly inadequate income maintenance—inadequate
by the measures of minimal needs as published by the U.S.
Bureau of Labor Statistics—virtually condemns millions of
children to conditions of existence under which physical, social,
emotional, and intellectual development are likely to be severely
handicapped.

A similarly destructive version of legally sanctioned abuse of
children on the institutional level is the experience of several
hundred thousands of children in foster-care, in training and
correctional institutions, and in institutions for children defined
as mentally retarded. That these settings of substitute child care
usually fail to assure optimum development for the children en-
trusted to them has been amply demonstrated and, thus, does
not require further documentation here.[3]

The massive manifestations of institutional child abuse in
schools, in the AFDC program, and in public child placement
go usually unchallenged by ardent advocates of child protection,
who tend to be deeply concerned about child abuse in the home,
although the abusive conditions and practices of public education,
public welfare, and child placement are endemic to these systems,
and are visible to all who care to see. Perhaps the enormity of
institutional abuse dulls our sensibilities in the same way that
the fate of inmates of concentration camps, or of populations
suffering from natural or man-made catastrophes, tends, after a
while, to arouse a lesser response than the killing of a single
individual with whom we are able to identify.

Institutional child abuse is linked intimately to the third level
at which child abuse is manifested, the societal level. This is the
level at which those social policies originate which sanction or
cause severe deficits between the actual circumstances of children

and conditions needed for their optimal development. As the direct or indirect consequences of currently prevailing social policies, millions of children in our society live in poverty and are inadequately nourished, clothed, housed, and educated; their health is not assured because of sub-standard medical care; their neighborhoods decay; meaningful occupational opportunities are not available to them, and alienation is widespread among them. No doubt, these destructive conditions which result, inevitably, from the normal workings of the prevailing social, economic, and political order, and from the value premises which shape that order and its human dynamics, cannot fail to inhibit severely the development of children exposed to them.

Of the three levels of child abuse discussed in this section, the societal level is certainly the most severe one. For what happens at this level determines not only how children fare on the institutional level, but also, by way of complex interactions, how they fare in their own homes.

LEVELS OF CAUSATION OR CAUSAL DIMENSIONS

Before discussing the causal dimensions of child abuse, it should be stressed that the conventional dichotomy between individual and societal causation of social problems distorts the multi-dimensional reality of human phenomena. We know that psychological forces which shape individual behavior evolve out of the totality of life experiences in specific historical, cultural, social, economic, and political contexts. Individual motivation and behavior are thus always rooted in a societal force field. Yet societal forces are always expressed, or mediated, through the behavior of individuals, for societies cannot act except through their individual members. Clearly then, any human phenomenon, at any moment, involves both social and individual elements. In real life, these elements are inseparable. Their separation in theory is merely a product of scholarly, or rather, pseudo-scholarly abstraction.

Based on this reasoning, all child abuse, at any level of manifestation, involves acts or inaction of individuals, on their own or as institutional agents, whose behavior reflects societal forces mediated through their unique personalities.

The most fundamental causal level of child abuse consists of a cluster of interacting elements, to wit, a society's basic social philosophy, its dominant value premises, its concept of humans;

the nature of its social, economic, and political institutions which are shaped by its philosophy and value premises, and which in turn reinforce that philosophy and these values; and, finally, the particular quality of human relations prevailing in the society, which derives from its philosophy, values, and institutions. For, in the final analysis, it is the philosophy and value premises of a society, the nature of its major institutions, and the quality of its human relations, which determine whether or not individual members of that society will develop freely and fully in accordance with their inherent potentialities.

To discern a society's basic social philosophy and values and its concept of humans, one needs to ascertain whether it considers everyone to be intrinsically of equal worth in spite of his or her uniqueness and, hence, entitled to the same social, economic, and political rights; or whether everyone in the society considers himself, and those close to himself, of greater worth than anyone else, and hence entitled to more desirable or privileged circumstances. The former, egalitarian philosophy would be reflected in institutional arrangements involving cooperative actions in pursuit of common existential interests. Every individual, and that includes every child, would be considered an equally entitled subject, who could not be deprived of his rights, exploited, and dominated by any other individual or group, and whose right to fully and freely develop his individuality would be assured and respected, subject to the same right of all others. The latter, non-egalitarian philosophy, on the other hand, as we know so well from our own existence, is reflected in institutional structures which encourage competitive behavior in pursuit of narrowly perceived, egotistical interests. Everyone strives to get ahead of others, considers himself entitled to privileged conditions and positions, and views and treats others as potential means to be used, exploited, and dominated in pursuit of his egotistical goals.

The quality of human relations and of human experience in a truly egalitarian social order would be essentially harmonious. A sense of true community and well-being would be shared by all. Economic institutions would be organized rationally, not for private profit and capital accumulation, but to satisfy everyone's real needs. Waste would be avoided, the environment protected, and natural resources preserved. Political institutions would be truly democratic and participatory; power would be equalized and decentralized; everyone would share equally in important decisions, and especially decisions affecting his existence. Clearly, all forms of domination and exploitation would be precluded, the scarcity and jungle mentality by which we now live would be overcome, and a true Commonwealth based on reason could evolve.

The quality of human relations and of human experience in non-egalitarian social orders is, typically, characterized by competitiveness and jealousies, individual isolation and loneliness, alienation, distrust, fear, and insecurity. These qualities are inevitable correlates of non-egalitarian, hierarchical, domineering, and exploitative social, economic, and political institutions, which tend to be controlled by huge, centralized, and dehumanizing bureaucracies. Under such institutional structures, individuals cease to be subjects, or masters, of their own lives, and are turned into means for objectives far beyond their true existential needs. Real liberty and true self-actualization are not feasible in such social orders, irrespective of their ideological stances or window-dressings, be that ideology "free-enterprise-capitalism" and pseudo-democracy as in the United States and the so-called "free" world, or be it "state-capitalism" and centralistic pseudo-socialism as in the Soviet Union and several other so-called "socialist" countries.

This brief sketch of contrasting social philosophies, societal institutions, and modes of human relations suggests that full and free development of every child's inherent potential may be possible only in a society organized consistently around egalitarian and cooperative value premises, since the equal right to self-actualization is implicit in an egalitarian philosophy, while such a right is incompatible with a non-egalitarian philosophy. In a society organized on non-egalitarian and competitive principles, full and free development for all children is simply impossible as, by definition, there must always be losers in such societies, whose chances to realize their inherent potential will be severely limited. Hence, there will be, in such societies, significant developmental deficits for large segments of their populations—or a high level of socially structured and sanctioned abuse of children.

A second, more specific, though related to the first, level of causation of child abuse may be intrinsic to the social construction, or definition, of childhood prevalent in a society. How does a society view its children, all its children, and how does it define their rights? How much obedience, submission, and conformity does it expect of children? Does it process children through caste-like channels of socialization into relatively closed and inflexible social and occupational structures, or does it encourage them, within limits of reason, to discover and develop their individuality and uniqueness, and to shape their lives accordingly? Obviously, optimal development of the inherent potential of all children is a function of the extent to which a society's processes of socialization are permeated with a commitment to such self-actualization for all. When this commitment is lacking altogether, or when it varies with such factors as sex, race, social and economic position of a family, etc., then different children will experience varying deficits in realizing their potential. Presently, in our society, social policies which sustain different levels of rights for children from different social and economic backgrounds are a major, direct cause of many forms of child abuse on the societal and institutional levels, and an indirect cause of abuse on the family level.

A further causal dimension of child abuse is a society's attitude toward the use of force as a legitimate means for attaining ends, especially in inbalanced, interpersonal relations such as master-slave, male-female, guard-prisoner, and adult-child. The long-established tendency to resort to the use of force for dealing with conflicts in our society seems to require no documentation here, nor does it seem necessary to document the specific readiness to use force, or the threat of it, as a means to maintain authority and discipline in adult-child relations in the public domain such as schools and other child care settings, and in the private domain of the family. The readiness to use physical force for disciplinary objectives is certainly endemic in our society, rather than a manifestation of deviance.

It should be noted that the readiness to use force in general, and in adult-child relations in particular, is intimately linked to a society's basic philosophy and value premises, and to its concept of humans and their rights. A non-egalitarian philosophy is much more likely to sanction the use of force than an egalitarian one, since the use of force against other humans constitutes the strongest possible negation of equality. The use of force toward children is also related to the manner in which childhood, and the rights of children are defined by a society, and in turn tends to reinforce that definition.

As mentioned earlier, the use of force toward children is widespread in our society on the institutional and family levels. Attempts to limit and outlaw it in public institutions have had so far only limited success. It may be noted, in this context, that due to the compatibility between the use of physical force and an in-egalitarian philosophy and competitive social, economic, and political institutions, corporal punishment and the threat of it may actually be highly functional in preparing children for adult roles in an inegalitarian and competitive social order. For, were our children reared in a harmonious fashion without threats, insults, and physical force, they might not be adequately prepared and conditioned for adult roles in our inegalitarian, competitive reality.

Whenever corporal punishment in child rearing is sanctioned, and even subtly encouraged by a society, incidents of serious physical abuse and injury are bound to happen, either as a result of deliberate, systematic, and conscious action on the part of perpetrators, or under conditions of loss of self-control. In either case, but especially in the latter, physical attacks on children tend to relieve tensions and frustrations experienced by the perpetrators. Clearly then, these attacks are carried out to meet emotional needs of the perpetrators rather than educational needs of the victims, as is often claimed by advocates of corporal punishment.

The next causal dimension may be referred to as "triggering contexts." These contexts operate jointly with the societal sanction of the use of physical force in adult-child relations. Adults who use force toward children do not do so all the time, but only under specific circumstances which serve as triggers for their abusive behavior. In general, abusive attacks tend to be triggered by stress and frustration which may cause reduction or loss of self-control. Stresses and frustration may facilitate abusive attacks even without causing a reduction or loss of self-control, as long as the appropriateness of the use of force in child rearing is accepted, an acceptance which was shown to be widespread in our society.

One major source of stress and frustration for adults in our society is the multi-faceted deprivations of poverty and its correlates, high density in overcrowded, dilapidated, inadequately served neighborhoods; large numbers of children, especially in one-parent, mainly female-headed households; and the absence of child care alternatives. Having identified poverty and its correlates as one important triggering context of child abuse in the home, we may now note that social policies which sanction and perpetuate the existence of poverty among large segments of the population, including millions of children, are thus indirect sources of child abuse in the home. It should be emphasized, though, that poverty, per se, is not a direct cause of child abuse in the home, but operates through an intervening variable, namely, concrete and psychological stress and frustration experienced by individuals against the background of culturally sanctioned use of physical force in child rearing.

Poverty is not the only source of stress and frustration triggering child abuse in the home. For such abuse is known to occur frequently in many homes in adequate, and even affluent, economic circumstances. One other, major source of stress and frustration in our society is the alienating circumstances in most workplaces, be the work manual labor, skilled and unskilled occupations, or administrative, managerial, and professional work through all levels and sectors of business, academic, and government bureaucracies. A recent report by a task force of the U. S. Department of Health, Education, and Welfare documented the seriousness of work alienation which is experienced by constantly growing segments of the working population.[4] This government report is certainly not biased against the economic system of the United States. And yet, it reached similar conclusions to those voiced by many severe critics of this system in recent years. These conclusions are that the prevailing competitive and exploiting human relations in the work place, and its hierarchical and authoritarian structures, tend to cause psychological stress and alienation for nearly every working person. These pressures may lead to various forms of deviant behavior such as alcoholism, drug addiction, mental illness, white collar crime, etc. Perhaps the most frequent locus for discharging feelings of stress and frustration originating in the formal world of work is the informal world of primary relations, the home and the family. Conflicts between spouses are one form this discharge may take. Child abuse in the form of violent physical outbursts is another. Here then, we identify once again a triggering context for child abuse on the interpersonal level, which is rooted deeply in societal forces, namely, the alienating quality of our society's economic and productive system complemented by the culturally sanctioned use of physical force in child rearing.

The final causal dimension of child abuse on the interpersonal level in the home and in child care settings is intra-psychic conflicts and various forms of psycho-pathology on the part of perpetrators. Child abuse literature is largely focused on this dimension and thus little needs to be said here to document it. However, what needs to be stressed is the fact that psychological disturbances and their manner of expression are not independent factors but are deeply rooted in, and constantly interact with, forces in the social environment of the disturbed individual. To the extent that psycho-pathology is not rooted in genetic and bio-chemical processes, it derives from the totality of the life ex-periences of the individual which are shaped by continuous inter-actions between the person and his social setting, his informal and formal relations in primary and secondary contexts. However, not only the etiology of intra-psychic conflicts and disturbances is conditioned, in part, by social forces, but also the manner in which these conflicts and disturbances are expressed in social relations is very much culture-bound. The symptoms of emotional disturbance and mental illness are not randomly generated phenomena, but derive from normal behavioral traits in a culture. These normal traits appear in exaggerated or negated forms in behavior which is considered deviant, neurotic, and psychotic. Hence, one may assume that in a society in which the use of physi-cal force in general, and toward children in particular, is not sanctioned, intra-psychic conflicts and psycho-pathology would less often be expressed through violence against children. It follows from these considerations that the "battered-baby syndrome" and other forms of child abuse which are associated with mental illness are not independent of societal forces, although the perpetrators of these acts may be considered to be emotionally ill individuals. We are thus again led to the conclusion that abusive acts and conditions, irrespective of the level of manifestation, cannot be understood in terms of one specific causal dimension, but only in terms of complex interactions among the several causal dimensions sketched in this section.

PRIMARY PREVENTION

According to a general conceptual model, primary prevention moves from identification toward elimination of the causal contexts from which specified, undesired phenomena derive. It needs to be realized that the prevention of undesired phenomena may result also in the elimination of other phenomena whenever such other phenomena derive from, or are part of, the same causal context. The likelihood of such simultaneous prevention of phenomena could lead to serious dilemmas in situations when some of the phenomena are desired, while others are considered undesirable, or when groups in a society differ in their respective evaluation of the desirability of the several phenomena. Decisions concerning primary prevention of social phenomena and of "social problems" are thus essentially political choices.

Turning now to the primary prevention of child abuse, we may begin by summarizing our conclusions so far. Child abuse, conceived of as inflicted deficits on a child's right to develop freely and fully, irrespective of the source and agents of the deficit, was found to occur on several related levels: on the interpersonal level in the home and in child-care settings, on the institutional level through the policies and practices of a broad array of child care, educational, welfare, and correctional institutions and agencies, and on the societal level, where the interplay of values and social, economic, and political institutions and processes shapes the social policies by which the rights, and the existential realities of all children, and of specific groups of children are determined. The causal dimensions of child abuse are, first of all, the dominant social philosophy and value premises of a society, the social, economic, and political institutions shaped by its philosophy and values, and the quality of human relations to which these institutions, philosophy, and values give rise; other causal dimensions are the social construction of childhood and the social definition of children's rights, the extent to which a society sanctions the use of force in general, and, more specifically, in the child rearing context, stress and frustration resulting from poverty and from alienation in the work place which may trigger abusive acts, and expressions of intra-psychic conflicts and psycho-pathology which in turn are rooted in the social fabric. While child abuse, at any particular level, may be more closely related to one rather than another causal dimension, none of these dimensions are independent, and they exert their influence through multiple interactions with each other.

This analysis suggests that primary prevention of child abuse, on all levels, would require fundamental changes in social philosophy and value premises, in societal institutions, and in human relations. It would also require a reconceptualization of childhood, of children's rights, and of child rearing. It would necessitate rejecting the use of force as means for achieving societal ends, especially in dealing with children. It would require the elimination of poverty and of alienating conditions of production, major sources of stress and frustration which tend to trigger abusive acts toward children in adult-child interaction. And, finally, it would necessitate the elimination of psychological illness. Because of the multiple interactions among the several causal dimensions, progress in overcoming the more fundamental dimensions would also reduce the force of other dimensions. Thus, transforming the prevailing inegalitarian social philosophy, value premises, and institutions—and the kind of human relations they generate—into egalitarian ones would also result in corresponding modifications of children's rights, elimination of poverty and alienation at work, and rejection of the use of force. It would indirectly influence psychological wellbeing, and would thus eliminate the processes which now trigger child abuse in interpersonal relations.

Effective primary prevention requires working simultaneously toward the transformation of all the causal dimensions. Fragmented approaches focused on one or the other causal dimension may bring some amelioration, but one should entertain no illusions as to the effectiveness of such piecemeal efforts. Even such important and necessary steps as outlawing corporal punishment in schools and other child care settings would have only limited, though highly desirable results. There simply is no way of escaping the conclusion that the complete elimination of child abuse on all levels of its manifestation requires a radical transformation of the prevailing injust, inegalitarian, irrational, competitive, alienating and hierarchical social order into a just, egalitarian, rational, cooperative, humane, and truly democractic, decentralized one. Obviously, this realization implies that primary prevention of child abuse is a political issue which cannot be resolved through professional and administrative measures.

Primary prevention of child abuse would result also in the prevention of other, equally undesirable and equally inevitable consequences or symptoms of the same causal context, including many manifestations of social deviance. However, it would also result in the complete transformation of the prevailing social, economic, and political order with which large segments of our society are either identified or drifting along, because this order conforms to their accustomed mental sets, and because they seem reluctant, due to inertia, to search actively for alternative social, economic, and political orders which might be more conducive to human fulfillment for all. Some or many members of our society may even be consciously committed to the perpetuation of the existing order, not realizing how destructive that order may be to their real human interests.

Whatever one's attitude may be toward these fundamental

political issues, one needs to recognize and face the dilemmas implicit in them and, hence, in primary prevention of child abuse. If one's priority is to prevent all child abuse, one must be ready to part with its many causes, even when one is attached to some of them, such as the apparent blessings, advantages and privileges of inequality. If, on the other hand, one is reluctant to give up all aspects of the causal context of child abuse, one must be content to continue living with this social problem. In that latter case, one ought to stop talking about primary prevention and face the fact that all one may be ready for is some measure of amelioration.

RESEARCH

In concluding this essay on the nature and prevention of child abuse from a holistic perspective, some observations seem indicated on implications for research. Research, to be meaningful in a social sense, should derive from socially meaningful issues and should pursue imaginative hypotheses aimed at solving these issues. Far too often, scarce research resources seem to be wasted on essentially irrelevant studies which explore insignificant, fragmentary issues and pedestrian hypotheses, often with the aid of highly sophisticated research technology. These critical comments on the state of social research apply to a large part of past and present research on child abuse and its prevention.

The discussion in this essay of the levels of manifestation and the causal dimensions of child abuse does suggest a series of socially meaningful issues which could be addressed through social research. Likewise, the discussion of primary prevention of child abuse suggests one comprehensive hypothesis which could be explored and tested by means of properly designed research. The issues to be investigated are the validity of the causal model of child abuse and its several dimensions and their multiple interactions. The hypothesis concerning primary prevention states that societies which overcame the causal dimensions of child abuse identified in this essay would gradually free themselves of child abuse. These issues and this hypothesis could be explored cross-culturally, historically, and experimentally. One could search for past and present societies and communities, whose philosophy, value premises, societal institutions, and human relations are relatively free of the posited causal dimensions of child abuse, and one could examine whether the incidence of child abuse on all levels of manifestation is indeed lower in these societies than in our own. Alternatively, one could stimulate and facilitate the emergence of communities organized on principles that preclude the hypothesized causal context of child abuse, and one could then observe whether the incidence of child abuse on all levels would decrease over time, and eventually cease altogether.

Less ambitious approaches to research are, of course, possible. However, if social research should guide us toward primary prevention, it needs to be designed around a causal model and a hypothesis concerning approaches to the elimination of the causal dimensions. Other types of research can guide only toward some form of amelioration, which may be all one is ready to engage in and which, of course, may have some utility as long as it is not misrepresented as a contribution to primary prevention.

Choices of foci for research turn out to be related to a scholar's fundamental social and political outlook, in the same way as attitudes towards primary prevention were shown to be essentially political. A researcher who accepts the prevailing social order is likely to select topics for study which will not threaten or challenge that order. On the other hand, a researcher who is committed to social justice for all, and who conceives of social science as a tool in the struggle for human liberation, will not hesitate to conduct studies of alternative social patterns and life styles which may thoroughly challenge prevailing assumptions, and which hold promise for a human existence freed of the many injustices of the prevailing social order, of which child abuse is merely one.

CHAPTER EIGHT

Common Roots and Functions of Warfare and Welfare

Warfare and welfare are usually assumed to serve contradictory ends and to be rooted in antithetical values, institutions and dynamics. In this essay, I propose to challenge this notion and to advance, instead, the thesis that, inspite of significant differences between them, warfare and welfare serve, nevertheless, identical and complementary functions, and are both rooted in identical societal values, institutions and dynamics.

As with other phenomena which are considered to be "social problems," such as poverty, crime, unemployment, inflation, mental illness, etc., but which are merely by-products of the "normal" workings of certain social systems, warfare and welfare can not be understood and overcome unless their philosophical and institutional roots and functions are first unraveled. This requires studying warfare and welfare from a holistic-evolutionary perspective which treats social, economic, political, psychological, and ideological dimensions of human societies as variables rather than as constants, settled once and for all. When warfare and welfare are explored in this fashion and are placed within the context of universal existential processes, the extent to which they tend to fit the internal logic of certain patterns of these processes should become discernable, and their presumed inevitability can then by demystified.

What, then, are the general functions of warfare and welfare, and from what philosophical roots and values do they derive? To explore these questions, I will focus first on welfare and then on warfare.

WELFARE AS A SOCIETAL INSTITUTION

In discussing welfare I am concerned primarily with formal, institutionalized practices as reflected in social policies and services of "welfare-states," whether the services are administered directly by units of government, or indirectly by government-chartered, "voluntary" agencies. I am only tangentially concerned with attitudes and acts of spontaneous and systematic cooperation and mutual aid within families and among friends, neighbors, and members of communities. There is historical and philosophical continuity and interaction between cooperation and mutual aid, and welfare-state policies and services. However for purposes of the present exploration, I am concerned with aspects of welfare state policies and services which differ, in a fundamental sense, from acts of cooperation and mutual aid. For these differences contain the clues to the philosophical roots and societal functions of welfare as an institution.

Acts of spontaneous and systematic cooperation and mutual aid represent transactions among individuals and groups of essentially equal social, economic and political standing. They derive from a sense of mutual caring and responsibility, a shared human and community identity, common perceptions of interests, and value positions tending toward equality, liberty, self-reliance, cooperation, and collectivity orientation. Implicit in these acts is respect for the autonomy and individuality of all those involved, helpers and helped alike. The function of spontaneous and systematic cooperation and mutual aid is to compensate individuals for temporary or extended handicaps or disadvantageous conditions inherent in certain stages of the life process, or caused by natural phenomena and by the vicissitudes of living. The aim of such cooperation and mutual aid is to assure normalization of circumstances and fullest possible integration and participation in community life of those affected by adverse circumstances.

Policies and services of welfare-states, on the other hand,

involve usually transactions among individuals and groups of essentially unequal social, economic, and political standing. While these services can be, and often are, administered in a humane fashion, and while they can, and often do, improve the circumstances of deprived and disadvantaged individuals and groups, their underlying function is, nevertheless, to serve as a balance-wheel for a social order based on injustice, privilege, force and structural violence. The values implicit in, and promoted by, welfare-state policies and services are inequality, domination, competition, and self-orientation.

To support these assertions concerning welfare in the welfare-state, one must examine the evolution, the structure and dynamics, and the social philosophy of welfare-states. Chart 1 below, a schematic representation of human social orders, should be useful in such an examination.

CHART #1 KEY VARIABLES OF SOCIAL ORDERS, SOCIAL POLICIES, & SOCIAL CHANGE

HUMAN NEEDS—the source of social orders (biological psychological, social)

- needs for security of provision of life-sustaining and enhancing goods and services;
- needs for meaningful, satisfying human relations: being cared about and acknowledged as an authentic, autonomous subject, and care about and acknowledge others in like manner;
- needs to engage in meaningful, self-directed, creative and productive work, conducive to self-discovery, self-expression and self-actualization.

SOCIAL INSTITUTIONS
Key domains for social institutions:
1. Resource management & control: selection, development, stewardship of natural and human designed and created resources, including all material goods and non-material products, such as knowledge, skills, technology, etc.
2. Division and organization of work: allocation of roles to people and people to roles; modes of production;
3. Distribution of all kinds of rights: social, psychological, economic, civil, political, etc. through entitlements, rewards, prerogatives, and constraints;
4. Decision making, conduct of public affairs, governance.

SYMBOLIC UNIVERSE
Psychological equivalents of social structure;

Consciousness of socially constructed reality;
Concepts of human nature, of nature, and of the super-natural;
Perceptions of individual interest and of collective interest;
Social policy relevant value dimensions:
   equality—inequality
   liberty—domination
   cooperation—competition
   collectivity—
      orientation—selfishness

legitimation
socialization
social control

Implicit in Chart 1 is the assumption that social orders are creations of the human mind and of human actions, or rather of the thoughts and actions of countless humans communicating and interacting through space and time. Social orders emerge through the gradual institutionalization of collective responses to existential imperatives intrinsic to the human drive to survive in natural settings which are always characterized by relative scarcities of life-sustaining resources, and which always require human work to secure such resources. Essentially then, different social orders are different solutions to the same existential problems, namely, to satisfy the biological, psychological, and social needs of their members. Societies can, therefore, be compared and evaluated in terms of the extent to which they succeed or fail to satisfy these needs.

Chart 1 lists four related existential domains for which social orders must evolve institutional structures and dynamics to assure their continuity and viability: management of resources, organization of work and production, distribution of rights, and governance. The Chart also shows that parellel to their institutional structures, social orders require a "symbolic universe" which interprets, justifies and sustains these institutions, shapes the consciousness of people, and also interprets nature, the supernatural, the concept of human nature, perceptions of interests and value positions relevant to the institutional order. Finally the Chart indicates that legitimation of the social order, socialization into it, and social control of individuals living in its orbit, are the result of mutually reinforcing interactions of a society's "material" institutions and "symbolic universe."

Before using the model of social orders in Chart 1 to sketch the emergence of institutionalized welfare within the context of the evolution of the welfare-state, some observations are indicated on the notion of self-reliance. Self-reliance is the opposite of dependence and thus the real antidote of welfare, since dependence is the condition which leads inevitably to the institutionalization of welfare measures. Self-reliance of individuals and of human groups is possible when they are in a position to satisfy their needs by producing for themselves life-sustaining and life-enhancing resources. In order to produce needed resources, individuals and groups must have free access to, and free use of, natural resources such as land, water, air, sunlight, minerals, wildlife, vegetation, energy, and human-created resources such as tools, scientific knowledge, technology and skills, for all production involves bringing together natural resources, human-created resources, and human capacities. Self-reliance then requires freedom to bring these components together in ever new combinations.

One further point to note is that self-reliance does not require that individuals or groups produce everything needed for their existence, for self-reliance is not the same as self-sufficiency or autarky. However self-reliance is predicated upon exchanges among different individuals and groups of their respective products on fair, non-exploitative, flexibly-egalitarian terms. Rough measures for fair exchanges are the equivalence of efforts invested in products, the importance of products in terms of a hierarchy of human needs, and the degree of scarcity of natural resources used in production.

Institutionalized welfare measures in the welfare state are rooted in human dependence, or rather in societal processes, structures and dynamics which first undermined, and eventually prevented all together, opportunities for genuine independence and self-reliance on the part of major segments of populations. The evolutionary process leading to this outcome will now be sketched.

The first and most fundamental step in the fateful process which eventually destroyed opportunities for self-reliance for the majority of individuals in many human groups, and which, then led via charity to the welfare state, was the establishment by individuals of claims to exclusive control over territories and natural resources on these. It may be noted already at this point that this step was also the beginning of a process leading to warfare and the warfare state. Appropriations for use by one individual and his family was one feasible, and sensible, approach to solving the issues of resources-management and provision during early stages of human evolution. The purpose of this solution was to assure owners and their relations a steady flow of life-sustaining, needs-satisfying provisions, and thus to reduce existential insecurity. This choice, at the dawn of human history, became gradually the root of the powerful institution, ideology and dynamics of private property, the archetype and core of many ancient and modern societies, cultures, and states.

The choice of individual appropriation of life-sustaining resources was by no means inevitable, nor is it inherent in human nature as is often erroneously assumed. There is ample evidence throughout history, all over the world, that many human groups created social orders using an opposite principle, according to which life-sustaining resources of nature should not be appropriated by individuals for exclusive use and control, but should be freely available for use by all members of a group to sustain and enhance everyone's existence. Hindsight suggests that this egalitarian, cooperative, collectivity-oriented approach to solving issues of resource management and provision constituted a far more sophisticated choice than appropriation for exclusive individual use of resources, especially when these alternative approaches are compared and evaluated in terms of the extent to which human needs are satisfied throughout a population, and in terms of efficient use of scarce resources.

The principle of private property as a basis for individual security has had significant institutional, ideological, psychological, and behavioral consequences for human groups who evolved their social systems around that principle. Since owning land and other natural and human-created resources was considered desirable, owning more such property came to be considered even more desirable. This attitude, and actions based on it, led to efforts to increase one's holdings, to the emergence of an acquisitive, selfish and competitive mentality, and to human relations shaped by these practices and mentality. As long as enough resources were available for everyone to appropriate a sufficient share to assure his existence, this system worked adequately. However, when all available resources had been appropriated the mentality and dynamics of acquisitiveness and competition caused people to try to increase their holdings by taking from others by force and cunning.

As the holdings of some people increased while those of others decreased a new, serious problem emerged: who would work with the natural resources to assure the continuous production of needed provisions? Up to that stage in evolution everyone had worked with his own resources preserving thus his independence and self-reliance. Yet as the holdings of some individuals increased they could no longer put them to effective use, working by themselves. Besides there was also the problem of guarding and defending the holdings amassed in competiton with others who constituted an ever present threat, especially since their own holdings were no longer large enough to sustain their existence through work. One ingenuous solution to these complementary dilemmas seems to have been to induce the losers in the competition for property to work on, and to guard, the property of the winners. In this way additional human capacities would be available to the owners of property, while the owners, in turn provided work opportunities and a limited share of life-sustaining products to those who had lost control of sufficient natural and human-created resources, to sustain themselves, and who had consequently nothing left but their own human capacities. This arrangement became the second major step on the road to dependence and welfare, for it gradually accomplished the complete structural separation of major segments of the population from the real sources of genuine freedom, independence, self-reliance, and self-determination through self-directed work, namely equal access to, and use of, productive natural and human-created. resources and facilities.

In passing mention should be made here of an early variation on the themes of increasing property holdings and recruiting a willing work force from among expropriated segments of the population. This variation was organized expeditions for the purpose of expanding control over territories and resources beyond the domain of one's own group and recruiting by force an enslaved work force from among the inhabitants of conquered lands.

An essential next step on the road to the welfare-state were efforts to condition and control the property-less and severely deprived masses of slaves and workers on whose work everyone, including the property owners, depended for survival. The solution to this difficult problem was found in hierarchical organization of work and authority which involved a fine gradation of privilege and power filtered down to workers as inducement for loyalty to their masters, the owners of property. This system resulted in multiple divisions of the work force into competing vertical segments and horizontal strata which received different material and symbolic rewards and power, exercised different levels of authority, and developed different interests, life-styles, aspirations, motivations, reference groups and loyalties.

One further important mechanism for solving problems of conditioning and controlling the workforce was to withhold opportunities for work and survival from a sizable segment of the work force, except in times of war. The ever present prospect of unemployment and its disastrous existential consequences posed a constant threat, especially to the lowest layers of the work force, those who were expected to perform the least desirable work. That threat, and the frequent experience of actual unemployment, developed not only into a major mechanism for disciplining the work force but also for keeping the shares of workers in the aggregate product of their work relatively low, ensuring thus the continuation of wealth accumulation on the part of owners.

The developments sketched here schematically, in an over-simplified manner, have taken thousands of years. They were far from smooth and were accompanied by fierce conflicts and struggles within and among various human groups. Empirical evidence of the stages mentioned in this sketch can be found throughout the history of many civilizations all over the globe. However, with time a societal pattern began to emerge with which we are now very familiar, a social order in which the ownership and control of natural and human-created wealth are concentrated in the hands of a small segment of the population while the rest of the people are essentially deprived of productive resources except for their human capacities which, in the case of most of them, are usually not fully developed. Those who own no property can not be self-reliant through self-directed work, the fruits of which they may enjoy proudly. They are forced instead to depend for their existence on work opportunities provided by property owners on terms that suit the owners' interests to further increase their wealth and control through profit-generating, rather than needs-satisfy-ing, use of productive resources. Furthermore, the property-less work force continues to be divided into countless layers and interest groups through differential rewards, opportunities, and penalties built into the system, and they are forced to compete among themselves to obtain the rewards and avoid the penalties. Sex, race, ethnicity, nationality, age, formal education, certifica-tion, and licensing are all used to increase the internal divisions of the work force, and to prevent its unification and organization around its underlying, true existential interest: to liberate the productive resources and facilities in order to achieve self-reliance, freedom and self-determination through self-directed work.

Most now existing social orders have come a long way from the earliest steps of appropriation of territories and natural resources. They evolved through many social, cultural, scientific, and tech-nological stages, from a gathering and hunting economy to agriculture and industry, and from slavery to serfdom and wage-labor. However the basic organizing principle of property rights and relations has remained relatively constant as the core of the changing social-economic orders. Those who managed to own and control productive resources appropriate for the time and develop-mental stage of their societies gained usually also political influence and power. This, in turn, enabled them to assure the legitimacy of the established divisions of wealth, division of labor and organization of production, and distribution of goods, services, civil and political rights, and social recognition and prestige. Those who gained political influence and power also created the concept, the institution and the ideology of the state, the central function of which became to assure and protect the status-quo of privilege, injustice, inequality, domination and exploitation in every sphere of life, which had emerged over hundreds of generations. The state defined the status-quo as "law and order" and thus legitimated the results of ages of lawlessness and disorder, injustice, force, violence, and cunning. The state was committed to maintain and defend the established order by all possible and necessary means, including covert and overt force, against any attempt to bring about significant changes in the prevailing distributional patterns, policies, and processes.

Certain aspects of the "symbolic universe" and of the consciousness and psychology of people, which evolved in interaction with the institutional developments sketched above, should now be noted. The emerging social orders came to be thought of as "natural" and as the only "right" orders. Eventually they were interpreted as the "will of God," and their rulers were believed to hold office "by the grace of God." Priesthoods, at first hesitatingly, and later enthusiastically, bestowed their blessings and full support on established orders and affirmed the sanctity of private property and its guardian, the state, in spite of contrary prophetic messages in the Scriptures and other sacred sources.

Humans were thought to be unique, at the peak of nature, apart from the rest of nature rather than harmoniously integrated into it, nature's masters designated by God. These notions led in time to an exploitative attitude toward natural resources, and to mindless waste and destruction. Human nature was thought to be evil, and, indeed, humans displayed evil attitudes toward one another, and tended not to trust others. Furthermore, humans came to be thought of as unequal in worth and as entitled to different rights, depending on the amount of property and power they managed to acquire. Success in the acquisitive drive was interpreted as indication of superior qualities, as evidence of virtue and of God's blessing, and hence, as a basis for social recognition and prestige. Conversely, failure in the acquisitive drive was interpreted as due to individual shortcomings, to sinful ways, to God's condemnation and rejection, and, hence, a basis for societal contempt, disapproval and rejection.

Life itself came to be viewed as a permanent contest in a zero-sum game, with everyone struggling "to get a larger piece of a finite pie." People developed selfish, inegalitarian and competitive attitudes toward one another and a jungle mentality of mutual fear, suspicion, and mistrust, envy and jealousy. They came to view themselves as subjects and everyone else as potential objects to be used and exploited. They manipulated one another pragmatically, in accordance with "the rules of the game" for their individual ends. They related to one another through formal roles rather than as whole, feeling and caring human beings. They became lonely, isolated and alienated. To compensate for their emotional deprivations they escaped into substitute gratifications, illusions, drugs, alcohol, and mental ills.

Attitudes toward work came to reflect the emerging institutional contradictions. Originally, work was respected as an important source of human wealth and as the means for human survival and for the enhancement of the quality of life. There was also pride in a well executed job and the resulting product, and enjoyment of the fruits of labor. These original and functional attitudes towards work, the original work ethic, were destroyed when people were expropriated, their access to resources and productive facilities was subjected to control by others, direction of their work was removed from them, and products were alienated from the producers, in short, when work became exploitative. These developments caused work to be viewed as an unavoidable chore and evil. The joy of creativity had gone out of it. Besides when owners of wealth began to withdraw from work and to develop a cult of leisure and an ethic of work-avoidance, according to which engaging in physical labor was debasing and demeaning of the person, negative attitudes toward work began to permeate the consciousness of the population. Henceforth, people tried to work as little as possible and to shift work onto others, especially when it was intrinsically unpleasant and dangerous. Gradually also, in order to increase output, profit, and efficiency measured by economic criteria, most work processes were structured in a manner that undermined the possibility of intrinsic gratification. Work became boring, mind-killing, and offensive to the senses. Using the worker's intellect at work became counterproductive, an obstacle to speed and efficiency. Furthermore, work took place within the general competitive context of the struggle for survival and advancement and within hierarchically structured huge bureaucracies. This too added to the oppressive experience of work and increased alienation from work and frustration from the unrewarding human relations of most work places.

Clearly institutional developments   had resulted in massive disincentives to work. To counteract these trends a work-ethic had to be resurrected on an illusionary base. The only real work incentive given the institutional reality and ideological developments, was the fear of starvation. To this a myth had to be added, according to which hard work was a direct road to success and wealth as well as an indirect road to salvation, for after all, work was "sacred". With the aid of this myth the commitment to work on the part of those who had to work was to be shored up. There was enough truth in this myth to render it believable in spite of overwhelming contrary evidence. And so the myth continued to survive and to sustain exploitative work processes of a production system where labor—a function of humans, is employed by capital—lifeless matter, in the interest of the owners of capital. This production system is a far cry from a mode of production fitting the original work ethic, a system where whole humans freely employ resources to advance their existential interests.

Having sketched the institutional evolution and the symbolic universe of social systems organized around privately owned and controlled productive resources and facilities, the functions of institutionalized welfare policies and services in such societies can now be spelled out. Essentially, institutionalized welfare fits into such social systems as a safety-valve or balance wheel. It constitutes an effective and even "efficient" line of last defense which can be adjusted flexibly to changing circumstances and to recurrent threats to the systems stability.[1]

Social orders fitting more or less the dynamics discussed here have caused throughout their evolution, and continue to cause at present, immense suffering of many millions of propertyless and income-less human beings. When people have no wealth and when their income ceases, or is insufficient to sustain a minimal existence because of age, illness, accidents, death of breadwinners, unemployment, low wages, lack of education and skills, discriminatory practices, etc., all of which are quite "normal" occurences in these societies, their very survival would be threatened, unless they received voluntary aid from relatives, peers, neighbors, and other caring individuals, or unless some formal institutional mechanisms are established to assist them. No doubt institutionalized charity and welfare are rooted partly in the neighborly, humanistic response to suffering, in a common human identity, in a collective sense of guilt, and in a desire to stop suffering and to satisfy human needs. Yet these humanistic elements were never strong enough to bring about an open challenge to the systemic roots and forces which render dependency and its correlates and consequences inevitable.

Yet institutionalized welfare does not merely refrain from confronting and challenging the structural obstacles to self-reliance and human liberation which are inherent in the social orders of welfare states. Being themselves created and maintained by these social orders, welfare institutions and their policies and services aid in many ways in the preservation of these social orders and their ideologies. A central function performed by the welfare system is the pacification of suffering and oppressed groups during periods of potential rebellion, a cooling off of potentially explosive moods. No doubt, were the entire welfare system to cease to function tomorrow, those now dependent upon it for sustenance and survival could not be stopped from rebelling and from severely threatening the prevailing social order. Clearly then, by assuring through the welfare system an utterly inadequate mode of existence for masses of deprived individuals and groups in the population, the privileged segments of welfare-states succeed to assure the maintenance of the existing, inegalitarian order at relatively little cost.

Further contributions which the welfare system makes to maintenance of the prevailing social order of welfare states are the socialization and control of marginal segments of the workforce. These people are blamed through the ideology of the welfare system for their failure to be self-supporting and self-reliant in a context which is structured to prevent them from ever becoming self-supporting and self-reliant.[2] They receive some minimal aid from the welfare system in a dehumanizing manner that tends to undermine their self respect. That aid is kept systematically below the level of the lowest going wages, and as soon as some undesirable jobs become available, assistance is withdrawn and people are forced back into the marginal positions of the productive system. This kind of assistance is actually an indirect subsidy to businesses who depend on this marginal work force. Frequently also, the welfare system provides more direct subsidies to businesses, through tax-cuts and wage support for "manpower" training programs, in accordance with a theory according to which benefits would "trickle down" to poor segments of the population from stimulation of business activity and greater profits.

The controls used to discipline the marginal segments of the work force reach, however, far beyond those directly affected. Segments of the work force slightly above these marginal segments live under the constant threat of being pulled down to the welfare level unless they work dilligently at their jobs. The treatment of those receiving welfare is designed to deter those slightly better off from ever applying for welfare and to differentiate themselves in any possible way from welfare recipients. The only way to stay off welfare and off unemployment compensation is to hold on tightly to available jobs, however frustrating these jobs might be.

It may be noted in support of the characterization of institutionalized welfare as serving primarily system-maintenance functions, that even progressive proposals for welfare reform such as ·massive income re-distribution do not challenge the principle of private ownership and control of productive resources, which is the central obstacle to human liberation and to the establishment of an egalitarian social order in which alone people can regain self-reliance and self-determination. Further evidence comes from welfare states with the most liberal welfare policies and services such as the Scandinavian countries. These societies too, maintain privileged segments within their populations and, although the circumstances of the non-privileged segments tend to be far more tolerable than in less developed welfare states, the fundamental issues of human liberation, namely, free access to productive resources, self-reliance, and equality of rights to free and full development and self-actualization through self-directed work, remain essentially unresolved.

Summing up the discussion of institutionalized welfare in the context of welfare states, we found that the key institutions of human existence in welfare state societies function in a manner which assures privileged conditions in all spheres of life for a small segment of the population at the top of a finely graded pyramidal social structure, and enforced dependence and severe deprivation for a fairly large segment of the population at the bottom of the pyramid. People between the group on top and that at the bottom find themselves in a continuous competitive race to move upward and to avoid being pushed downward.

The severe deprivation experienced by those at the bottom has often been interpreted as violence inherent in the very structure of the system, a form of violence that does not destroy life with a single blow, but which obstructs the full and free development of the life potential of many millions of people through the "normal" processes of the social order. Many minds and souls are slowly being killed as one of the externalities of the workings of welfare-states. Moreover, not only the most severely deprived segments suffer from this "violence of peace". The whole order seems to be maintained in balance, and everyone's development seems inhibited, by ever-present, latent force and by ideological indoctrination. It is highly unlikely that human beings would otherwise submit themselves voluntarily to conditions of severe injustice which prevent the full actualization of everyone's human potential.

The policies and services of institutionalized welfare in the welfare state were shown to fit into this system like a hand fits into a glove. Welfare is an essential component of a broad range of mechanisms through which the inegalitarian, oppressive and covertly violent social orders of welfare states pacify, condition, and control their populations, and defend and perpetuate their social systems. Clearly these systems could not survive without elaborate defenses. The conclusion is inevitable: a central function of institutionalized welfare is the defense of privilege, the perpetuation of dependence and injustice, and the prevention of genuine self-reliance. Its roots are a philosophy, consciousness, values and dynamics of inequality, acquisitiveness, selfishness, domination and competition.

WARFARE AS A SOCIETAL PROCESS

While welfare tends to destroy human life potential slowly and somewhat covertly, warfare employs overt, destructive force and violence for the same objectives, the attainment and defense of privilege at home and abroad. Warfare, although its dynamics and ideology are not less complex and contradictory than those of welfare, may nevertheless be less difficult to comprehend, since its roots, functions, and values are usually less disguised.

As indicated, when discussing the evolution of the welfare state, claims to exclusive ownership and control of territories and natural resources are likely to have been first steps on a course that has often led to warfare. Such claims by individuals and groups of humans imply the establishment of a privileged position in relation to others. If others respect such claims, and if similar claims by others are also respected, no conflicts leading to warfare need arise, especially if every group manages to sustain its existence on the territory it claimed, and if exchanges of goods and raw materials take place among different groups on fair, egalitarian terms.

History suggests, however, that relations among humans and human groups all over the globe were frequently defined and perceived in conflict terms and many groups permitted their conflicts to erupt into "cold" and "hot" warfare, rather than settle them by attempting to redefine the context in common human interest terms.

Conflicts that led to warfare were always related to efforts to defend or increase existing privileges with respect to control over territories or natural and human resources, to establish such new privileges, or to challenge privileges and claims established previously by other groups. It seems that the declared causes of warfare were hardly ever valid in an objective, absolute sense. Rarely if ever, was warfare the only available course toward survival and enhancement of the quality of life for the groups involved. However, in the subjective perception of those involved warfare usually was viewed as the only alternative open to them.

Warfare is more likely to be initiated by human groups who developed internally in accordance with inegalitarian and acquisitive institutional patterns and values, than by egalitarian and cooperative societies. Warfare in such cases is an extension outward of the behavioral patterns and the mentality that shape internal human relations and institutions. Inegalitarian, acquisitive groups, as we have seen, are divided and polarized internally and will often engage in internal "civil" wars. Extrapolating the conflict model of human relations and of the life context unto external relations appears to them perfectly logical and natural. When those in power in such groups present an external war as being in the interest of the whole group, or in the "national interest," they are consciously or unconsciously distorting reality. While they may believe their own claims, warfare is unlikely to ever be in the true existential interest of those who are induced or forced to do the actual fighting. Those who derive advantages from warfare are less likely to do the actual fighting. The only ones who tend to come out of warfare with advantages and increased privileges are rulers, planners, commanders, providers of war supplies, and owners of productive resources. The fighting men, the ones who take the risks and losses, are usually members of propertyless groups who also tend to be deprived and oppressed during "peaceful" periods at home.

External warfare may also be used to deflect public consciousness from internal grievances and from intense internal conflicts between small, powerful, dominant elites, and the rest of the population. At such times, phrases like "national security" and "national interest" become important codewords and myths.

Illusions of "national unity" are fostered and people's minds become confused as to the real dynamics of the situation. Appeals to nationalism, prior to and during times of war, usually succeed to interrupt efforts concerned with real internal problems of a population, partly, also because warfare tends to eliminate unemployment and thus can create illusions of prosperity.

Presumed threats to the national security and suspicion of foreign secret agents, and of foreign enemies, are also handy excuses for secret, and, at times, open repressive measures at home, and for equating internal critics and opponents with foreign enemies which makes it more easy to deal with them as enemies.

This brief discussion of selected aspects of warfare suggests that it is always related to the creation, maintenance and protection of privilege, occasionally for an entire group, but usually for the privileged segments of groups organized on inegalitarian, acquisitive principles, and guided by conflict and zero-sum models of human relations and human existence. Such human groups are usually organized as formal states, and they are thus the very same social systems we encountered under the label "welfare-states" in the preceding discussion. Clearly, warfare serves indentical and complementary ends to welfare and both derive from the same roots, dynamics, values and ideology. Both have also domestic and foreign versions. In the case of welfare, the foreign version is called "foreign aid" which never comes without strings, the strings being protection of the selfish interests of the donors and their privileged circumstances. In the case of warfare, the domestic version is forceful repression of rebellious groups and civil wars, which are intended to maintain the status-quo of privilege at home.

Warfare and welfare interact in many ways and thus reinforce each other as they pursue their common objectives, at times jointly, at other times separately. It is perhaps not mere coincidence that the warfare establishment and the welfare establishment operate through similarly structured bureaucracies, that they tend to use a similar vocabulary, e.g. target populations, intervention strategies, war on poverty, etc., and that top officials will move in the United States, a leading example of the warfare-welfare state, from the Department of State, to the Department of Defense, and from there to the Department of Health, Education and Welfare and finally to the Department of Justice, the one that defines institutionalized injustice as the "law of the land."

Warfare and welfare are designed to perpetuate inequality and injustice among humans at home, and among the peoples of the world abroad. They are employing a multi-dimensional approach to defend the privileged circumstances and the corresponding power relations which emerged over generations through systematic elaborations on the simple principle of private ownership and control of scarce productive resources.

EPILOGUE

What suggestions can be derived on the basis of this depressing analysis of the roots, functions, dynamics, values, and ideology of warfare and welfare?

Problems of welfare can not be fully comprehended, nor overcome effectively, within the context of the current definitions of welfare which treat the fundamental organizing principles of the social order as constants. Welfare reform, however comprehensive, merely introduces new variations on the underlying theme of managing dependence and preventing genuine self-reliance. Such reforms cannot solve the fundamental problems, although they may ameliorate deprivation and are thus desirable in these limited terms.

Real solutions to welfare must begin with a radical redefinition of issues, goals and values. Dependence must be related to its causes, the manner productive resources are now owned and controlled, work and production are organized, rights and responsibilities are distributed, and decisions are made and implemented. There is only one solution to welfare: to abolish its institutionalized version by liberating productive resources and assuring access to these resources to all humans on equal terms so that they may become free, independent, productive, and self-reliant citizens of self-directing, democratic and cooperative communities.

Problems of warfare too cannot be overcome without fundamental redefinitions of the issues. Here too amelioration that moves toward disarmament or reduction of war threats is desirable, but is only a temporary answer. Issues of warfare cannot be solved by degrees but only by qualitative changes. Like in the case of welfare the underlying causes must be confronted and eliminated. The causes were identified as competitive pursuit of privilege at home and abroad. Hence the answer is the elimination of all privileges and equalization of access to the world's resources for all the world's people within a context that stresses the underlying, common, existential interests of all humans everywhere. Not surprisingly, the solutions to warfare and welfare are identical since their roots, functions, dynamics, and values were found to be identical.

Finally, it seems that solutions to issues of warfare and welfare require the gradual transformation of the welfare state and its alter-self, the warfare state, since states are the guarantors of privilege and injustice. The competing welfare-warfare states which now dominate the world with disastrous consequences for the quality of life of all humans, including the most privileged segments, and which threaten the chances of survival of humankind, will have to be transformed into a coordinated, egalitarian, cooperative federation of self-reliant, free communities, each directing its own affairs and life-style through genuine democratic processes, each guaranteeing to its members equality of rights and responsiblities, and all participating in exchanges of raw-materials and human-created goods and knowledge on fair, egalitarian terms.

To avoid any misunderstandings, it should be noted, that the designation welfare-warfare states as used above refers not only to free-enterprise, oligopoly-capitalist, pseudo-democratic nation states, but also to state-monopoly-capitalist, pseudo-socialist nation states. In both types of states humans are neither free, nor equal, nor self-reliant, for societies in these states are organized into pyramids of privilege and power.

These then are the logical conclusions of reasoned analysis. Transforming this logic into new existential possiblities, in spite of overwhelming odds, is the crucial task for political practice by humanistic movements committed to genuine liberation and self-actualizaton for humans everywhere.

CHAPTER NINE

An Egalitarian—Humanistic Perspective on the Conflict in the Middle East

In the following essays, written originally for THE JUSTICE, the student newspaper of Brandeis University, I applied an egalitarian-humanistic perspective to the analysis of a current international conflict, and to the development of a framework for its solution. As with other conflicts among human groups, a durable solution to the conflict in the Middle East seems predicated upon a radical redefinition of the issues in terms of the underlying common existential goals and interests of all the parties to the conflict.

Zionism and Palestinian Rights*

One is more likely to miss the real issues behind the Middle East conflict and crisis when one attempts to understand them by focussing merely on their latest phase than when one attempts to unravel their historical roots. Let me, therefore, present briefly some fundamental aspects of the long-standing conflict in the Middle East, and of what appear to me logical approaches to its solution derived from principles of justice and fairness.

*Reprinted from *The Justice*, Brandeis University, Nov. 7, 1973.

BASICS

• Jewish people have lived in Palestine uninterruptedly for over 3000 years. Descendants of Jewish people who were exiled from that country at various times tended to maintain a strong cultural relationship with it, and have attempted repeatedly to return there. The right of Jewish people to live in Palestine and govern their own affairs there seems, thus, in my view, beyond question.

• Non-Jewish people of different origins (including some of Jewish origins) have also lived in Palestine for thousands of years, some even prior to the first Jewish conquest of that land. Over the last 1300 years, since the Arab conquest of Palestine, the non-Jewish population increased considerably. Late in the 19th century, when modern Jewish immigration started, the dominant character of the country and its population was Arab, Christian and Moslem, with small Jewish communities in Jerusalem, Safed, Tiberias, Jaffa, and a few other locations. There can be, in my view, no question whatsoever concerning the equal rights of the non-Jewish "Palestinian" people to live in Palestine, to return to it when exiled, and to govern their own affairs there in the same way as the Jewish people.

ZIONISM

• The modern Zionist movement began as a political movement among European Jews late in the 19th century. Its founders and leaders redefined the historical relationship of the Jewish people with Palestine in modern, political, nationalistic terms. This was a period during which many modern nation states were founded, and Zionism, following the tendencies of the period, defined its political objective as the reestablishment of Palestine as a Jewish state.

From its beginning, Zionism thus disregarded the basic rights of the Palestinians by aiming for exclusive Jewish sovereignty in Palestine, a privileged, dominant position for Jewish people. During that period European nations tended to consider themselves superior to Asian and African people whom they treated arrogantly as "primitive natives."

Zionism shared this attitude toward the Palestinian population, and considered the Jewish settlers as outposts and defenders of "European civilization and progress" in the Middle East. Rather than seeking mutually satisfactory arrangements with the Palestinians, Zionist leaders negotiated with European governments in order to obtain an international charter for the establishment of the Jewish State. They usually disregarded the existence of the politically weak and unorganized Palestinian population, and pursued their goals within the context of European, and later American, power politics.

They claimed Palestine "a land without a people for a people without a land." It may also be noted here that from the early days of Zionist colonization many Arab tenant farmers were displaced from the land on which they lived and worked, when that land was sold to Jewish settlers by absentee landlords, and that Jewish settlements tended to pursue a policy of exclusion against non-Jewish workers and products.

SOVEREIGNTY

• Political Zionism and its claim for Jewish exclusive sovereignty gradually led to the emergence of nationalistic consciousness and equally extreme counter-claims among the Palestinians, and thus became the source of the destructive conflict which has flared up repeatedly into armed confrontation over the past 75 years.

The Zionists were usually successful politically, diplomatically, and militarily throughout these conflicts. They had the advantages of better organization, modern education, and know-how, vast resources, and technology.

The Jews are a committed, creative, imaginative and hard-working people, and they were desperate because of persecution and suffering in Europe. Yet, the more successful Zionism became, because of its growing might and skillful powerplay, the stronger became the resistance of the Palestinians, who gradually came to understand the Zionist political aim of dominance. They fought back to assure their rights to self-determination in their homeland, and gradually succeeded to obtain political support from Arab and Muslim nations around Palestine, and from many other Asian and African nations.

The states who came to the aid of the Palestinians probably had, and have, their own political calculations and objectives, in the same way in which various nations who supported the Zionist cause always had their own perceived interests in mind.

SOLUTIONS

• The current situation is complex, and solutions are not easy to come by. Essentially, there seem to be two ways to search for solutions. One is to disregard the past and to continue the pragmatic power play where "might is right", irrespective of considerations of justice and fairness, and of historical realities. Such an approach aims to obtain formal legitimation of facts created by force, diplomacy, and power.

An alternative approach is to reject legitimacy derived from the use of force and successful political power play, and to develop solutions which recognize the real needs and rights of the people involved, and which conform to principles of justice, equality and fairness.

I opt for the second approach, not only because it is right in an ethical sense, but also because, in the long run, it seems to be the only way to a lasting peace, and hence to security and survival for Jewish and Palestinian people in their common land.

The widely used arguments concerning Israel's needs for buffer territories to defend herself against Egyptian and Syrian attacks and threats of annihilation seem valid only within the frame of reference of pragmatic power politics,—that is, as long as Israel refuses to explore solutions which guarantee the full and equal rights of the Palestianians along with the same rights for the Jews.

I am aware that searching within the context of equal rights for both people opens up the question of the continued existence of Israel as a nation state in its present form. This question must be faced squarely.

In my view what is important is not a particular political form, but the existential substance, which means arrangements that will assure to both Jews and Palestinians the best chance for peaceful co-existence, security, liberty, self-governance, and social, economic and cultural development and cooperation. Therefore, different forms of political models such as two separate states, a federation, a con-federation, a bi-national state, or a secular single state ought to be considered.

The form and symbols seem far less important than the substance, as long as the form eventually agreed upon by Jews and Palestinians incorporates the principles of equality, justice and liberty for both people, and for all individuals and groups among the Jewish and Palestinian peoples. In this context let us not forget that, historically, states have usually been instruments for the legitimation and enforcement of privileged positions, inequalities, and injustice at home and abroad.

In this brief essay I have sketched some important points. I have also left out other important points of which I am aware, and some others of which I may not be aware. What seems to be needed in terms of a meaningful contribution to the solution of the Middle East conflict are intellectual efforts to deepen our understanding of its roots. In such a search we must avoid superficial and ad hominem arguments. We also must avoid a tribal perspective, and must attempt to view the situation from the perspectives of all parties to the conflict.

It seems to me that if the circumstances of the Jewish and Palestinian people were suddenly reversed (a possibility which could occur if we continue on a collision course) the Jews would be as unwilling, as the Palestinians are now, to recognize as legitimate a state of affairs resulting from the use of force and skillful diplomacy and power play.

It would be preferable for the Jewish people to adopt a position based on principles of justice while they are strong rather than postpone such a philosophical shift until the balance of power is reversed.

Security or Peace*

Efforts toward peace in the Middle East seem to have failed in the past because Israelis and Palestinians have searched for solutions from a narrow, ethnocentric perspective, which disregards the real needs and rights of the other party to the conflict.

Genuine peace in the Middle East, and anywhere else, seems predicated upon a commitment of all parties to a conflict to acknowledge the real needs and rights of everyone involved. Proposed solutions which do not meet this requirement can only lead to illusions of peace, enforced perhaps through a temporary balance of military and diplomatic power, but not to lasting peace, chosen freely, and adhered to, by the parties. Genuine peace will never emerge from military and/or diplomatic maneuvers and power plays, but only from the elimination of the injustices at the roots of a conflict.

What then is the source of the conflict in the Middle East that must be acknowledged and overcome? Essentially this source has always been, and still is, the reluctance of the Israelis and the Palestinians to recognize each other's existence, real human needs, and equal rights to meet these needs in Israel/Palestine. The basic condition for real peace is, therefore, an unequivocal commitment by both peoples to respect and uphold the equal right of each to

*Reprinted from *The Justice*, Brandeis University, Feb. 25, 1975.

live securely, and to develop autonomous communities and social and cultural institutions throughout their common homeland, free of political domination and economic exploitation by the other.

Different political formulae can be devised and evolved by Israelis and Palestinians in conformity with this basic principle, such as two federated states, or an egalitarian, democratic, bi-cultural commonwealth. Yet, whatever political formula is eventually chosen, what is essential is the affirmation of the equal right of all Palestinians and all Jews to live, if and when they wish, in their historical homeland, as masters of their own destiny. Obviously also, lands occupied in war would have to be returned to the neighboring nations so that they may join in a peace settlement for the entire region. The sooner Jews and Palestinians realize that mutual recognition of their equal rights is a *sine-qua-non* for peaceful survival and development, and for real prosperity, the closer will they have come to a workable solution of their common suffering, and to a realization of their real interests.

Zionism and Racism*

The recent United Nations resolution declaring Zionism a form of racism is an oversimplification which nevertheless contains elements of truth. Like many political slogans emerging in a forum of contesting nation-states who are more concerned with power than with justice, it distorts meanings and contributes little towards a just solution of tragic conflict. Yet the elements of truth in the resolution must be confronted rather than simply drowned in a flood of emotions and denied by equally oversimplified defensive statements.

Zion is a hill in Jerusalem on which Jews erected a temple thousands of years ago dedicated, in the words of their prophets, to the pursuit of peace through justice for all peoples. Zion has come to symbolize the cultural roots of Jews and their identity. It also symbolizes the land where they once lived in independent communities, from which they were expelled by force, and to which many Jews have returned to live again in self-directing communities.

Racism is the negation of equal worth and equal rights of all people, and the belief of some to be superior to others. It is reflected in the political act of domination and exploitation. Racism is not intrinsic to Zionism any more than it is intrinsic to being German,

*Reprinted from *The Justice*, Brandeis University, Nov. 25, 1975.

English, Chinese, African, black or white. Yet any people, including Jews, may develop in the course of its history racist political positions.

Modern political Zionism, which developed in 19th century Europe in response to racist persecution of Jews, did indeed incorporate racist elements by sharing the mentality and practices of European colonial settlers and their attitude of superiority toward non-European and non-white peoples. Political Zionism aimed to establish Jewish dominance in Palestine over the local Palestinian population and realized this aim when the State of Israel was created. Unfortunately, in that State the non-Jewish, Palestinian population has never enjoyed full equality in political, social, and economic terms.

The Jewish people must overcome the racist elements of political Zionism and of the State of Israel which are a blatant contradiction to the true meaning of Zion and which threaten Jewish physical and cultural survival. To overcome these elements Jews need to recommit themselves to the original meaning of Zion, peace through justice and equality for all peoples including the Palestinians. In political terms this means affirming the equal rights of Jews and Palestinians to return to their common homeland and to live in a multi-ethnic commonwealth of self-directing, cooperating communities throughout the land of Zion-Palestine, with neither people dominating and exploiting the other.

PART
III

INQUIRY INTO
POLITICAL PRACTICE

CHAPTER TEN

Thoughts on Political Practice toward an Egalitarian, Humanistic, Democratic Social Order*

I present this essay as a contribution to a theory of political practice. It suggests several hypotheses for a political strategy aimed at establishing an egalitarian, humanistic, and democratic social order and sketches several criteria for developing and testing such a strategy. Implicit in the suggestions given here are also certain questions concerning widely held strategy assumptions among revolutionary social movements.

SOME COMMENTS ON VALUE PREMISES AND GOALS

Considerations of political strategies need to start with a specification of the goals which are to be attained, and the value premises which underlie these goals. The value premise implicit in the discussions in this book is that all humans everywhere, in spite of individual and cultural differences and uniqueness, are intrinsically of equal worth, and are, hence, entitled to equal social,

* Reprinted from *Discussion Bulletin*, #7, (May-June 1974), of the New American Movement, a democratic-socialist movement in the United States.

economic, civil, and political rights. The political goal derived from this value premise is the establishment of a social order on local, national, and world-wide levels, based on the principle of full equality. In such a social order every human being is a subject rather than a means for someone else's goals, and hence, all forms of exploitation of one human by another would be eliminated. Such an order must be based on knowledge and reason rather than on supersitition, prejudice, and force; it must be based, as pointed out above, on collective ownership and rational preservation, and on utilization of all life-sustaining and life-enhancing resources, rather than on competition, acquisitiveness, and pursuit of narrowly perceived self-interest resulting in thoughtless exploitation of resources and lopsided concentration of wealth. Many people are coming to realize the utter futility of achieving existential fulfillment under the prevailing "capitalist" system and its social, psychological, economic, and political dynamics with their intrinsic irrationalities and contradictions, and the resulting loneliness and alienation of isolated individuals, each struggling to survive and maximize his own illusions of well-being.

Labels to characterize political goals invariably lead to oversimplifications of complex issues, and to misunderstandings. However, for the sake of brevity, I will refer to these goals as radical and revolutionary, since the social order implicit in them involves a radical departure from the organizing principles of the prevailing order; they are radical, further, since, in my view, the establishment of the new order is predicated upon a cultural revolution in our viewing of humans, their relations to each other, and the meaning of life, as well as being predicated upon revolutionary restructuring of our social, economic, and political institutions (so as to adjust them and their dynamics to the principles of equality, cooperation, collectivity orientation, and rationality).

CRITERIA FOR AN EFFECTIVE POLITICAL STRATEGY

Any political strategy is essentially a set of untested hypotheses specifying means assumed to be effective in transforming a given existing social order into an alternative one. It is important in this context to keep in mind that all currently proposed revolutionary strategies are essentially untested, and hence, unproven. This suggests that all those who agree roughly on goals should be tolerant of each other's strategy proposals, for no one can be certain of the validity and effectiveness of proposals as long as such validity and effectiveness have not yet been demonstrated.

For a revolutionary strategy to meet the test of logic and reasoned analysis, it must satisfy certain requirements. Foremost among these is the identification and interpretation of forces which sustain, perpetuate, and defend the prevailing social order, for it is these very same forces which a revolution must overcome if a new order is to be established. A further requirement of an effective strategy is that the means it proposes to employ should not inadvertently result in an increase of the forces which defend the *status-quo* and resist the revolution. Obviously, such an outcome of a revolutionary strategy would be counterproductive, as it would merely increase repression of the revolutionary movement, and increase the suffering resulting from oppression.

One must be reasonably confident that the means one selects for a revolutionary strategy should not be inherently antithetical to the very value premises, principles, and goals of the revolution. If they are so antithetical, the strategy would contain within itself the seeds of destruction of the new order; it would thus be doomed to failure even though it might achieve a temporary appearance of success. Another crucial consideration in shaping a revolutionary strategy is implicit in the questions: who is to benefit from the revolution? Whose interests are to be served by it? Hence, who would or should, support it?

APPLYING THE CRITERIA TO STRATEGY CONSIDERATIONS

Starting with this last set of questions, it is my premise that a revolution establishing an egalitarian, humanistic, democratic social order is for the benefit of all human beings everywhere; it would assure that the fundamental, intrinsic human needs and interests of everyone would be met in perpetuity through a system of rational and balanced development, distribution, and preservation of resources on a global scale and the system would assure to everyone equal access to social, economic, and political positions; it would thus involve equal rights and responsibilities for all. In accordance with this premise the revolution should not be viewed as a zero-sum game where some win at the expense of others who would be losers. In an egalitarian, humanistic revolution, everyone is to be a winner. For the result of such a revolution is not that today's "wretched of the earth" will be its new masters or dictators, nor that "today's poor will inherit the kingdom of heaven". Rather, the result is the elimination of any social, economic, and political class differentiation, and hence, the avoidance in perpetuity of privilege and of one human's subordination to another. Implicit in this concept of the revolution is the apparent paradox that the dis-accumulation and liberation of privately controlled wealth and power, and their transfer to collective control for everyone's equal benefit, is in the true human interest; it is not only of true interest to the currently deprived individuals and groups, but to everyone, including those who now command a disproportionate share of wealth and of social, economic, and political power. The validity of this apparently paradoxical proposition becomes evident when one analyses the existential and concrete costs of maintaining and defending the prevailing order of worldwide inequality, injustice and irrationality for those who supposedly benefit from this order. The tremendous costs of defending and perpetuating inequality, injustice, and irrationality at home and abroad, costs which are reflected in widespread alienation and social and psychological pathology among affluent and non-affluent segments of capitalist societies everywhere, and also in constant international tensions and wars, absorb, as we all know, vast amounts of material resources and human potential.

If there is validity to the proposition that the revolution will benefit all, then, at least theoretically, everyone is a potential member of the revolutionary movement; it is necessary of course that everyone overcome misconceptions concerning the real meaning of the prevailing order and of the revolution. The major obstacle to the spreading of revolutionary consciousness, and hence, to the revolutionary movement, is the prevailing constantly regenerated and reinforced false consciousness of nearly all population segments in capitalist societies; it matters not whether they be actual or potential owners of wealth, oppressors or oppressed, "ruling class" or "working class".

When a revolutionary movement disregards these subjective aspects of social reality, and conceptualizes the revolutionary effort simply as a struggle between the "ruling" and "working" classes, it actually contributes indirectly to the perpetuation of the prevailing false consciousness concerning present and revolutionary reality; it may thus unintentionally strengthen the forces resisting the revolution. Such a movement, by dichotomizing and over-simplifying a complex objective and subjective reality, and by opting for a simple conflict model of revolutionary strategy, may actually destroy revolutionary prospects. This error in theory seems to be one important source of past failings of revolutionary movements.

When a revolutionary movement persists in conceptualizing the revolutionary effort in conflict of interests or in zero-sum terms, groups in the population who are to be losers by the *movement's* definition of the revolutionary process will do everything in their power to prevent such a revolution. Hence, as such a revolutionary movement gains strength, society tends to become fiercely polarized, the class structure tends to rigidify, and the movement's class analysis tends to turn into a self-fulfilling prophecy. Such a process also tends to lead to a philosophical justification of physical force and violence as appropriate means for dealing with the conflict. Violence is used first in defense of the status-quo by those who feel understandably threatened as a result of the movement's definition of the revolutionary process. However, sooner or later the movement tends to be drawn into a vicious cycle of mutual violence.

Once physical force is accepted as an appropriate means toward a revolutionary goal, that goal may become unattainable, not only because of the greater capacity for violence on the part of the defenders of the "legitimate" status-quo, but also because of the contradictions between the revolutionary goal of social equality and the intrinsic dynamics of institutionalized violence. Brevity prevents me from articulating this important contradiction in detail. Yet I can refer to an ample literature on the issue of force and violence and on the logical necessity of correspondence between means and ends; note especially the writings of Mahatma Gandhi, Martin Luther King, and Martin Buber.

ELEMENTS OF A NON-VIOLENT, DEMOCRATIC REVOLUTIONARY STRATEGY

What conclusions can be drawn for an effective revolutionary strategy and practice toward an egalitarian, humanistic, and democratic social order from the foregoing considerations? Since the major obstacle to the realization of such an order seems to be an all-pervasive, "false consciousness" concerning the realities of the existing social order and of possible alternatives, the revolutionary strategy must be so designed as to constantly pierce and counteract that false consciousness and the dynamics of its regeneration and reinforcement. The fact that existing social, economic and political institutions are the prime sources of the consciousness of the population makes the changing of this consciousness while these institutions continue to exist a very complex task. Changing these institutions without changing the consciousness that sustains them is no easy task. The answer to this dilemma may be a simultaneous effort to change consciousness and to create through practice alternative, egalitarian institutions. These simultaneous change efforts can and should reinforce each other. Once in motion, they could develop into expanding movements, of individuals and groups engaged in political practice designed to overcome the system-shaped consciousness of growing segments of the population while at the same time creating in their own lives egalitarian, cooperative, self-reliant and self-directing institutions and communities which would gradually evolve into federations for mutual social, economic, political and cultural support.[1]

Such federations of movement collectives could be the beginning of a new institutional order parallel to, and within, the existing order. They would demonstrate by their very existence the feasibility of an alternative, humanistic-democratic reality conducive to the self-actualization of its members. Such a demonstration should in turn enhance the effectiveness of the movement in the ongoing political-cultural struggle to transcend dominant consciousness. Eventually, as these federations grow in size and strength they would begin to engage in non-armed resistance and civil disobedience toward the established order, and they could organize movements for refusal to cooperate with and providing resources for the order's oppressive, exploitative and dehumanizing institutions. In later stages of this process these institutions would be taken over, transformed thoroughly and operated directly by the people working in them. Systematic, non-violent practice along these lines should gradually undermine the functioning of the now existing order and bring about its transformation and absorbtion into an emerging alternative, humanistic society.

What is it about the prevailing, dominant consciousness that must be challenged. At the risk of over-simplifying a highly complex phenomenon, what needs to be challenged and overcome through revolutionary counter-education is the belief that the prevailing social, economic, and political systems and their competitive, self-centered, and in-egalitarian principles and dynamics are conducive to a satisfying human existence and that alternative social, economic, and political systems based on co-operative, collective, and egalitarian principles and dynamics are not conducive to such an existence. There are many other related aspects to the deeply ingrained, distorted view of reality which characterize consciousness in capitalist societies, yet it is not necessary to go further into this complex issue. The revolutionary strategy which seems to me most promising over the long haul, involves constant and consistent efforts to challenge the dominant definitions of reality in theory and eventually in practice, to clarify their fallacious nature, and to substitute more valid definitions and humane institutions in their place.

Evidence of reality distortions are all around us, and the process of redefinition and reinterpretation can therefore be pursued in relation to any subject and in any context, be it occupational, social, or private. In this way members of the revolutionary move-ment can also overcome the prevailing split between the political, occupational, social, and private spheres of life. All aspects of living can gradually be integrated as one becomes a politically aware and responsible individual. Revolutionary practice and political organizing would then no longer be limited to "special projects" as they would become a way of life.[2]

The revolutionary effort to challenge and overcome false con-sciousness has to be directed toward everyone affected by it ir-respective of a person's or a group's social and economic position. One should   include in such efforts privileged and advantaged segments of the population since, due to the prevailing shape of the distribution of power and wealth, changing the consciousness of these segments could have more far reaching consequences for the revolutionary process. If large numbers of the privileged could realize that their existential interests would be enhanced through revolutionary restructuring of the social order, they would have the power to implement the necessary social, economic and political changes. We should include privileged groups in a comprehensive strategy of political re-education and counter-definition, rather than concentrate all our efforts on deprived and severely oppressed groups.

The issue of selecting target groups for revolutionary, political education and organizing is linked also to the choice between cooperative versus conflict strategies. I reject the interest-group, zero-sum conception of revolutionary benefits, and opt instead for a universal benefit revolutionary concept. Hence, the appeal to join the revolutionary movement should be addressed to every individual and to every group. Such a strategy choice is in my view also implicit in the notion of a truly democratic approach to political action, organizing, and revolution.

The political strategy suggested here in general terms avoids the personalizing of enemies. In accordance with this approach, the enemies of social equality, justice, and reason are not specific individuals and groups, but the principles and dynamics which shape the social, economic and political institutions of the existing order and which are reflected in acquisitive, competitive, exploitative, and self-centered attitudes and behaviors on the part of nearly everyone living under these institutions. By avoiding the theoretical error of declaring and treating certain groups and individuals as "enemies", the chance they will act as enemies of the revolutionary movement is reduced, and the chance that they too will join the movement is enhanced, especially when the movement is committed to help them understand the existential benefits which they can expect from the revolution. The overall chances of a revolutionary movement are enhanced as the number of its potential enemies is reduced and the number of its supporters grows.

The final comments to be made in this brief discussion of revolutionary strategy concern the fit between means and ends. The primary means suggested here are creation of alternative, egalitarian institutions within the existing institutional context. They include intellectual encounter by way of reasoned, critical analysis of reality aimed at transcending system-shaped, dominant consciousness, and include also non-armed resistance to, and refusal to participate in, existing, oppressive institutions; the aim is of course to eventually paralyze, transform, and take over these institutions. This is intrinsically a democratic, egalitarian, non-exploitative, and non-violent approach, in harmony with the goal of the revolution. Yet, not only is this approach in harmony with the projected goal; it can also become intrinsically liberating long before the goal is achieved. The very process of freeing one's own mind and of helping others to overcome the distorted images of reality which are now clouding their consciousness can have liberating consequences, in existential terms, for those engaged in that process long before the comprehensive institutional revolution is accomplished. This process, when engaged in systematically by members of a growing movement, the growth of which accelerates constantly as its membership increases, is likely to become a source of irresistible strength. This process itself is a cultural revolution spearheading the transformation of all social, economic, and political institutions into a truly egalitarian, humanistic, democratic world order, based on reason and on the potentialities of humankind.

CHAPTER ELEVEN

Comments on Means and Ends: A Critique of the Political Perspective of the New American Movement*

Political discussion in a democratic movement working toward liberation, equality, and justice, should search for valid strategies toward these goals, irrespective of whether or not proposed strategies conform to principles once considered valid. Statements of political perspectives reflect thinking at a point in time, and possess no more intrinsic validity than critical thinking in the present. They contain no safeguards against errors. Hence they should always be open to critical re-examination, and should never constrain the intellectual freedom of thinking humans in the present.

The New American Movement is a significant, radical movement but its political perspective involves errors in theory which are reflected in contradictions between means and ends and which may, therefore, prevent the attainment of our humanistic and egalitarian goals. These errors in theory include:

    a. the emphasis on "class-consciousness" and class-conflict as central strategic concepts;

*Reprinted from *Discussion Bulletin* #8, (July-Sept. 1974) of the New American Movement.

182

    b. the related notion of "working-class control" as an ob-
       jective of socialist revolution, referred to often as "taking
       state power";

    c. the omission of an unequivocal commitment to non-
       violent action as the sole means toward fundamental
       social transformation.

In accordance with its political perspective, NAM aims ". . . to create a society . . . in which full and free development of every individual will be the basic goal." Such a society is unlikely to come into being through strategies rooted in class-consciousness and class related conflicts of interests, and aiming to take state power and establish working class control. Only strategies which conform in every respect to the humanistic and egalitarian goals of the movement can be expected to bring about the emergence of social, economic, and political institutions conducive to the full and free development of every individual. The means must reflect and contain the ends, if the ends are ever to be attained. Clearly, an unequivocal commitment to non-violent action is a *sine-qua-non* of a valid strategy for human liberation,[1] for any form of violence directed against humans, be it physical force or subtle political manipulation, constitutes the very negation of liberty, equality, self-actualization, and human authenticity. Hence it would defeat the attainment of such humanistic ends.

A valid strategy toward the creation of a social and world order conducive to everyone's full and free development needs to reflect the essential attributes of such an order. Hence the development of strategy must begin with a specification of these attributes. Foremost among these attributes is the sharing, by individuals and groups in such a society, of a non-divisive, unifying, humanistic consciousness, rooted in the recognition of the underlying, common interests of all humans, everywhere, irrespective of current social position. Only a society whose members will achieve such insights and such consciousness, will be ready to eliminate all forms of domination, oppression, and exploitation, and to consider all humans, in spite of their uniqueness, of equal worth, and thus entitled to equal rights, liberties, and responsibilities. Individuals in such a society would come to realize that everyone's true interests can be served best, when equal social, economic, and political rights are accorded to all, and when resources and energy are not wasted and destroyed in efforts to defend and perpetuate irrational, socially constructed, inequalities. In organizing its institutions such a society would, therefore, avail itself of the following fundamental principles: mutuality, cooperation, individuality in the context of collectivity, and above all reason. By employing these principles it would transcend the fallacious conflict and scarcity models of human reality, and could work towards meeting real human needs in a rational and egalitarian fashion.

A social and world order rooted in a unifying, humanistic consciousness would constitute the antithesis of many past and present social orders, irrespective of their modes of production, distribution, and governance, and their levels of cultural, scientific, and technological development; be they slave-holding, feudal, capitalist, or so called socialist societies and states. For these social orders are characterized by divisive, segmented consciousness rooted in narrowly defined conflicts of interests among individuals and various groups, all fiercely competing with each other on local, trans-local, and worldwide levels. Human relations in such societies, inevitably, involve exploitation, domination, and oppression. Their fundamental organizing principles are selfishness, competition, and all-pervasive inequalities in social, economic, and political spheres.

The foregoing observations suggest that the crucial difference between societies that would be conducive to the full and free development of every individual, and societies that tend to inhibit or obstruct such full and free development, is the content and the quality of the dominant consciousness of the citizenry, and the principles underlying the organization of a society's social, economic, and political institutions which shape that consciousness, and, in turn, are reinforced by it in a perpetual process of interaction. Hence, if NAM's aim is indeed to create a society in which all humans will develop freely and fully, then we must adopt strategies which will facilitate the emergence of a non-divisive, unifying, humanistic consciousness—strategies which are not directed against individuals and social classes in the prevailing order, but against the dominant consciousness of that order and the principles that shape its institutions and determine the human dynamics within it. In political education we would have to stress the underlying, real, common interests around which all humans, everywhere, irrespective of class and other group characteristics, can, and must unite, if the growing, world-wide, social, economic, and political crises are to be overcome, and if humankind is to use its powers of reason to shift from its present, irrational, and suicidal course toward one assuring survival, liberation, and fulfillment to all. Our strategies will have to reject, rather than to promote, the prevailing, dominant, divisive and fragmented consciousness, which derives from a world view of inevitable, perpetual conflicts among groups competing for survival in a context of scarcities. NAM must work for the acceptance of the organizing principles of all-inclusive human cooperation and equality in the pursuit of "life, liberty, and happiness" for all—the real common human interests. No other set of principles can assure the emergence of a non-divisive, humanistic consciousness, and of a just social order reflecting that consciousness. We must renounce all strategies involving any form of domination, control, and exploitation in human relations among individuals, groups, and social classes, irrespective of which individuals, groups, or classes would assume the dominant and controlling roles.

To the extent that these arguments follow logically from NAM's basic goal of full and free development for all humans, the emphasis, in the political perspective, on class-consciousness and class-conflict as central strategic concepts and organizing principles, and the related notion of working class control, however broadly that class is defined, must be rejected as fallacious, and as serious obstacles to the emergence of a non-divisive, inclusive, humanistic consciousness. Liberation strategies rooted in class-consciousness, class-conflict, and in working-class control involve an implicit acceptance of social fragmentation and of interest conflicts as the basis for organizing society and human relations. Thus instead of negating, these strategies merely sustain new variations of ancient, fallacious themes, which have shaped many past and present, dehumanizing social orders. Clearly, these strategies are self-defeating as they offer no hope of escape from the vicious cycle of absurd social systems and destructive world orders which, invariably, emerge from arbitrary divisions among humans, and from irrational conflicts of interests rooted in a fallacious scarcity model of the world. I am aware, that according to Marx, strategies fostering working-class consciousness and working-class control would eventually lead to a classless society. Yet I find this hypothesis unsupported in history and faulty in logic. Fragmented consciousness and conflict of interests models will always result in fragmented, competitive, and hierarchically structured social orders. Only an inclusive human consciousness rooted in the recognition of underlying, common, human interests can result in a cooperative and egalitarian social and world order. It may be noted here also that a "working-class-consciousness" is not a reality in a competitive society. The working class is of course, seriously divided, and its many segments are fiercely competing among themselves, reflecting thus the general dynamics of a social order shaped by the conflict model and committed to the perpetuation of multiple inequalities. Liberation movements that undertake the educational task of unifying the internally torn working-class and of creating class-wide consciousness among working people, could instead concentrate their efforts on promoting a world-wide human consciousness as a basis for unifying all humans around their real interests, and on overcoming the false consciousness rooted in the conflict model of reality.

The image of a socialist revolution leading to working-class control contradicts another image, that of a truly liberated society free of all control, except self-control on the part of autonomous, authentic human beings, associating freely and spontaneously in small collectives or affinity groups,[2] each determining its own activities and life style, all living in an egalitarian context in a decentralized, world-wide commonwealth of democratically integrated communities, engaged in rationally designed production, exchange, and consumption, all geared to satisfying everyone's real needs. If this latter image reflects the real existential goals of NAM, and I believe it does, for only in such a society can everyone develop freely and fully, then we must renounce all notions of control and domination by any class, and of "taking state power". These notions simply cannot co-exist with human freedom, equality, and self-actualization.

CHAPTER TWELVE

*Systemic Constraints and Radical Practice in Education**

The purpose of this essay is to present an analysis of the functions of education from a broad perspective—social, economic, and political—and to derive from this analysis suggestions for a political strategy. Teachers may pursue this strategy in efforts to promote an egalitarian, democratic, social order. The analysis summarizes conclusions reached over the years by many observers and critics of society in general, and of education in particular.

One major source of misunderstanding the nature and dynamics of social institutions (education, religion, economy, etc.) is that they tend to be studied and interpreted by "insiders" whose perspective is likely to be too narrow and affected by vested interests. Students of social institutions are gradually realizing that in order fully to comprehend any specific institution one needs to study its interactions with the total societal context in addition to exploring its internal dynamics. We have come by now to accept that the economy and defense are too important to our existence

* Prepared for the Task Force On Education, New American Movement, and published in its newsletter *Chalkboard*, Issue #1, Winter 1973/74.

to be left in the hands of professional economists and soldiers. The same logic seems to apply to the study and interpretation of education.

Teachers, when examining their profession, tend to be concerned primarily with aspects of the educational process which involve interaction with individual students or groups of students. Their orientation to educational processes is atomistic, and they lose sight of the aggregate function, dynamics, and outcomes of education as a social institution. They are aware, so to speak, of single trees but have no sense of the forest. This atomistic orientation may, however, have its own social function. It enables teachers to maintain their sanity by holding on to the illusion that they are engaged in the meaningful activity of furthering the fullest possible development of their own students. Were they fully conscious of the naked truth concerning the aggregate outcome of education, they probably could not carry on, for that truth flies in the face of their cherished notions concerning the nature of the educational process.

What, then, is that naked truth and on what evidence is it based? Macro-level analysis of the aggregate output of the educational enterprise in any society, at any time, reveals that irrespective of the efforts and capacities of individual teachers and students, and irrespective of what actually goes on in individual schools, be they "progressive" or "conservative", "free" or "public", any generation of students will fill at the termination of its formal education the array of "work" and "non-work" positions existing in society, whatever the nature of this array may be. The educational process then constitutes one of society's principal mechanisms for reproducing the prevailing social division of labor by sorting out, preparing, and channelling generation after generation of students into the prevailing work organization. Consequently, what educational systems produce in the aggregate is determined ultimately by the prevailing modes of production, consumption, distribution, and work organization of a society rather than by what educators like to call the philosophy, values, methods, content, structure, and procedures of the education system. Closer analysis reveals, of course, that the philosophy, values, methods, content, structure and procedures of educational systems are not independently designed by philosophers of education and by Schools of Education, but are constantly shaped and reshaped by the changing modes of production, consumption, distribution, and work organization of society, and by the value premises and ideology implicit in these modes and organization. Hence, significant changes of important aspects of education cannot be evolved independently within the educational system. The only effective way to obtain such changes is by restructuring the modes of production, consumption, distribution and work organization. The educational process will then change almost automatically by generating the necessary modifications or "educational reforms" to assure the fit between its output and the demands of the restructured modes of production, consumption, distribution and work organization. In the simplest possible terms then, it is the social context which determines the nature, dynamics, and outcome of the educational process. Formal education as an institutionalized social process reproduces the social context but does not change it.

Educators throughout history have tended to disregard the foregoing causal relations and have pursued the illusion of educational omnipotence, hoping, in spite of consistent evidence to the contrary, that if they only improved their methods they could change the prevailing social order. Siegfried Bernfeld, a well known socialist educator, unravelled the futility of these illusions of the educational profession in an insightful essay entitled, quite appropriately, "Sisyphos—or the Limits of Education"[1].

The general proposition that the educational system of a society in its entirety reproduces the prevailing social order and its corresponding division of labor requires, of course, many additional specific propositions if the educational process is to be fully comprehended. Space limitations preclude here such a complete analysis. However, it should at least be noted that the general function of an educational system as a whole, namely the reproduction of the total social order is usually divided into segmental functions, namely the reproduction of certain definable segments of that order. Hence different units of educational systems are geared to the preparation of specified segments of the next generation. Efficiency in accomplishing the segmentation of a generation of students into the strata of a social order and the division of labor is, of course, enhanced by such procedures as segregation, tracking, biased testing and grading procedures, ritualistic examinations, certification requirements, etc. Not all differences in educational content and method are, however, meaningless. Some differences are valid in terms of the differential preparatory needs of specific segments of the social order and the division of labor. Yet, it should be noted in this context that the social and economic origins of individual students and of groups of students are known to be no less important determinants of the eventual roles these students will fill in the social order and in the division of labor than differences in their school experiences. As a matter of fact, these social and economic characteristics of students tend to be important determinants of the kind of educational experiences to which they will be exposed. Family background thus interacts with specialized educational experiences to reinforce the reproduction of the stratification systems.

A crucial question implicit in the proposition that educational systems are segmented along social strata is whether by exposing all students to the "best" possible educational experiences (assuming we know from independent sources what "good education" really is), all will attain "good" positions in the division of labor and a correspondingly "good life". Merely spelling out this question reveals its nonsensical nature. Clearly, as long as production and consumption are organized hierarchically and competitively, and as long as profit and exploitation are essential aspects of the social-economic order, some individuals and groups will occupy more desirable positions than others, and some will be left without any positions, even when all are exposed to the same educational experiences. By merely equalizing education without eliminating the hierarchical, alienating, competitive and exploitative social order, and without generating and assuring meaningful and equally rewarded positions for all, education would simply be deprived of the sorting-out and channeling function for the social order, and some other mechanism would be devised to accomplish that function. Some evidence for such a change in function can already be observed as a result of the "open admission" policy of public universities. The more students enter colleges and attain college degrees, and the more diversified their socio-economic backgrounds are, the less important becomes the possession of college degrees for entry into desirable positions, and new, arbitrary entry requirements are established. Also, as college attendance is more widely distributed, qualitative standards are reduced in the "non-elite" schools. High School education passed through a similar process of qualitative devaluation several decades ago when school attendance was made compulsory up to age 16 or 18, the result being that an average high school education in 1970 is probably not superior in educational achievement to an average grade school education in the 1920s.

Similar arguments are relevant in relation to current efforts by parent groups, teachers, and schools to "improve" the quality of education in their neighborhood schools through various mechanisms including "free schools", "open schools", "ghetto academies", etc. These efforts have a certain intrinsic validity for oppressed groups in the context of a competitive and exploitative social order. However, the meaning and consequences of this approach in terms of changing the social system as a whole are negligible. The aggregate consequences will obviously be zero as long as the total system remains unchanged. What actually happens is that the children of some groups will become more competitive in the market at the expense of the children of some other groups. Essentially this is merely a game of musical chairs with desirable positions being shifted around, but the ratio of desirable to undesirable positions remaining unchanged. Thus these efforts may reflect the cooptation into the capitalist mentality of additional groups. Also, the intensity of competition and conflict among various deprived minority groups is likely to be intensified along with these efforts as those now accustomed to fill preferred positions are not planning to vacate them. There simply is no magic solution to the demand for social equality by modifying the educational system, while maintaining the competitive and exploitative social order intact. There can be only new illusions until a society moves to replace that competitive, exploitative order with an egalitarian, democratic one, involving equal social, economic, and political rights and responsibilities for all.

Does the essentially conservative function of educational systems suggest the conclusion that working within such systems is utterly meaningless and futile for teachers committed to the establishment of an egalitarian, democratic society? The answer to this question depends on one's overall views concerning political strategy.[2] My own position is that in spite of its nature and dynamics, the field of education offers considerable scope for revolutionary practice provided the results of the foregoing analysis are taken into consideration, and the implicit limits of education as a formal social institution are not disregarded. In order to clarify this apparently paradox position the analysis of the function of education has to be pursued a bit further. Such an exploration reveals that education does not merely reproduce the social order and its division of labor. It also transmits from generation to generation the value premises, ideology, and consciousness which assure "voluntary" adaptation and conformity to, uncritical acceptance of, and emotional loyalty to, the established social order, on the part of a significant majority of the population, irrespective of the nature and quality of that order and of the extent to which it actually meets the existential needs of its members. The dominant consciousness of a population is, of course, a major source of stability of any social order, and hence it is not surprising that the educational system, the primary function of which is the reproduction of the established social order, has a complementary function, namely, the transmission of the kind of consciousness which emanates from, reflects, and assures the continuity and stability of, that order. Nor is it surprising that the educational process tends to inhibit the development of those human capacities by which individuals may question and challenge the dominant consciousness of their society. Hence education tends to stifle the natural curiosity of students, their urge for critical questioning and analysis of reality, their free intellectual development and creativity, and their impulse toward self-assertion. It should be noted that education achieves these results primarily through the total experience and the structure and quality of human relations to which students are exposed, and only marginally through the cognitive content of teaching. Consciousness is absorbed, to a considerable extent, directly from the educational environment rather than through communication of specific intellectual content. The latter merely supplements the attitudes and orientations which are communicated through the "vibrations" of the system. It should also be noted that formal education is not the only source of consciousness transmission and reinforcement. The family, the neighborhood, the peer group, the church, the media of communication and entertainment, signals from business and government spokesmen, etc., all participate in massive continuous efforts of generating an all-pervasive common consciousness supportive of the status quo and hostile to any questioning of the prevailing order.

Yet, just because of the crucial importance of consciousness for the stability and perpetuation of any social order, it also happens to be the Achilles heel of all oppressive and exploitative social orders, and hence a preferred focus for revolutionary practice. If a revolutionary movement could enable sufficiently large segments of a population to liberate themselves from the distorted consciousness with which they were inculcated, and to achieve a more accurate comprehension of the oppressive aspects of their social reality, then the people could use their newly gained insights to organize movements for their own liberation, and to transform an existing, exploitative social order into an egalitarian, democratic one.

This far too brief sketch of certain revolutionary dynamics brings us back to the role of teachers in this process. It seems, on the basis of our analysis, that individual teachers simply cannot expect to change the primary function of an educational system, the reproduction of the existing social division of labor. However, they can, individually, and as a growing movement, aim to subvert the conventional processes of reproducing the dominant societal consciousness. This can be done systematically by appropriately restructuring the experiences of students in classrooms, and by changing the nature and quality of teacher-student, and teacher-parent relations, as well as by suitably modifying cognitive and intellectual interactions with students, parents, and colleagues. In this manner they can use the educational process toward liberating rather than thwarting the minds of students, to further their capacity for critical thought, and to stimulate thus the emergence of a counter-consciousness.[3]

No doubt this kind of educational practice is not easy to develop in current school environments, nor is such practice free from personal risks. It requires imagination, tact, and conviction on the part of teachers and also a large measure of understanding and tolerance for the opinions of colleagues, parents, students, and administrators, who have not yet extricated themselves from the dominant consciousness. It is important to forego "movement jargon", code words, and slogans, and to communicate in a style and manner calculated to reach those who do not accept a radical position. Provocative behavior and language are clearly contraindicated, for the purpose of radical practice is not to be expelled from the system, but to stay within it, and become a focal point of a counter definition right inside the system. We must remember that we do not aim to communicate only with those who already agree with us but to reach and challenge the consciousness of the vast majority who have not reached our insights. Obviously, we must talk in their language and use concepts they are familiar with and committed to.

These brief comments on radical practice merely suggest principles which require elaboration and testing through actual educational practice. Yet the purpose of this essay was mainly to suggest a theoretical basis for politically conscious practice in education. Using this theoretical basis, individual teachers need to develop their own classroom style and content so as to further the growth of critical consciousness among their students, the students' parents, and colleagues. By joining with other colleagues in a democratic, egalitarian movement they can accelerate the development of theory and practice of counter education, and draw support from each other in their lonely and at times frustrating work. Developing such an organized movement of like-minded teachers will also enhance their ability to protect themselves against ostracism and hostility from unconvinced colleagues, and against repressive measures which powerful institutions are likely to use against teachers pursuing the course advocated here.

CHAPTER THIRTEEN

Practice in the Human Services as a Political Act *

I develop here a rationale for, and an approach to, the conscious integration of a political component into professional practice and illustrate this approach in services on behalf of children. The proposed approach reconceptualizes professional roles in the human services as potentially powerful means of a radical, revolutionary, political strategy; the aim of this strategy is to eliminate the systemic sources and dynamics of social, economic, and political inequalities, the major underlying causes of the entire array of social problems with which the human services profess to be concerned. It should be stressed that the terms "radical" and "revolution" are not synonymous with violence. Violence is merely one possible means of revolutionary struggle, and, in my view, on both theoretical and practical grounds, not a very appropriate means. As used here, these terms reflect a theoret-

* Reprinted with permission from the *Journal of Clinical Child Psychology,* Volume III, No. 1, Winter-Spring, 1974; and the Journal of Sociology and Social Welfare, Vol. III, No. 4, March 1976.

An expanded version of this paper was presented at the 19th Annual Program Meeting of the Council on Social Work Education, San Francisco, California, February 27, 1973.

ical position according to which professional intervention should identify and attack the roots rather than the symptoms of social problems; hence, it should promote the transformation of the existing dysfunctional, alienating social order into one conducive to the fulfillment of the needs of all people, rather than facilitate the adaptation of people to the systemic requirements of the prevailing order and the vested interest groups that dominate it.

Politicizing professional roles is not an innovation but merely an effort to do consciously what happens anyway without sufficient awareness. It is known that one latent function of professional practice is to stabilize the prevailing social order and, hence, such practice has political implications and consequences whether we intend it that way or not. The notion that professional practice is politically neutral is, therefore, erroneous and is, itself, a politically powerful myth that serves the interests of groups benefiting from the existing social order by effectively neutralizing potential challengers of that order, and by contributing, thus, to its perpetuation and to the perpetuation of social problems intrinsic to it.

A CONCEPTUAL MODEL FOR THE STUDY OF SOCIAL POLICIES AND SOCIAL PROBLEMS.

Human services professionals and others interested in overcoming social problems by eliminating their sources and dynamics in the fabric of society must first attempt to identify these sources and dynamics. They may be aided in such attempts by a model of social policies, the central proposition of which is that social problems are not natural phenomena but are inevitable consequences of policies designed, or choices and decisions made, by humans. Viewing social policies and the problems they generate as "natural phenomena" tends to result in apathetic acceptance of existing problems as exemplified in the notion, "The poor will always be with you." However, realizing that humans do play a decisive role in shaping the policies by which they live implies that it is within their collective power to redesign existing policies whenever they prove not conducive to the pursuit of "life, liberty, and happiness" for all. This, by the way, is the central message of our "Declaration of Independence" a most eloquent argument on behalf of the principle of revolution.

In accordance with the proposed conceptual model, social policies determine (1) the overall quality of life in a society, (2) the circumstances of living of individuals and groups, and (3) the nature of all intra-societal human relations. These universal "output variables" of social policies are shaped by the following key processes which are known to operate in any human society:

1. The development of material and symbolic, life-sustaining and life-enhancing resources;
2. The "division of labor," or the channelling of individuals and groups into specific positions ("statuses") within the total array of societal tasks and functions;
3. The distribution to individuals and groups of specific rights to material and symbolic, life-sustaining and life-enhancing, resources.[1]

The key processes of social policy interact with various natural and societal forces. Of special significance among these forces are the dominant value premises or ideology of a society—its basic organizing principles—which tend to constrain the malleability of social policies. Not all the numerous values of a society are, however, equally relevant to the shaping of its policies. Since social policies involve primarily developmental, allocative, and distributive decisions, the following value dimensions which bear directly upon these types of decisions are most relevant in this context: equality vs. inequality, collectivism vs. self-centeredness, and cooperation vs. competition. Thus, a society which values "rugged individualism" and competitiveness in pursuit of self-interest and which considers inequality of circumstances of living a "natural" order of human existence will tend to exploit its natural and human resources and to preserve structured inequalities through its processes of resource development, status allocation, and rights distribution. Conversely, a society which values co-operation in pursuit of collective interests and which is truly committed to the notion that all humans, irrespective of their individual differences, are intrinsically of equal worth and dignity and hence, are entitled to equal social, economic, civil, and po-litical rights, will tend to develop social policies involving rational development, utilization, and preservation of natural and human resources, equal access to statuses, and equal rights to material and symbolic life-sustaining and life-enhancing resources.

THE SOURCES AND DYNAMICS OF SOCIAL PROBLEMS IN THE FABRIC OF CAPITALISM.

Having identified through the conceptual model the universal key processes and functions of social policies, and having stressed the crucial role of policy-relevant value premises or basic organizing principles of a society, we are now ready to explore the sources and dynamics of social problems. Let us examine as an illustrative case the poverty syndrome, no doubt, one of the most disturbing and pervasive social problems.

Using the conceptual model it is easy to recognize the social-structural dynamics of poverty in systematic inequalities in the allocation of statuses, and in the distribution of social, economic, and political rights and liberties, as well as in the patterning of resource development which derives from and in turn, reinforces the existing unequal distribution of rights. Government statistics reveal a stubborn stability of these inequalities over many decades. Thus, the distribution of income, an important index of the distribution of rights, has maintained the following characteristic shape ever since World War II in spite of the "war on poverty" and hosts of other "anti-poverty" programs. The lowest fifth of families ranked by income receive about five percent of aggregate income, while the highest fifth receive over 40 percent, and the top five percent receive about 15 percent. The distribution of wealth, perhaps a more significant index of rights than the income distribution, is even more lopsided than the distribution of income.[2]

The distributions of income and wealth are, in any society, *functions* of the prevailing economic and political systems. Accordingly, we are led to conclude that poverty and its complex social and psychological correlates in the United States are inevitable consequences of the economic and political dynamics of capitalism and its derivative versions, national and multi-national, oligopoly capitalism. It is, therefore, to the essential features of capitalism that we must turn next in our efforts to unravel the sources and dynamics of poverty and related social problems.[3]

Capitalism, as an economic-political system, is organized around the value premises of rugged individualism, competition in pursuit of self-interest, and inequality of human worth and rights. Its basic institutional principle is private ownership of, and control over, the economic sources of life, including land, other natural resources, and means of production.

The central driving force or source of energy of capitalism is the profit motive, which is reflected in the constant drive to maximize the profits of individual and corporate entrepreneurs, the owners of various forms of capital, through competition and collusion in the marketplace. This acquisitive thrust, which is aided greatly by the inheritance principle and by a broad range of tax and other policies in support of private business activities, results over time in constantly increasing accumulation and concentration of economic resources and in corresponding concentration of political power and influence.

The values, principles, and dynamics of capitalism give rise to several kinds of exploitation. First of all, there is the exploitation of the workers-producers, the large segment of the population who own and control little or no capital and who, in order to survive, must sell their labor in the market for a mere fraction of the value of the products they create. For the profits of capitalists, the returns on their investments (rent, interest, and dividends) are nothing but parts of the fruits of labor of which the workers-producers are deprived under prevailing institutional arrangements. A second form of exploitation is closely related to the former. This is the retail business profit, that part of market prices of goods and services which exceeds their real production and distribution costs, and which workers-producers must pay in their roles as consumers when buying back their own products. Other aspects of the profit-motivated exploitation under capitalism are evident in the thoughtless destruction of natural resources such as land, forests, wild animals, mineral deposits, water, and air; and in the immense waste implicit in various economically irrational practices such as built-in obsolescence, annual model changes, marginal, nonfunctional differences among equivalent products, packaging, non-utilitarian frills on products, emphasis on production of luxury goods in spite of large-scale unmet needs for essential basic goods, competitive and deceptive advertising, massive diversion of human and material resources to military production, wars, and space spectaculars, etc.

Exploitation is implicit also in qualitative aspects of "efficient" production processes. Workers have little control over the usually dehumanizing nature of these processes, or over the nature of the very products they create. They are viewed and treated as means or "factors of production," rather than as ends or "masters of production." These aspects of the production context have resulted in widespread psychological alienation of production, service, and office workers, and, of late also, of management personnel.[4]

The capitalist drive for profit and its corollary, exploitation, show little respect for national boundaries. The large scope of worldwide, economic, and political penetration by U.S. business interests, which is often perceived as a modern form of colonialism and imperialism, is reflected in a recent report of the U.S. Department of State.[5] According to this report, the U.S. controls nearly 30 percent of the "Planetary Product" though the U.S. population is less than six percent of mankind. Obviously, there is a significant linkage between the expansionary tendencies of U.S. capitalism in search of profit and the imperialistic tendencies of U.S. foreign policies. Logical by-products of these tendencies are overt and covert military adventures and other forms of foreign intervention all over the globe, including support of many "anti-communist," oppressive, military dictatorships, and subversion of and economic sanctions against elected socialist governments, as well as the far-reaching influence in our own society of the military-industrial complex.

In reviewing briefly the essential features of capitalism we noted that efforts to maximize profits tend to be the overriding considerations in business decisions, although this may not always be evident in certain short-range decisions. According to theoretical models of capitalistic market economies, under conditions of perfect competition (which have never been realized in any modern, industrial society), the profit-oriented decisions of numerous, competing, individual enterprises should automatically result, in the aggregate, in the most efficient allocation and utilization of the human and material resources of a society. Moreover, these uncoordinated, separate decisions of entrepreneurs in competitive free markets are also supposed to assure the satisfaction of the needs of the entire population. Anyone familiar with the prevailing modes and priorities of resource allocation and utilization in American society, and with the actual level of satisfaction of even such basic human needs as food, shelter, clothing, transportation, health care, and education, need not be told that the capitalist theories and promises of smooth and efficient self-regulation of supply and demand, of prices, and of resource allocation, by Adam Smith's "invisible hand," are merely a cruel hoax. Capitalism never intended to satisfy, nor succeeded to satisfy, the basic and more complex needs of entire populations, for doing so would preclude profits and exploitation. Rather than organizing production and distribution to satisfy the real needs of all people, capitalism, in its constant drive for ever larger profits, tends first to *generate*, and then to cater to, distorted needs. Widespread, constant poverty and deprivation, cyclical depressions, and wasteful, high rates of unemployment and underemployment which exceed by far officialy reported levels, and which would be even higher but for our vast military production and repeated involvement in wars, clearly demonstrate the mythical character of prevailing capitalist economic models, theories and ideologies.

The conceptual model presented earlier enables us to recognize the fallacies of capitalist theories. To summarize, capitalism as an economic and political system is a cluster of related social policies shaped by the values and dynamics of competitive pursuit of narrowly-perceived self-interest and by an implicit concept of humans as intrinsically of unequal worth. The three key policy processes of resource development, status allocation, and rights distribution conform to the profit-oriented, exploitative, and non-egalitarian tendencies of capitalism, according to which natural resources and humans are objects of exploitation for privately controlled capital rather than subjects in their own rights. On the "output" side of the capitalist policy cluster we find, consequently: (a) gradual deterioration of the overall quality of life in rural, suburban, and urban environments: (b) great differences in the circumstances of living of various population segments with masses of people living in abject poverty, deprivation, and apathy, a constantly striving, hard-pressed, discontented, and insecure middle class, living in pseudo-affluence, and a small, isolated upper class, living in wasteful luxuries; and (c) an intensely pathological quality of human relations characterized by alienation, insecurity, anxiety, loneliness, isolation, escapism, superficiality, self-centeredness, competitiveness, hostility, exploitation, mistrust, and nearly complete absence of truly meaningful mutual bonds.

A REVOLUTIONARY STRATEGY FOR THE HUMAN SERVICES PROFESSIONS.

Our study of the sources and dynamics of the poverty syndrome has led to the conclusion that this social problem is an inevitable, structural consequence of the economic, political, and ideological dynamics of capitalism. At the same time, we also realized that many other social problems, such as psychological alienation, are intrinsic to capitalism. Having identified these causal links, the requirements of an effective strategy for the elimination of the poverty syndrome seem now self-evident. Such a strategy must aim to replace an economic and political system of which poverty is an intrinsic aspect with an alternative system which is so constituted as to preclude poverty as a structural possibility.

Such a system would be shaped by alternative value premises of cooperation in pursuit of collective interests, and by an implicit concept of humans as intrinsically of equal worth, irrespective of their individual differences, and as entitled to equal social, economic, civil, and political rights and liberties.

The key processes of social policies, and through them, the political and economic institutions in such an alternative social order would conform in their operations to these alternative value premises and concepts. Land, other natural resources, and means of production would be owned collectively and controlled democratically and would be developed, utilized, and conserved in a planful, rational manner so as to meet the real needs of all people and to preclude waste and destruction. Access to statuses would be open on an equal basis, and rights and liberties would be distributed equally, as universal entitlements, irrespective of individual statuses. It should be noted in this context that equality as conceived here, following R. H. Tawney's eloquent exposition[6] would not be achieved through monotonous uniformity but through thoughtful and flexible consideration of individual differences and needs. Exploitation in any form would be prevented through appropriate institutional arrangements in production, distribution, consumption, and governance, and psychological alienation would thus be gradually overcome. The overall quality of life would gradually improve as circumstances of living would become equal for all and as human relations took on a healthy, constructive, caring and positive quality.

Clearly, then, poverty cannot be eliminated without a total revolution of our existing social and economic order, a "cultural" revolution of value premises, organizing principles, and basic concepts of man and a corresponding "structural" revolution of social, economic, and political institutions. That does not mean that the scope of poverty could not be reduced within the existing order. Such a reduction is possible through significant reforms. We should realize, however, that such reforms within the capitalist system cannot overcome the dynamics and the corresponding alienating and dehumanizing attitudes of self-centeredness, competition, and of socially-structured inequalities, the very roots of the poverty syndrome and many other social problems. We thus are faced with a simple choice. If we are committed to preserve the capitalist system and are unwilling to replace it with a humanistic, egalitarian alternative, we must get used to living with the inevitable by-products of capitalism. On the other hand, if we find these by-products utterly unacceptable, we have no choice but to eliminate their source, capitalism.

We are now ready to consider the integration of a conscious, radical, political component into professional practice in the human services and the transformation of this practice from an instrument of systems maintenance into one of revolution. However, before articulating the specific contributions professional practice can bring to a revolutionary strategy, my views on the general principles of such a strategy need to be sketched.

Replacing the prevailing alienating, competitive, capitalist social order with a humanistic, egalitarian, cooperative one seems to be in the true interest of nearly everyone in our society, since the existing order oppresses not only deprived groups but prevents the vast majority of citizens from leading meaningful, harmonious lives and from realizing their inherent human potential. If, then, the revolution is in nearly everyone's true human interest, it does not seem valid to view it as a zero-sum game, where currently deprived population segments would be "winners" and the current middle and upper classes "losers". Rather, the revolution is to be viewed as a truly liberating process for all with everyone coming out a "winner" in humanistic terms. Though acknowledged theoretically by past and present revolutionary movements, this concept has not been integrated adequately into revolutionary strategy.

The major obstacles to a revolutionary transformation of our society at the present time are the existing social, economic, and political institutional arrangements and the corresponding, dominant consciousness of nearly all groups in the population according to which the capitalist system either already serves their interests or will eventually do so. Most groups are ready to struggle for their perceived interests within the existing system and fail to see that such struggles can obviously not succeed for everyone. Not only must there always be losers in a competitive economic and political marketplace, but the "winners" cannot achieve a meaningful existence because of the intrinsic social and psychological dynamics of that system. Further obstacles to the revolutionary process are uncertainty about the reality of an alternative social order for the United States, and, related to this, a vague fear of the unknown. There is also fear and rejection of the little that is known from selective and often biased information about various past and ongoing revolutions against capitalist systems.

In view of these considerations it seems that a revolutionary strategy should aim to overcome the prevailing misconceptions or "false consciousness" concerning the complex realities and the real, economic and social "costs and benefits" of capitalism and of humanistic, egalitarian, alternative social systems. Such educational or rather, re-educational, efforts must be directed at every segment of the population rather than merely at oppressed groups, for, as suggested above, the revolution is to be for everyone, as it is in everybody's truest human interest. Accordingly, no groups or individuals, whatever their current social positions, should be cast in the image of enemies of the people and of the revolution, for such images tend to turn into self-fulfilling prophecies. They prevent communication to important and powerful segments of the population and undermine the potential for consciousness change among those labeled enemies. Such labeling also tends to invite and mobilize action in defense of the status quo through repressive resistance to the revolutionary process. The false consciousness of powerful groups is thus merely reinforced. Although "personalizing the enemy" and expressing hostility toward him may unify oppressed groups and aid in overcoming their false consciousness, it seems counterproductive in terms of an effective overall revolutionary strategy. Revolutionary interpretation and re-education as conceived here should, therefore, identify the "enemy" not in specific individuals and abstract groups, such as the "ruling class", but in the non-egalitarian, competitive, oppressive, and exploitative value premises and organizing principles of the prevailing social order, in the institutional arrangements and social policies derived from these values and principles, and in the destructive, interpersonal and intergroup relations and conflicts generated by these arrangements and policies. Such an interpretation should also reveal how we all, oppressed and oppressors alike, are trapped in, and act in accordance with, the same dehumanizing, irrational arrangements which humans have created and continue to maintain, and hence, how the liberation of every group depends on the liberation of all groups from the shackles of the existing order.[7]

The revolutionary strategy which I advocate is thus based primarily on reason and on man's capacity to use his intellect critically and creatively. Judicious use of civil disobedience, and dynamic, non-violent resistance would be appropriate means in terms of this strategy. However, the use of physical force and violence seems contraindicated on various ethical, theoretical, and practical grounds, as force and violence are not only intrinsically incompatible with the revolutionary aims, but are also unlikely to change the perceptions and consciousness of people.

Summing up these thoughts on strategy, a true revolution seems to require fundamental changes of consciousness concerning the social reality and the perceptions of self-interest on the part of large segments of the population. A true revolution is, therefore, a cultural change process and not merely an institutional and structural one. These two change processes are, of course, very closely related to, and constantly interact with, each other. To advance such comprehensive, cultural, and institutional change processes in the United States, in spite of the prevailing, mind-crippling, and indoctrinating influences of our educational systems and our media of mass communication and entertainment, we need to organize a dynamic, nonviolent, revolutionary liberation movement. A majoi unction of such a movement would be to unravel and demystify, by means of systematic counter-communications and reeducation, the illusions and distortions disseminated perpetually by the dominant communications media which tend to reinforce the prevailing misconceptions and false consciousness of the population concerning capitalism and possible alternative systems.

Professional practice in the human services could become an important factor of such an evolving liberation movement if large numbers of practitioners in health, education, and welfare services would redefine their individual and professional roles in political terms. Professional practice seems particularly well suited for counter-communication functions aimed at overcoming false consciousness, as its primary operational mode is communication and interaction around basic human needs and service-programs, with individuals, groups, organizations, communities, or even larger and more complex human aggregates. The quality, content, and thrust of professional practice must, of course, be modified significantly if it is to unmask, rather than sustain, existing illusions; to unravel, rather than to cover up, the causes of social problems, and to promote identification with a liberation movement, rather than adjustment to the status quo.

The conceptualization of practice in the human services suggested here involves politicizing this practice by consciously integrating into it counter-communications aimed at overcoming false consciousness and thus, at attacking social problems at their roots. Obviously, this practice is incompatible with the now-prevailing systems-maintenance orientation of the human services.

Professionals in these services have, of course, been aware for many decades of their systems-maintenance and social control functions and have struggled in vain with the dilemmas implicit in this situation. To ease the burden of these intrinsic contraditions of the human services context, professionals have tried to overcome them by depoliticizing practice. The political context of social problems, and, hence, of primary prevention, was recognized but was split off from professional practice, and this arbitrary split was then rationalized conceptually. Accordingly, systems change efforts were assigned to social action units of professional agencies and organizations and to political activities of individual professionals functioning as private citizens, while professional practice was naively defined as politically neutral. Yet, as pointed out above, the notion of political neutrality of professional practice is an illusion, since political neutralization of a large professional group constitutes, in itself, a significant, though covert, political act in defense of the status quo. The conceptualization of professional practice as a conscious political act attempts to overcome this dysfunctional, status quo-serving, political neutralization of practice by restoring the essential political component to the very center of practice. Obviously, there are personal dilemmas and organizational conflicts implicit in the approach proposed here, and various difficulties may be expected in translating this philosophy into actual practice.

As for the personal dilemmas and the organizational conflicts inherent in the integration of a political reeducation function into professional practice in the human services, considerable resistance may be expected from organizations employing these professionals, as these organizations are linked, directly or indirectly, into the existing social order, its policies, and value premises. The solution to these dilemmas derives from the notion of individual responsibility for ethical action. In contrast with "organization-men" such as Lieutenant Calley at My Lai and Adolph Eichmann at Auschwitz, professionals are expected not to identify with organizational philosophies and not to follow blindly organizational directives when these philosophies and directives clash with basic human rights and social justice which they are committed to promote. This means that those who accept the conceptualization of an integrated, conscious, political-professional role will have to act thoughtfully in accordance with their ethical commitments in spite of organizational resistance, and will thus become focal points in a network of an emerging counter-culture bent upon transforming the existing institutional system from within.

Politically informed practice in the human services, as conceived here, should be clearly distinguished from indoctrination and manipulation. Such practice is meant to be truly liberating in the fullest sense of this concept, for it aims to open up new vistas of choice for individuals and groups even while facilitating maximum utilization on their part of now-available resources and services. Practice with an integrated revolutionary perspective involves consistent attempts to bring into consciousness the multiple causal links between specific personal and social issues or problems addressed by a given service and the dynamics of the prevailing social, economic, and political order. Beyond thus fostering awareness of the true, causal context of issues and problems, such practice would also facilitate insights into options available to individuals and groups for organizing themselves and others into a liberation movement against the systemic causes of their specific problems and the existing, general oppression and exploitation.

APPLICATIONS TO CHILDREN.

A very simple illustration of the integrated political-professional approach will now be described. I have selected for this purpose a field with which I am familiar, child welfare, and, more specifically, protective services for children. In a recent study of child abuse all over the country,[8] I was led to conclude that abuse inflicted upon children by society by far exceeded in scope and destructive consequences their abuse by parents. Moreover, I also realized that societal abuse and neglect, which is reflected in abject poverty, malnutrition, developmental deficiencies, ill-health, inadequate education, social deviance, etc., among millions of children and families, is a major factor in abuse and neglect by individual parents. In spite of these facts, many public child-protective services throughout the country tend to convey a punitive, threatening, guilt-producing message to parents. The essence of this message is that parents are "bad", for if they were not, their children would not be abused and neglected. Furthermore, unless parents were going to correct their "unacceptable" childrearing patterns, their children would be taken away. Implicit in this message is the notion that society is "good", concerned about children, and, hence, free of guilt regarding their conditions. Reality, unfortunately, tends to be the reverse. Society, as now constituted, is "guilty" of child abuse since prevailing social policies doom millions of families to conditions which make adequate child care impossible. Many human service workers might not be able to offer any more adequate care to children than poor parents do, were they living in similar circumstances.

In accordance with the integrated, political-professional approach, protective services workers, in working with parents around the well-being of neglected children, should be straightforward about the question of "societal guilt", and should facilitate the parents' understanding of the social dynamics underlying the child's neglect. Once parents comprehend these systemic roots of the neglect situation, workers could help them to discover possibilities for organizing with others in struggles for a just social order. This very exploration and clarification can contribute to a growing sense of self and of liberation on the part of parents, since they are not being threatened, blamed, and burdened with guilt as happens so often in conventional child welfare practice.

Of course, not all child abuse and neglect are due to poverty and societal neglect. Yet, all child abuse and neglect has its roots in the social fabric, and the child welfare worker should always unravel the specific causal context in given cases and then share this insight with the parents.

The model for professional intervention sketched here is, in a certain sense, analogous to the psychoanalytic approach according to which the discovery and adoption of more satisfying and constructive patterns of living is facilitated by bringing into consciousness repressed intrapsychic conflicts—the covert dynamics of destructive patterns of living. Our practice model extrapolates this psychotherapeutic principle to the level of sociotherapy in that it deals with destructive social patterns and processes by making conscious the societal conflicts and dynamics underlying them, and by facilitating the discovery and choice of alternative, potentially conflict-free patterns. In view of this analogy, politically informed professional practice could be described as "socioanalysis and sociosynthesis".

The broad range of social issues, problems, and programs in which professionals in the human services are involved requires, of course, considerable flexibility, imagination, and creativity in adapting the general, political-professional intervention model to specific situations. To work out these adaptations for different fields and levels of practice is the challenge now facing the human services professions. By meeting this challenge, in spite of resistance this revolutionary thrust will arouse from defenders of the status quo, the human services professions could become truly relevant in terms of their original mission as conceived by Socrates and Plato—to serve the good of mankind rather than their own narrow self-interest.

NOTES TO CHAPTER ONE

1. Shaw, Bernard, *The Road to Equality*, Boston, Mass.: Beacon Press, 1971.
2. Tawney, R. H., *Equality*, London: George Allen and Unwin, Ltd., 1964.
3. For an exposition of the futility of such claims see: Kropotkin, Petr, *Mutual Aid - A Factor of Evolution*, Boston, Mass.: Porter Sargent, 1956.
4. Benedict, Ruth, "Synergy - Patterns of the Good Culture," *Psychology Today,* June 1970.
5. Budd, Edward C. (ed.), *Inequality and Poverty*, New York: W. W. Norton & Co., 1967. Kolko, Gabriel, *Wealth and Power in America, An Analysis of Social Class and Income Distribution*, New York, Washington, London: Praeger Publishers, 1962.
6. An illustration of these inequalities is the United States of America. Its population in 1971 was less than six percent of the world's population, but it consumed about 40 percent of the world's production.
7. Lakey, George, *Strategy for a Living Revolution*, San Francisco, Cal.: W. H. Freeman and Co., 1973.
8. "A Blueprint for Survival," *The New York Times*, February 5, 1972. Meadows, Dennis L., et al., *The Limits of Growth*, Washington, D.C.: Potomac Associates, 1972. Heilbroner, Robert L., *An Inquiry Into the Human Prospect*, New York: W.W. Norton & Co., 1974.

NOTES TO CHAPTER TWO

1. For a detailed discussion of policy analysis and development see the author's book, *Unravelling Social Policy*, Cambridge, Mass.: Schenkman Publishing Co., 1973, revised edition, 1976.
2. See Chart 1 on page 19.
3. See the essay "Practice in the Human Services as a Political Act," in Part 3 of this volume.

NOTES TO CHAPTER THREE

1. For a comprehensive discussion see: David G. Gil, *Unravelling Social Policy*, Cambridge, Mass.: Schenkman Publishing Co., 1973; Peter L. Berger and Thomas Luckmann, *The Social Construction of Reality*, Garden City, N.Y.: Doubleday & Company, Inc., 1966.
2. Theodorson and Theodorson, *A Modern Dictionary of Sociology*, New York, N.Y.: Thomas Y Crowell Co., 1969.
3. Erich Fromm, *Man For Himself*, New York, Toronto: Rinehart and Company, 1947.

NOTES TO CHAPTER FOUR

1. William Ryan, *Blaming the Victim*, New York: Pantheon Books, 1971.
2. Peter L. Berger and Thomas Luckmann, *The Social Construction of Reality*, Garden City, New York: Doubleday & Co., 1970.
3. The discussion of types of human needs is based in part on Abraham Maslow's concept of need hierarchy. See his book: *Motivation and Personality*, New York: Harper and Row, 1954; revised edition, 1970.
4. Petr Kropotkin, *Mutual Aid—A Factor in Evolution*, Boston, Mass.: Porter Sargent, 1956, originally published in 1902; Martin Buber, *Paths in Utopia*, Boston, Mass.: Beacon Press, 1958; Rosabeth M. Kanter, *Commitment and Community*, Cambridge, Mass.: Harvard University Press, 1972.
5. R.H. Tawney, *The Acquisitive Society*, New York: Harcourt, Brace & Co., 1920.
6. Frances Fox Piven, Richard A. Cloward, *Regulating the Poor: The Functions of Public Welfare*, New York: Pantheon Books, 1971.
7. Ruth Benedict, "Synergy," *American Anthropologist*, 1970, pp. 320-333; reprinted in *Psychology Today*, June 1970, pp. 51-77.
8. Karl Hess, *Dear America*, New York: William Morrow, 1975.
9. e.g., for more recent works, see Robert L. Heilbroner, *An Inquiry Into the Human Prospect*, New York: W.W. Norton, 1975; Barry Commoner, *The Closing Circle*, New York: Alfred Knopf, 1971; Nicholas Georgescu-Roegen, "Energy and Economic Myths," *Southern Economic Journal*, January 1975; Mihajlo Mesarovic and Eduard Pestel, *Mankind at the Turning Point*, New York: Dutton & Co., 1974; George Wald, "Arise Ye Prisoners of Extinction," 20th World Conference Against A & H Bombs, 1974, also in *New York Times*, 8/17/74; E.F. Schumacher, *Small Is Beautiful*, New York: Harper & Row, 1973.
10. Andre Gorz, *Strategy for Labor*, Boston: Beacon Press, 1967; idem, *Socialism and Revolution*, Garden City, N.Y.: Anchor Press/Doubleday, 1973.

NOTES TO CHAPTER FIVE

1. David G. Gil, *Unravelling Social Policy—Theory, Analysis, and Political Action Toward Social Equality* (Cambridge, Mass.: Schenkman Publishing Co., 1973; Revised edition, 1976).
2. *Profiles of Children*, 1970 White House Conference on Children (Washington, D.C.: Government Printing Office, 1970), p. 147, Table 107.
3. Seth Low, *America's Children and Youth in Institutions 1950-1960-1964*, U.S. Department of Health, Education, and Welfare, Children's Bureau (Washington, D.C.: Government Printing Office, 1965), p. 31, Table 2.
4. Low, *America's Children*, p. 32, Table 3.
5. Low, *America's Children*, p. 2.
6. U.S. Bureau of the Census, *Statistical Abstract of the United States: 1971* (Washington, D.C.: Government Printing Office, 1971), p. 23, Table 21.
7. Donnell M. Pappenfort, Dee Morgan Kilpatrick, and Alma M. Kuby, *A Census of Children's Residential Institutions in the United States, Puerto Rico, and the Virgin Islands: 1966*, 7 vols. (Chicago: The University of Chicago, The School of Social Service Administration, Social Service monographs, 2d ser., 1970).
8. Shirley A. Star and Alma M. Kuby, *Number and Kinds of Children's Residential Institutions in the United States*, U.S. Department of Health, Education, and Welfare, Children's Bureau (Washington, D.C.: Government Printing Office, 1967).
9. Bernard Greenblatt, ed., "Residential Group Care Facilities for Children," in *State and Local Public Facility Needs and Financing, Study Prepared for the Subcommittee on Economic Progress*, Joint Economic Committee, 89th

Cong., 2d sess. (Washington, D.C.: Government Printing Office, 1967), see especially section on "User Charges," pp. 633–634.
10. Low, *America's Children*, p. 8.
11. Low, *America's Children*, pp. 8–9.
12. Low, *America's Children*, p. 9.
13. Low, *America's Children*, p. 9.
14. Low, *America's Children*, p. 10.
15. Alfred Kadushin, *Child Welfare Services* (New York: Macmillan, 1967), p. 528. Reprinted by permission of Macmillan Publishing Co., Inc. from *Child Welfare Services* by Alfred Kadushin. Copyright © 1967 by Alfred Kadushin. See also Henry S. Maas and Richard E. Engler, Jr., *Children in Need of Parents* (New York: Columbia University Press, 1959); Shirley Jenkins and Mignon Sauber, *Paths to Child Placement* (New York: Community Council of Greater New York, 1966).
16. Kadushin's three quotes are from U.S. Congress, Senate, *Hearings before the Public Health, Education, Welfare and Safety Subcommittee on the District of Columbia*, 89th Cong., 1st sess., May 10, 1965 (Washington, D.C.: Government Printing Office, 1965).
17. Robert H. Bremner, ed., *Children and Youth in America, A Documentary History, Vol. 1, 1600-1865* (Cambridge, Mass.: Harvard University Press, 1970), p. 74.
18. Bremner, *Children and Youth in America, Vol. 1*, pp. 74–75.
19. Bremner, *Children and Youth in America, Vol. 1*, pp. 438–439, 547–558.
20. Bremner, *Children and Youth in America, Vol. 1*, p. 439. This quote refers to Indian and also to black children.
21. Bremner, *Children and Youth in America, Vol. 1*, p. 72.
22. Bremner, *Children and Youth in America, Vol. 1*, pp. 76–78.
23. Bremner, *Children and Youth in America, Vol. 1*, pp. 319–322.
24. Robert Francis Seybolt, *The Private Schools of Colonial Boston* (Westport, Conn.: Greenwood Press, 1970), pp. 11–13, 16, 17, 24, 29, 32, 34–37, 40, 41, 43, 44, 49, 52, 57.
25. Bremner, *Children and Youth in America, Vol. 1*, p. 85.
26. Bremner, *Children and Youth in America, Vol. 1*, pp. 91–93.
27. Clarence E. Lovejoy, *Lovejoy's Preparatory School Guide* (New York: Simon and Schuster, 1971).
28. See for instance Porter Sargent, *The Handbook of Private Schools—An Annual Descriptive Survey of Independent Education*, 52nd ed. (Boston, Mass.: Porter Sargent, 1971). *Private Independent Schools—The American Private School for Boys and Girls* (Wallingford, Conn.: Bunting and Lyon, Inc., Publishers, 1971); Lovejoy, *Lovejoy's Preparatory School Guide; The Vincent Curtis Educational Register* (Boston, Mass.: Vincent Curtis Educational Register, published annually).
29. For more detailed historical information on institutional care for dependent children, readers should consult Bremner, *Children and Youth in America, Vol. 1*, pt. 1, chap. 3; pt. 2, chap. 4; pt. 3, chap. 5; *Vol. 2*, pt. 3; "Child Welfare: Institutions for Children," in *Encyclopedia of Social Work*, vol. 1, ed. Robert Morris et al. (New York: National Association of Social Workers, 1971), pp. 120–128; Kadushin, *Child Welfare Services*, pp. 518–521.
30. David J. Rothman, *The Discovery of the Asylum—Social Order and Disorder in the New Republic* (Boston: Little, Brown, 1971).
31. Martin Wollins and Irving Piliavin, *Institution or Foster Family—A Century of Debate* (New York: Child Welfare League of America, 1964).
32. Kadushin, *Child Welfare Services*, pp. 520–521. Quoted by permission of Macmillan Publishing Co., Inc.
33. Alexander Liazos, "Processing for Unfitness—Socialization of 'Emotionally

Disturbed' Lower-Class Boys Into the Mass Society" (unpublished Ph.D. diss., Brandeis University, 1970).

34. For a historical perspective on residential institutions for dependent children see Bremner, *Children and Youth in America.* For a recent journalistic exposition of conditions in residential children's institutions which reflect the built-in expectation and acceptance of failure see Howard James, *Children in Trouble—A National Scandal* (New York: David McKay, 1970).

35. Low, *America's Children,* Appendix A, Census Definitions and Explanations, pp. 25–29.

36. John Bowlby, *Maternal Care and Mental Health* (Geneva, Switzerland: World Health Organization, 1951); *Deprivation of Maternal Care—A Reassessment of its Effects* (Geneva, Switzerland: World Health Organization, 1962); *Maternal Deprivation* (New York: Child Welfare League of America, 1962).

37. David G. Gil, "Thoughts on Social Equality", See Part One of this volume.

38. Oskar Lewis, *The Study of Slum Culture—Backgrounds for La Vida* (New York: Random House, 1968); Edward C. Banfield, *The Unheavenly City* (Boston: Little, Brown, 1970); Edward C. Banfield, "The Cities: The Lower Class," *New York Times,* October 12, 1970; Richard Todd. "A Theory of the Lower Class," *The Atlantic,* September 1970.

39. Stephen M. Rose, *The Betrayal of the Poor, The Transformation of Community Action* (Cambridge, Mass.: Schenkman Publishing Co., 1972).

40. Roland Warren, "The Model Cities Program—An Assessment," in *The Social Welfare Forum, 1971* (New York and London: Columbia University Press, 1971).

41. William Ryan, *Blaming the Victim* (New York: Pantheon Books, 1971).

42. See for instance Howard W. Polsky, *Cottage Six* (New York: Russell Sage Foundation, 1962); Lydia F. Hylton, *The Residential Treatment Center, Children, Programs, and Costs* (New York: Child Welfare League of America, 1964); Rosemary Dinnage and M. L. Kellmer Pringle, *Residential Child Care—Facts and Fallacies* (New York: Humanities Press, 1967); Liazos, "Processing for Unfitness."

43. Pappenfort *et al., Census.*

44. Pappenfort *et al., Census,* p. 33, Table 24.

45. Pappenfort *et al., Census,* p. 53, Table 42.

46. Pappenfort *et al., Census,* p. 81, Table 70; p. 85, Table 74; p. 89, Table 78; p. 93, Table 82.

47. Kadushin, *Child Welfare Services,* p. 535.

48. Pappenfort *et al., Census,* p. 97, Table 86; p. 101, Table 90; p. 105, Table 94.

49. Pappenfort *et al., Census,* p. 127, Table 114.

50. Pappenfort *et al., Census,* p. 137, Table 124.

51. Pappenfort *et al., Census,* p. 141, Table 128.

52. Pappenfort *et al., Census,* p. 147, Table 134; p. 149, Table 136.

53. Pappenfort *et al., Census,* p. 155, Table 142; p. 157, Table 144.

54. Pappenfort *et al., Census,* p. 151, Table 138; p. 153, Table 140.

55. For details see Pappenfort *et al., Census,* pp. 166–229, Tables 153–216.

56. Polsky, *Cottage Six;* Irving Piliavin, "Conflict Between Cottage Parents and Caseworkers," *Social Service Review,* 37 (March 1963).

57. James, *Children in Trouble.*

58. Pappenfort *et al., Census,* pp. 238–245, Tables 225–232.

59. Quoted in James K. Whittaker, "Group Care for Children: Guidelines for Planning," *Social Work,* 17, no. 1 (January 1972), 60.

NOTES TO CHAPTER SIX

1. Henry D. Kempe et al., "The Battered Child Syndrome," *Journal American Medical Association* 181 (17), 1962.
2. David G. Gil, *Unravelling Social Policy*, Cambridge, Mass.: Schenkman Publishing Co., 1973; Revised Edition 1976; see also Part 1 of this Volume.

NOTES TO CHAPTER SEVEN

1. William Ryan, *Blaming the Victim*, New York: Pantheon Books, 1971.
2. *Child Abuse Prevention Act, 1973*, Hearings before the Sub-Committee on Children and Youth of the Committee on Labor and Public Welfare, U.S. Senate, 93rd Congress, 1st Session, on S. 1191, Washington, D.C.: Government Printing Office, 1973, p. 14.
3. See the essay "Institutions for Children" in this volume.
4. Task Force to the Secretary of HEW, *Work in America*, Cambridge, Mass.: The MIT Press, 1973.

NOTES TO CHAPTER EIGHT

1. Frances Fox Piven and Richard A. Cloward, *Regulating the Poor: The Functions of Public Welfare*, New York: Pantheon, 1971.
2. William Ryan, *Blaming the Victim*, New York: Pantheon, 1971.

NOTES TO CHAPTER TEN

1. Martin Buber, *Paths in Utopia*, Boston, Mass.: Beacon Press, 1958.
2. George Lakey, *Strategy For A Living Revolution*, San Francisco, Cal.: W. H. Freeman, 1973.

NOTES TO CHAPTER ELEVEN

1. Gene Sharp, *The Politics of Nonviolent Action*, Boston, Mass.: Porter Sargent Publishers, 1973.
2. Murray Bookchin, *Post-Scarcity Anarchism*, San Francisco, Cal.: Rampart Press, 1971.

NOTES TO CHAPTER TWELVE

1. Bernfeld, Siegfried, *Sisyphos-oder die Grenzen der Erziehung*, Wien: Internationaler Psychoanalitischer Verlag, G.M.B.H., 1925.
2. For some general observations on strategy, see the essay: *Thoughts on Political Strategy*, in Part Three of this volume, and the Epilogue in my book *Unravelling Social Policy*, Cambridge, Mass.: Schenkman Publishing Co., 1973; Revised Edition, 1976.
3. Freire, Paulo, *Pedagogy Of The Oppressed*, New York: Herder & Herder, 1970.
   Freire, Paulo, *Education For Critical Consciousness*, New York: Seabury Press, 1973.
   Illich, Ivan, *De-Schooling Society*, New York: Harper & Row, 1971.

NOTES TO CHAPTER THIRTEEN

1. For a discussion of the conceptual model of social policies and its utilization in the analysis and synthesis of policies, see the author's book: *Unravelling Social Policy: Theory, Analysis and Political Action Toward Social Equality*, Cambridge, Mass.: Schenkman Publishing Co., 1973. See also the author's article: "Theoretical Perspectives on the Analysis and Development of Social Policies," in Part One of this volume.

2. Letitia Upton and Nancy Lyons, *Basic Facts: Distribution of Personal Income and Wealth in the United States*, Cambridge, Institute, 1972.

3. For a systematic study of capitalism see: Howard Sherman, *Radical Political Economy*, New York & London: Basic Books, Inc., 1972. Richard C. Edwards, Michael Reich, Thomas E. Weisskopf, eds., *The Capitalist System*, Englewood Cliffs, N.J.: Prentice Hall, Inc., 1972. Paul A. Baran & Paul M. Sweezy, *Monopoly Capital*, New York: Monthly Review Press, 1966.

4. See the recent H.E.W. study *Work in America*, Washington, D.C.: Superintendent of Documents, 1972. See also: Andre Gorz, *Strategy for Labor*, Boston: Beacon Press, 1969.

5. U.S. Department of State, Bureau of Intelligence and Research, *The World's Product at the Turn of the Decade: Recessional*, RESS-54, Sept. 12, 1972.

6. R. H. Tawney, *Equality*, London: George Allen and Unwin Ltd., 1964. (First published in 1931).

7. Paulo Freire, *Pedagogy of the Oppressed*, New York: Herder and Herder, 1970.

8. David G. Gil, *Violence Against Children*, Cambridge, Mass.: Harvard University Press, 1970. (Revised paperback edition: Harvard University Press, 1973.) See also the essays "Violence Against Children," and "Holistic Perspective on Child Abuse And Its Prevention" in Part Two of this volume.

Index

Aged, 13; protection of the, 15, 56; homes for the, 88

Aid to Families with Dependent Children (AFDC), 133

Alcoholism, 10, 116, 117, 118, 128, 139, 154

Alienation, 10, 25, 52, 53, 66, 69, 76, 136, 154, 174, 176, 190, 196, 201, 202, 203; of workers, 38, 54, 139, 141, 142, 199; of youth, 26, 54

American Indians, 82, 90, 94, 97-98, 120

Arabs, 154-165

Beliefs, Societal, *See* Value Premises

Benedict, Ruth, 6

Bernfeld, Siegfried, 189

Boarding Schools, Private, and affluent, 86, 90-92, 94-95, 97; for American Indians, 82, 90, 94, 97-98; as institutions, 81-82, 93, 96; quality of life in, 102-103

Buber, Martin, 64, 177

Bureacracy, 57, 59, 61, 66, 128, 136, 139, 154, 160

Cabot-Lodge, George, 64

Capitalism, 174, 184, 204; mythical character of models of, 61, 75, 200-201, 205; reforms in, 62, 179, 202-203; as source of social problems, 176, 197-203; systems of provision of, 53-61 *pass.*; values of, 6, 55, 136, 162, 198-201

Centralization, 53, 54, 66, 73, 136

Charity, 52, 58, 82, 86, 92, 149, 155

Child Abuse, 101, 104, 105, 131; caused by individual or by Society, 105-107, 128, 134-141, 207-208; characteristics

of legally reported, 109-111; and child-rearing patterns, 110, 120-122; conceptual model of, 118-123, 130-131; definition of, 107-108, 129-130; and families, 111-112, 131-132; incidents and circumstances surrounding, 112-114, 131-134; on institutional level, 131-133, 137; investigations of, 105-115, 128; official actions following, 114-115, 123-124; prevention and reduction of, 106, 123-127, 130, 141-143; and research recommendations, 143-144; scope of, 108-109; and social policy, 106, 123-129 *pass.*; on societal level, 133-141, 207, 208

Child Rearing, 110, 120-125, 132, 138, 141, 207

Children, 56, 80, 194; American Indian, 90, 94, 97, 98; delinquent, 83-88, 92, 95, 98-102; dependent and neglected, 79-104 *pass.*, 116, 130, 132, 134; education of, 104, 131-134, 141, 207; equality of, 102-103, 126, 130, 135-136, 142; and families, 80, 83, 86, 87, 90-94, 103, 105-107, 109-118, 121-125, 131-132, 137; handicapped, 79-81, 83-85, 87, 89, 92, 98-99, 110, 132, 133; institutionalization of, *See* Institions; Orphaned, 87, 92; and preparation for adulthood, 138; services for, 15, 106, 207; 1970 White House Conference on, 79

Civil Liberties, *See also* Rights, 32, 33, 34, 38, 41

Class, 7, 70, 87, 176; conflict, 182-183, 185, consciousness,